WITHDRAWN
UTSA LIBRARIES

P9-CJV-603

RENEWALS: 458-4574

DATE DUE

NOV 19	DEC 1 9		
FEB 10	NOV - 8		
MAR 04	OCT 1 1		
APR 1 9			
MAY 06			
MAY 07			
NOV 2 4			
SEP 2 7			
NOV 2 8			
NOV 2 7			
MAR 2 0			
MAR 2 6			
FEB 1 9			
MAR 2			

Demco, Inc. 38-293

VIOLENT DEATHS IN THE UNITED STATES

VIOLENT DEATHS
IN THE UNITED STATES

An Epidemiologic Study of Suicide, Homicide, and Accidents

PAUL C. HOLINGER, M.D., M.P.H.
Rush–Presbyterian–St. Luke's Medical Center

FOREWORD BY JAN FAWCETT, M.D.

THE GUILFORD PRESS
New York   London

© 1987 The Guilford Press
A Division of Guilford Publications, Inc.
72 Spring Street, New York, N.Y. 10012

All rights reserved

No part of this book may be reproduced, stored in a retrieval system, or
transmitted, in any form or by any means, electronic, mechanical,
photocopying, microfilming, recording, or otherwise, without written
permission from the Publisher

Printed in the United States of America

Last digit is print number: 9 8 7 6 5 4 3 2 1

LIBRARY OF CONGRESS CATALOGING-IN-PUBLICATION DATA

Holinger, Paul C.
    Violent deaths in the United States.

    Bibliography: p.
    Includes index.
    1. Suicide—United States.   2. Homicide—United
States.   3. Accidents—United States.   4. Violent
deaths—United States.   5. Psychiatric epidemiology—
United States.   I. Title.   [DNLM: 1. Accidents—
occurrence—United States.   2. Death, Sudden—
occurrence—United States.   3. Homicide—occurrence—
United States.   4. Suicide—occurrence—United
States.   5. Violence.   W820 H732v]
    RC569.H65   1987   1304.6'4'0973021   87-10720
    ISBN 0-89862-672-2

LIBRARY
The University of Texas
at San Antonio

TO PAUL H. HOLINGER, M.D.

Scientist, bronchoesophagologist, father, and friend

ACKNOWLEDGMENTS

This book has emerged slowly over the past several years, and I owe a great deal to the many who have helped in a variety of ways during that time. Special thanks go to those with whom I had the pleasure of coauthoring various chapters: Elaine H. Klemen, M.S.W.; Kevin W. Luke, M.D.; Paul Montes II; Daniel Offer, M.D.; Sonia Perez; and Jay Sandlow. I am also particularly indebted to four people who read the entire manuscript in its various stages and gave invaluable suggestions: Katie Busch, M.D.; Elaine H. Klemen, M.S.W.; Jane Murphy, Ph.D.; and Daniel Offer, M.D. In addition, I am extremely grateful for the support and help given throughout this project by the following persons: Michael Franz Basch, M.D.; William P. D. Cade; Pamela C. Cantor, Ph.D.; Jan Fawcett, M.D.; Marlene Goodfriend, M.D.; Shirley G. (Mrs. Louis S.) Hardin; Dorothy P. Holinger, M.S.; William J. Holinger, M.A.; Leo Levy, Ph.D.; Cynthia Pfeffer, M.D.; Howard Sudak, M.D.; Seymour Weingarten; and Robert Zadylak, M.D. Finally, profound gratitude goes to Betty Melton and her staff for their skill, patience, and good humor regarding the editorial, technical, and secretarial aspects of the book.

Appreciation is expressed for permission to reprint excerpts of the text and figures from the following previously published material:

Holinger PC: Violent deaths as a leading cause of mortality: An epidemiologic study of suicide, homicide, and accidents. *American Journal of Psychiatry* 137: 472–476, 1980. Copyright 1980 by the American Psychiatric Association. Reprinted by permission.

Holinger PC, Klemen E: Violent deaths in the United States, 1900–1975. *Social Science and Medicine* 16: 1929–1938, 1982. Copyright 1982 by Pergamon Press. Reprinted by permission.

Holinger PC, Offer D: Prediction of adolescent suicide: A population model. *American Journal of Psychiatry* 139: 302–307, 1982. Copyright 1982 by the American Psychiatric Association. Reprinted by permission.

Holinger PC, Offer D: Toward the prediction of violent deaths among the young. In *Suicide in the young* (Sudak HS, Ford AB, Rushforth NB, eds.). Copyright 1984 by PSG Publishing Company, Inc. Reprinted by permission.

Holinger PC, Holinger DP, Sandlow J: Violent deaths among children in the United States, 1900–1980. *Pediatrician* 12: 11–19, 1983–1985. Copyright 1985 by S. Karger AG, Basel. Reprinted by permission.

Holinger PC, Offer D, Ostrov E: Suicide and homicide in the United States: An epidemiologic study of violent mortality, population changes, and the potential for prediction. *American Journal of Psychiatry*, 1987, in press. Copyright 1987 by the American Psychiatric Association. Reprinted by permission.

This study was supported in part by the Center for Suicide Prevention and Research, Rush–Presbyterian–St. Luke's Medical Center, and by the Harold W. Schloss Memorial Fund. This work was, in part, conducted at and supported by the Harvard University School of Public Health, Boston, Massachusetts.

P. C. H.

FOREWORD

This book illustrates the power of epidemiologic studies at their best, in that it achieves many of the potentials of the use of epidemiologic data. For the social planner who advises government on the priorities for problems that require prevention and intervention, it provides the data to allot a very high priority for further research and preventive programs on accidental death, suicide, and homicide as causes of violent death. For the clinician who views the tragic outcome of suicide, homicidal death, or accidental death in terms of the individual's characteristics, the epidemiologic approach highlights the important trends common over a number of occurrences and helps separate those data which are pertinent to the prevention of such outcomes from the welter of other important, though perhaps not as central, clinical data.

As clinicians, we are invariably confronted by problems of suicide and other manifestations of self-destructiveness in our patients. In our day-to-day work with patients, we often tend to overlook the larger scene. Dr. Holinger, as both clinician and researcher, reminds us in this book that if we take suicide prevention seriously, we must look at this larger picture. To accomplish this enhanced understanding of self-destructiveness, he presents the longitudinal trends of not just suicide but homicide and accidents as well, emphasizing the importance of age, period, and population effects.

Enlarging our horizons with respect to violent deaths and self-destructiveness is of critical importance in psychiatry. As this book demonstrates, there have not been any successful preventive interventions in the United States that have led to a decrease in suicide and homicide rates on a large-scale, public health level. Rather, period, age, and cohort effects, not intentional intervention effects, have dictated the trends in these rates during the 20th century. With accidental deaths, the picture is somewhat different. Some data suggest that changes in speed limits and increased seat-belt use have decreased motor-vehicle-accident deaths in certain age groups. Yet for mental health professionals, it would seem that large-scale effective intervention and prevention of these forms of violent death should command a high priority. In countries outside the United States, there are only two examples of possibly effective public health interventions to decrease suicide rates: the shift from toxic to less-toxic gas in England, and the legislated decrease in the amount of prescribed sedatives in Australia. Even in these two instances, the data are extremely conflicting with respect to whether or not these interventions have, in fact, led to a sustained decrease in suicide rates.

Violent Deaths in the United States makes it clear that we must improve our efforts in intervention and prevention. To this end, perhaps the most intriguing part of the book emerges. In his attempt to bridge clinical and epidemiologic data and hypotheses, Dr. Holinger presents a series of studies on the relationship between population shifts and violent death rates. The importance of this work lies in the potential for prediction of violent death rates. With this predictive model comes the possibility of effective intervention and prevention of suicide, homicide, and accidents. Thus the epidemiologic realm is seen to influence us profoundly on a clinical level. Such an attempt at intervention and prevention is well worth our most serious attention.

Violent death is almost always needless death. Violent death in youth is a double tragedy. The relative loss of individuals whose lives seem to be full of potential by virtue of their physical health, energy, and the endless opportunities available to them cannot be tolerated in a progressive society. This work by Dr. Holinger and his colleagues helps us not only to see the importance of preventive intervention in the areas of suicide, homicide, and accidental death, but also to understand the important interface between social forces and individual dynamics which influences these outcomes and which must be further recognized and counteracted in order to avoid the tragic waste of potential creative life that we see today.

Jan Fawcett, M.D.
Professor and Chairman
Department of Psychiatry
Rush–Presbyterian–St. Luke's Medical Center

CONTENTS

VIOLENT DEATHS IN THE UNITED STATES

SECTION ONE

RATIONALE AND METHODOLOGY

Section I describes the purpose, literature, and methodology of the study. Violent deaths (suicide, homicide, and accidents) are the leading cause of number of years of life lost in the United States and the third leading cause of death. The purpose of this study is essentially to examine the following three issues: (1) the epidemiology of violent deaths; (2) the extent to which all forms of violent deaths may reflect self-destructive tendencies; and (3) the potential prediction of violent death trends in populations. The literature review (Chapter 2) focuses on these three issues: epidemiologic studies of violent deaths, clinical and epidemiologic data regarding self-destructive aspects of violent deaths, and the prediction of violent death trends in populations. Chapter 3, on methodology, examines the type of data utilized in this study and the problems involved. National mortality rates are the primary type of data used, and the methodologic problems determining the number of deaths and the population figures are discussed. Misclassification errors, national changes in classification over time, and concepts such as comparability ratios and age-adjusted rates are presented.

1

INTRODUCTION*

RATIONALE

Violent deaths (suicides, homicides, and accidents) are the leading cause of death of people aged 1–39 in the United States. More lives are lost to violent deaths during the first half of the normal life span than to heart disease, cancer, diabetes, or any other cause. In addition, violent deaths are the leading cause of expected life lost in this country. Overall, for all ages, violent deaths are the third leading cause of death, behind cardiovascular disease and cancer, respectively (Holinger, 1980). It is no exaggeration to suggest that this violent death aggregate represents a serious social and public health problem in the United States. The purpose of this book is to examine three aspects of this problem: the epidemiology of violent deaths; the self-destructive quality of violent deaths; and the potential for the prediction of violent deaths.

Scientists have long been interested in self-destructive tendencies among human beings. Most studies of self-destructiveness, however, have tended to concentrate only on suicide, that is, overt self-destructiveness (exceptions to this include Menninger, 1938;

*Two issues regarding the data in this book should be noted at the outset. First, while most of the data include the years 1900–1980, some of the data begin after 1900 or end prior to 1980. The reasons for these differences are explained in the text, and usually relate to the dates of the beginning of national compilation of various data. In other instances (especially Chapters 11 and 12) the national mortality data through 1980 were not available at the time of the statistical studies, and in those cases the most recent data were used. Second, the graphs presented in this book are often quite complex and "busy." Inasmuch as the book is oriented to discerning major trends (i.e., especially fluctuations of rates over decades and those age, race, and sex groups at highest and lowest risk) rather than to following minute changes in a single age group, the decision was made not to split the graphs up by age or to exclude certain data to make them less "busy"; rates for specific age, race, and sex groups can be found in the appendices if the graphs do not provide sufficient information.

Farberow, 1979; Wolfgang, 1959; and clinical data and research on accidents; see Chapter 2). The organizing principle of this book involves a curiosity about the nature and degree of self-destructiveness among human beings, and particularly the role such self-destructiveness may play in suicides, homicides, and accidental deaths in populations. An attempt will be made to show that the patterns of violent deaths in populations are not random, but rather have understandable patterns; and that while the behavior of an individual may be unpredictable, the violent death patterns for populations may be predictable. Essentially, three issues are presented in this book: (1) the epidemiology (distribution and frequency) of violent deaths (suicides, homicides, and accidents); (2) the extent to which all forms of violent deaths reflect self-destructive tendencies; and (3) the prediction of violent death patterns for populations.

A variety of questions will be addressed by examining these three major issues:

1. What are the epidemiologic patterns of violent deaths in the United States? What are the age, race, and sex patterns for suicides, homicides, accidents (total), motor-vehicle accidents, and non-motor-vehicle accidents? How are the patterns for suicide, homicide, and accidents similar and how are they dissimilar?
2. How do epidemiologic patterns of suicide (overt self-destructiveness) relate to patterns for homicides and accidents? What are the epidemiologic trends for violent deaths when studied in aggregate?
3. What variables seem to correlate most closely with violent death patterns? Is there any way to predict the suicide rates and other violent death rates for specific age groups in specific populations?

The term "violent deaths" has been used here as elsewhere (Weiss, 1976) to refer to suicides, homicides, and accidental deaths. There are at least two reasons for studying these forms of death in aggregate as violent deaths. *Webster's* (1977) defines the term "a violent death" as "caused by force: not natural." Thus, the first reason relates to the sense that these causes of mortality are often considered to be "unnatural" as compared with, say, cancer or heart disease: They do not involve the deterioration of the body's internal organs, but are imposed from without. Second, clinical evidence suggests that homicides and accidents, as well as suicides, may be self-inflicted: the victim to some degree provokes his or her own death by being in the wrong place at the wrong time. The idea of risk taking is relevant here, people who take more risks being in greater danger of dying by accident or homicide. It should be stressed that homicide data, that is, deaths by homicide, refer to those who are killed, not to those who kill. One study of several hundred homicides (Wolfgang, 1959, 1968) demonstrated that about 25% of all homicides were provoked by the victim, and Wolfgang termed these "victim-precipitated homicides." Certainly a perpetrator is necessary in homicides and in some accidents, but in this book the focus is on the victim. Suicide, homicide, and accidents, in this framework, are seen as related in that all may represent some expression of self-inflicted mortality, with suicide being the most overt, and homicide and accidents being more subtle manifestations of self-destructive tendencies and risk taking.

In order to clarify this notion of viewing violent deaths as reflecting self-destructive tendencies, it is necessary to discuss briefly perception and consciousness. How is it that homicides and accidents, as well as suicides, can be conceived of as self-inflicted and self-destructive? It is most important to view the brain as an extremely powerful perceptual organ, the task of which is to perceive and organize stimuli. There is an increasing amount of evidence to suggest that the brain perceives far more than scientists initially thought it did. For instance, studies of so-called subliminal stimulation (stimuli whose registration is outside conscious awareness), negative hallucinations, and tachistoscopic data demonstrate the massive amount of stimuli that the brain does receive and process (Klein, 1959; Basch, 1975). Basch (1975) has noted that most current evidence suggests that all perception is unconscious, that is, outside conscious awareness. Then the important issue for study is why and under what conditions various unconsciously perceived stimuli are permitted to reach consciousness. For example, suppose a person trips over a crack in the sidewalk. Given the brain's enormous perceptual capacity, there can be little doubt that the crack in the sidewalk was perceived on some level. But the question arises: Why was this perceived information not permitted into consciousness to prevent the person from tripping? Similarly, suppose someone is making a sandwich in a familiar kitchen and bumps his head on the overhanging cabinets. Again, clearly the brain has perceived the cabinets and their distance from one's head. Yet such information is not permitted into conscious or preconscious awareness in order to stop the accident from occurring. One has only to consider the brain's magnificent capacity for evaluating and organizing stimuli such as distance and speed (e.g., all the perceptual elements that go into a baseball player's catching a difficult fly ball or hitting a difficult pitch) to appreciate the nature of the block or distortion of the information flow to consciousness. Freud, although using a somewhat different perspective, dealt with this problem of accidents being psychologically determined as early as 1901 (Freud, 1901).

How, then, does this issue of perception by the brain and admission of such perceptions into consciousness help toward an understanding of the nature of homicides and accidental deaths, as well as suicides? Several clinical vignettes will be presented to bring the above discussion on perception back into the realm of violent deaths.

Clinical Vignette: Homicide

A 27-year-old woman in the midst of severe marital problems began going to bars in an area of the city known for its high crime rate. Despite being beaten up one night in that neighborhood, and against the urgings of her parents and husband, she continued her evenings in that area. One morning she was found murdered in that neighborhood. Witnesses said she had become rather obnoxious and provocative with two men the night before who were then seen following her out of the bar.

Clinical Vignette: Accident

A 31-year-old woman whose business was not going well was driving home from a business meeting and got on to a two-lane highway which she thought was part of an expressway with all lanes going her way. The car she was behind, as well as a semi-trailer up ahead in the lane next to her, both appeared to be moving in the same direction as she was. She pulled out to pass the slower-moving car ahead of her. As she was passing the car, she looked over and saw a horrified look on the driver's face. "This was the first time I realized that things were not quite right," she said. She looked ahead and then realized that the semi-trailer was coming toward her. She was hit by the truck, the car sheared in half, but she was not seriously hurt. However, the truck tipped over, falling on another car and killing the driver. About 4 years later, the same woman, now an insurance agent in the midst of a distressing divorce, was driving to an appointment when she ran a red light and hit one of the many cars which had begun to pull out into the intersection. She said she was sure the light had been green or that there had been no light. All witnesses said she ran a clearly visible red light. She later said she had not been wearing her contact lenses, a particularly risky omission, she admitted, given the amount of driving she does for her work. After dealing with the police and other driver, she canceled her appointment and began driving home (having put in her contact lenses). On the way home, driving on a two-lane highway with traffic moving in both directions, she moved out to pass a car ahead of her. She passed, but had not given herself enough time to get back into her lane before the oncoming cars reached her. The oncoming cars were forced to swerve onto the shoulder to avoid hitting her, and she was able to get back into her own lane without having another accident.

Clinical Vignette: Accident

A 30-year-old man who had been in analysis for several years and was becoming increasingly aware of his rage toward his mother went out jogging following an argument with her. Quite unusually, he slipped on some ice, hitting his head and causing a concussion. Later that evening he and his mother reconciled their differences primarily through the mother's attentiveness to the patient's injury. The next day the patient continued to be aware of his chronic rage at his mother and was increasingly anxious driving to work inasmuch as he felt certain he was going to be unable to control his car and would have an accident.

Clinical Vignette: Accident

The patient, a 36-year-old woman, became increasingly excited and overstimulated as she and the man she was dating became closer to each other and, in short, more and more loving. She began feeling so excited that she could scarcely contain herself, describing the feeling as "too much of a good thing." Finally, the tension of her overstimulation became intolerable, and one night she started drinking, sexually teased her male friend, and got into an argument with him which ended in door slamming; shortly thereafter she cut her legs severely while shaving.

In these vignettes, serious perceptual blocks or distortions led to death or severe injury. In the homicide case, the young woman did not allow herself conscious awareness (or, if she did have such awareness, chose not to act on it) of the realistic dangers of the neighborhood she was in or of the verbal warnings emphasizing the dangerousness of her actions. In the first accident vignette, the woman twice made severe perceptual distortions (seeing the semi-trailer as moving away rather than toward her and seeing a green rather than a red light), as well as engaging in serious risk taking in the second accident by not wearing her contact lenses which were necessary for accurate eyesight while driving. These vignettes also raise two other issues that are, for the most part, beyond the scope of this book, namely, the motivations and mechanisms that lie behind perceptual blocks and distortions and account for so many violent deaths; and the complex theoretical formulations used to explain perceptual blocks and distortions (such as repression, disavowal, splitting of the ego, and so on).

PURPOSE

The purpose of this book, then, is to address systematically the essential questions raised above. This work represents an attempt to look carefully at the data in an important area, that is, violence and violent deaths, which is often dominated by opinions rather than data. Furthermore, it is hoped that this endeavor will demonstrate that these data are comprehensible, that some sense can be made out of violent death patterns in populations.

This book focuses intentionally on the self-destructive perspective in examining suicides, homicides, and accidents. This is not to deny the importance of aggression or the existence of a perpetrator in homicides and some accidents; neither does it excuse the perpetrator of a homicide from responsibility. The decision to examine carefully the self-destructive perspective (e.g., the victim, risk-taking behavior) is merely a conscious choice to see if anything new can be learned or understood about violent deaths using such a microscopic focus. It appears that human beings generally tend to repress or disavow their self-destructive thoughts and impulses (e.g., consider society's abhorrence of suicide, even considering it a crime in some locations) and that the self-destructive perspective has not been adequately addressed by scientists. A second focus of the book is on the epidemiology of self-destructiveness rather than the intrapsychic motivation behind such a tendency. In other words, in this presentation the epidemiologic patterns are of most concern; the intrapsychic forces underlying such patterns (e.g., masochism, narcissism and grandiosity, perceptual distortions, issues in group psychology, etc.) will be the subject of future communications. Finally, the present work focuses on populations rather than individuals. The particular concern is on violent deaths in the United States, divided into categories of age, race, and sex. Intrapsychic, clinical data on violent deaths and self-destructiveness in individuals will be addressed insofar as they can aid in conceptualizing an understanding of violent death patterns in populations.

However, two large steps in the study of violent deaths may not yet be entirely possible; namely, a comprehensive theoretical understanding of the intrapsychic mechanisms underlying such ubiquitous self-destructiveness; and the understanding of self-destructiveness on a population, rather than an individual, level: Is there a qualitative difference in the patterns of violent deaths when one examines groups and larger populations as opposed to individuals? The first question must be answered primarily in the realm of psychoanalysis and clinical work with individuals. The second question involves the fields of sociology, psychiatric epidemiology, psychoanalysis, and clinical psychiatry. Most likely our understanding of violent deaths in populations will arise from a hybrid of or communication among those disciplines. Gedo and Goldberg (1973) have cogently warned against inappropriately using metapsychological models derived from psychoanalytic data to explain phenomena in social psychology. However, adequate models do not yet exist for understanding violent deaths on population levels. This book attempts a small step in the direction of providing such conceptualizations.

The book is divided into five sections. Section I (Chapters 1–3) describes the rationale for and methodology of the study as well as providing a literature review. Section II (Chapters 4–8) is a straightforward presentation of the epidemiology of the suicide, homicide, and accidental death patterns in the United States, 1900–1980. Section III (Chapters 9 and 10) utilizes the epidemiologic data to address the question of whether violent deaths reflect self-destructive tendencies. Section IV (Chapters 11 and 12) examines specific variables that may aid in predicting violent death patterns. Section V (Chapter 13) summarizes the epidemiologic findings and examines the explanatory power of the self-destructive perspective. Readers interested primarily in the rationale and summary of the study would do best to look at Chapters 1 and 13. Those involved in epidemiology and interested in the more detailed descriptions of the violent death patterns of the United States, 1900–1980, could focus on Sections II and III. Finally, those whose interest lies primarily in prediction and effective intervention may find Section IV of particular value.

THE IMPORTANCE OF VIOLENT DEATHS AS A LEADING CAUSE OF MORTALITY

An effort has been made to show that suicides, homicides, and accidents are not unrelated and that there are compelling reasons for studying them in aggregate as violent deaths. All are somehow seen as "unnatural," and all may represent self-destructive tendencies in part: Evidence exists that many homicides are victim-precipitated and represent suicides; "accidental" deaths may be due to accident-proneness and risk taking that reflect depression and suicidal tendencies. With this background to why violent deaths are studied in aggregate, we must examine the often-unrecognized fact that violent deaths are one of the leading causes of death in the United States. It would not be an overstatement to suggest that this aggregate represents a major public health problem in this country. The importance of violent deaths as a leading cause of mortality will be examined from three perspectives: trends in violent deaths over time; violent deaths as a leading cause of mortality by age; and amount of expected life lost through violent deaths.*†

Trends in Violent Deaths over Time

Violent deaths can be studied as a cause of mortality over time, keeping in mind both the comparability problems with the categories of national mortality data as well as changes in the age structure of the population (Holinger, 1980). The mortality rates for violent deaths have tended to decrease from 1900 to 1975, and they tend to parallel the increases and decreases found in suicide rates, even though suicide rates make up less than 20% of the violent death rate. The age-adjusted mortality rates for violent deaths also showed a decrease between 1900 and 1975 (see Figure 1-1). In 1900 violent deaths were only one of many important causes of death, with the age-adjusted mortality rate for violent deaths ranking behind the rates for major cardiovascular diseases, influenza and pneumonia, tuberculosis, gastritis and enteritis, and

*Figures 1-1 and 1-4 refer to causes of death and disease category numbers of the 8th revision of the International Classification of Diseases (ICD), adapted (World Health Organization, 1965), as follows: influenza and pneumonia (470–479, 480–486); tuberculosis (010–019); major cardiovascular diseases (390–448); malignant neoplasms (140–209); violent deaths (suicide, E950–E959; homicide, E960–E978; accidents, E800–E949; deaths due to injuries undetermined whether accidentally or purposefully inflicted, E980–E989, a category begun in the United States in 1968). For Figures 1-1 and 1-4 and Tables 1-1 and 1-2, the sources of data on the number of deaths, death rates, population for rate derivation, and age-adjusted death rates are noted by Holinger (1980), and unpublished data from the National Center for Health Statistics. Age-adjusted death rates were computed by direct method, using as the standard population the age distribution of the total population of the United States in 1940. In Figure 1-1, the age-adjusted death rate for violent deaths does not include E980–989; the mortality rates for E980–989 had a range of 2.1–2.6 per 100,000 population over the years 1968–1975 (unpublished data, National Center for Health Statistics).

†The data presented here included violent deaths that occurred in all U.S. states that participated in federal registration of deaths (death registration states), 1900–1932, and violent deaths that occurred in all U.S. states, 1933–1975 (with Alaska added in 1959 and Hawaii in 1960).

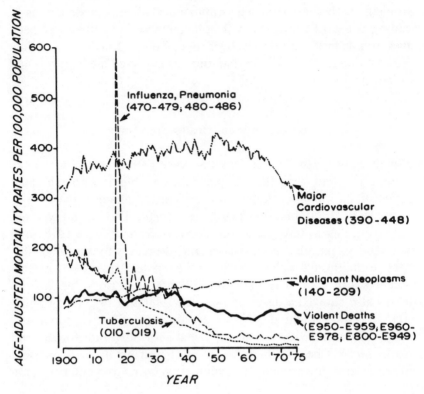

Figure 1-1. Age-adjusted death rates for the leading causes of death in the United States, 1900–1975. *Sources of data*: See text; Holinger (1980, Figure 2).

nephritis and nephrosis. Throughout the 20th century, as other causes of mortality have been more successfully controlled, violent deaths have emerged as one of the three leading causes of death. Cardiovascular diseases have ranked first (initial increase after 1900, subsequent leveling off, then a decline since the 1960s); malignant neoplasms, second (increase slowly since 1900); and violent deaths, third (decrease since 1900).

Mortality trends over time have shifted markedly for the separate components of violent deaths, that is, suicides, homicides, and accidents. Figure 1-2 presents the time trends of the various forms of violent deaths in the United States, 1900–1975. Figure 1-3 demonstrates the age patterns of suicide, homicide, motor-vehicle accidents, non-motor-vehicle accidents, and accidents (total), each averaged over the years 1900–1980. Suicide rates have increased in years of economic depression (especially during the early 1930s), decreased during World Wars I and II, decreased during the 1950s, and recently increased (Figure 1-2). Race and sex breakdowns (see Section II) show that suicide rates for men increase with age and are higher than those for women by a ratio of 2–3 : 1. In contrast, the highest suicide rates for women are in the middle-age period (35–64 years). Suicide rates for whites tend to be higher than those for nonwhites. Homicide rates gradually increased from very low levels in 1900 to peaks during the Depression of the 1930s, decreased during the 1950s, and then increased so that current homicide rates for most age groups of both sexes are as high or higher than those previously recorded in the United States (Figure 1-2). Homicide rates for men are consistently higher than those for women (ratio of about 4 : 1), and for both sexes the 25- to 34-year-olds have the highest homicide rates, followed by 35- to 44-year-olds and 15- to 24-year-olds, respectively. The homicide rates for nonwhites have been about 8 to 15 times greater than those for whites. Mortality rates for accidents are higher than those for suicide and homicide. Mortality rates for motor-vehicle accidents have gradually increased during the 20th century, while death rates for accidents excluding motor vehicles have shown a slow decrease (Figure 1-2). (However, despite these apparent differences in mortality patterns between suicides, homicides, and accidents, the similarities and parallels are even more striking, as the graphs and positive correlations in Chapter 9 show.) Accident rates for men have been consistently higher than those for women (ratio ranging from 5 : 1

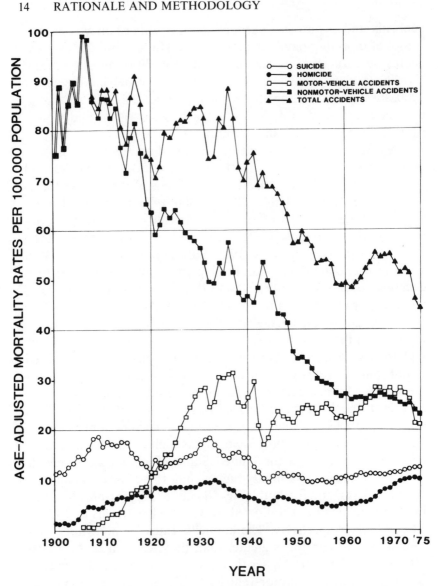

Figure 1-2. Age-adjusted violent death rates by type of mortality, United States, 1900–1975. *Sources of data*: See text; Holinger and Klemen (1982, Figure 1); *Vital Statistics—Special Reports* (1956) (for 1900–1953); Grove and Hetzel (1968) (for 1954–1960); *Vital Statistics of the United States* (1961–1975) (for age-adjusted motor-vehicle accident and non-motor-vehicle-accident mortality rates, 1961–1975); *Vital and Health Statistics* (1974) (for age-adjusted total accident, suicide, and homicide mortality rates, 1970–1975).

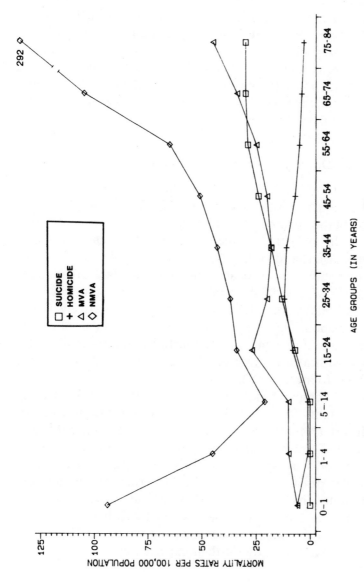

Figure 1-3. Age patterns of violent deaths by type of mortality, United States, 1900–1980. *Sources of data: Vital Statistics—Special Reports* (1956) (for 1900–1953); Grove and Hetzel (1968) (for 1954–1960); *Vital Statistics of the United States* (1961–1978) (for 1961–1978); unpublished data, National Center for Health Statistics (for 1979 and 1980).

in the younger groups to 2 : 1 in the older groups); accident rates for nonwhites tend to be higher than those for whites.

Trends in violent deaths among the young are of particular interest. The rate of violent deaths among 15- to 24-year-olds is now higher than ever recorded for this age group in the United States (Holinger, 1981). Over the 15-year period 1961–1975, the suicide and homicide rates for 10- to 24-year-olds more than doubled and were as high or higher than ever previously recorded. However, death rates for motor-vehicle accidents and accidents excluding motor vehicles among those age groups showed little overall change from 1961 to 1975.

Violent Deaths as a Leading Cause of Mortality by Age

With respect to violent deaths as a leading cause of mortality by age, in 1975 violent deaths were the third leading cause of death in the United States, behind cardiovascular disease and neoplasms, respectively. In 1975 the number of deaths from cardiovascular disease, neoplasms, and violent deaths were 971,047; 365,693; and 156,241, respectively. The death rates (per 100,000 population) were 445.8; 171.7; and 73.4, respectively. The age-adjusted death rates (per 100,000) were 291.4; 130.9; and 67.9, respectively. Other causes were responsible for far fewer deaths; the number of deaths from influenza and pneumonia, the fourth leading cause of death, was 55,664, with a death rate of 26.1 and an age-adjusted death rate of 16.6 (Holinger, 1980).

Table 1-1 compares violent death rates with the other leading causes of mortality for ages 1–39. In some young age groups, violent deaths are a tenfold greater cause of mortality than the next leading cause of death. Figure 1-4 shows the three leading causes of death for 1975 by age groups. This figure demonstrates that cardiovascular disease and neoplasms kill primarily middle-aged and older adults, that is, those who have already lived much or all of their expected life. Violent deaths, on the other hand, have relatively greater impact on adolescents and young adults, that is, persons who have lived little of their expected life.

Amount of Expected Life Lost through Violent Deaths

Another measure of the importance of various causes of mortality is the amount of expected life lost by specific causes of death. As

Table 1-1. 1975 U.S. Mortality Rates per 100,000 Population for the Three Leading Causes of Death among People Aged 1–39

Cause of death	Age (years)							
	1–4	5–9	10–14	15–19	20–24	25–29	30–34	35–39
Violent deaths (E950–E959, E960–E978, E800–E949, E980–E989)[a]	31.8[1][b]	18.6[1]	21.0[1]	76.5[1]	101.5[1]	88.3[1]	76.0[1]	74.9[1]
Congenital anomalies (740–759)	8.9[2]	2.4[3]						
Malignant neoplasms (140–209)	5.5[3]	5.4[2]	4.3[2]	6.0[2]	7.6[2]	11.4[2]	19.2[2]	35.5[3]
Major cardiovascular diseases (390–448)			1.7[3]	3.4[3]	5.4[3]	8.9[3]	18.1[3]	43.0[2]

Sources of data: See text.

[a]Disease category numbers of the 8th revision of the International Classification of Diseases, adapted (World Health Organization, 1965), appear in parentheses.

[b]Rankings of leading causes of death appear in brackets.

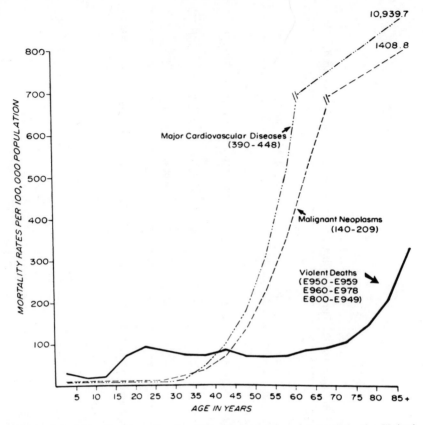

Figure 1-4. Mortality rates for the three leading causes of death in the United States in 1975, by age group. *Sources of data*: See text.

inating causes of infant mortality (Lalonde, 1974). Using 1975
n example, Table 1-2 shows that violent deaths are responsible
more years of expected life lost than any other cause of mortal-
. There are no major changes in the pattern of the data in Table
2 if infant mortality (ages 0–1 year) is retained, except that con-
enital anomalies are then ranked fourth.

Lalonde (1974) noted, the causes of deat
overwhelming impact on total figures and thu
significance of deaths that come before their
termed "amount of expected life lost" helps to a
those causes that tend to kill people before they h.
prime of life and those causes that tend to kill pe
completed an average life span. The amount of exp
therefore, highlights the diseases of the young, that i:
have most of their life ahead of them. This indicator is p
important in suggesting directions for health services and
programs.

To ascertain and measure the principal cause of early
calculations have been made of the years of potential life losi
to each cause, measured against a life expectancy of 70 years i

Table 1-2. Total Years of Expected Life Lost in 1975 in the United States, by Cause of Death

Cause of death	Years of life lost[a]
Violent deaths (E950–E959, E960–E978, E800–E949, E980–E989)[b]	4,651,738.5
Major cardiovascular diseases (390–448)	3,602,498
Malignant neoplasms (140–209)	2,723,431.5
Cirrhosis of liver (571)	454,876.5
Influenza and pneumonia (470–474, 480–486)	278,337.5
Congenital anomalies (740–759)	195,651.5
Diabetes mellitus (250)	181,698.5
Bronchitis, emphysema, asthma (490–493)	125,057
Nephritis and nephrosis (580–584)	60,710

Sources of data: See text.

[a]Years of expected life lost are measured against a life expectancy of 70 and calculated for ages 1–70. Mortality figures are reported by 5-year age intervals, and the number of years of expected life lost for the average year of a given interval is multiplied by the number of deaths in the interval to give the number of years of expected life lost. (e.g., for 1,000 deaths in the 20- to 24-year interval, 22 is the average age, 70 years is the life expectancy, so there are 48 years of expected life lost. 48 years lost × 1,000 deaths = 48,000 years of life lost for the 20- to 24-year interval). The years of expected life lost for each 5-year age interval from 1–70 (i.e., 1–4, 5–9, 10–14) are then added to give total years of expected life lost for the cause of death being studied.

[b]Disease category numbers of the 8th revision of the International Classification of Diseases, adapted (World Health Organization, 1965), appear in parentheses.

CHAPTER TWO

LITERATURE

There is a massive literature on the topics of suicide, homicide, and accidents. No attempt will be made at an exhaustive literature review in this chapter; rather, the objective is to convey a sense of the type of articles and data available in the literature and focus on those works that are most specifically relevant to the task at hand. The literature review will be divided into three sections, corresponding to the three major issues taken up in this book: the epidemiology of violent deaths; violent deaths as reflecting self-destructive tendencies; and the prediction of violent deaths.

Violent deaths have been researched from various perspectives, using many different kinds and levels of data. One must be careful to avoid the serious conceptual problems involved in trying to understand the data and findings of one scientific discipline. The literature and data on violent deaths ranges from psychoanalysis and clinical psychiatry, with their emphasis on intrapsychic and small group data, to epidemiology and sociology, with their focus on larger groups and population data. Frequently investigators derive hypotheses from one field and test them in another, sometimes mindful of the pitfalls and sometimes not. This literature review is organized by topic, rather than by type of data. However, an attempt will be made to note the kind of data and level of abstraction involved and to mention the conceptual problems when they arise.

THE EPIDEMIOLOGY OF VIOLENT DEATHS

Literature dealing with the epidemiology of violent deaths can be roughly divided into three parts, with some overlap: descriptive, etiologic, and studies dealing with the relationships among suicides, homicides, and accidents.

Descriptive

The descriptive literature essentially presents the frequency and distribution of violent deaths, that is, the numbers (or rates) of violent deaths, their location, and the age, race, and sex of the victim. The descriptive literature is somewhat falsely distinguished from the etiologic literature, inasmuch as any listing of the number and location of violent deaths begins to imply causality. The descriptive studies include national as well as local data, but most do not present data over time for all age, race, and sex combinations; in addition, most of the descriptive work is simply in tabular rather than graphic form, thereby hiding some important findings. For these and other reasons, then, Section II of this book has been included to give a rather complete and graphic presentation of suicides, homicides, and accidents, over time, in a variety of age, race, and sex combinations.

The bulk of the descriptive studies and research comes from the government, public health services, and insurance companies. The most comprehensive annual compilation of data is *Vital Statistics of the United States*, which presents rates and raw figures in mostly tabular form. Brooke (1974) and Klebba (1975), writing in the public health literature, have recently given summaries of national suicide and homicide time trends, respectively. Books on suicide (e.g., Dublin, 1963; Lester, 1972; Stengel, 1964) tend to be more common than those on homicide and accidents. Kramer, Pollack, Redick, and Locke (1972) present their descriptive suicide data in a useful graphic fashion (utilized in Section II of this book) by separately plotting male and female suicide rates by 10-year age intervals over time, thus allowing for age, sex, and historical variables to be included in one graph. Epidemiologists, in attempting to describe and understand patterns of suicide, homicide, and accidents, have utilized local as well as national data, and have studied the distributions of violent deaths in terms of time (e.g., what days and time of year have higher death rates) and location (e.g., in what parts of the nation, state, or city the deaths most common) (Lester, 1979; Rogot, Fabsitz, & Feinleib, 1976; Constantino, Kuller, Perper, & Cypess, 1977). In an article unusual for its discussion of the descriptive data of suicides, homicides, and accidents together, Weiss (1976) showed that since 1960 all those forms of death (except non-motor-vehicle accidents) had been increasing among young adults. He used the term "violent deaths" to refer to the suicide, homicide, and accident triad.

Etiologic

Durkheim's *Suicide* (1897) is classic example of using descriptive data to form hypotheses about the etiology of suicide on both social and individual bases. Studying suicide data in relation to religious affiliation, marriage and the family, and political and national communities, Durkheim suggested there were three categories of suicide. "Egoistic" suicide results from lack of integration of the individual into society; the stronger the forces throwing the individual onto his or her own resources, the greater the suicide rate in the society in which this occurs. "Altruistic" suicide results from taking one's own life because of greater integration of the individual into society, that is, religious sacrifice or unthinking political allegiance. "Anomic" suicide results from lack of regulation of the individual by society, that is, economic crises having an aggravating effect on the suicidal tendency. Lester's work (1966, 1972, 1979) relating suicide rates to sibling position, temporal variation, and so on also provides an example of the overt use of descriptive epidemiologic data to better enhance the understanding of etiology of violent deaths. Etiologic studies such as Durkheim's and Lester's also raise questions about the use of population data to provide explanations of individual acts such as suicide.

Relationships between Suicide, Homicide, and Accidents

There are a few studies that specifically address the nature of the relationships among suicide, homicide, and accidents. The type of data used ranges from population to small-group data; they are not clinical or intrapsychic data. Perhaps the best-known work examining these relationships is Henry and Short's *Suicide and Homicide* (1954). This study utilized data that included suicides, homicides, and aggravated assaults for specific localities over time spans of a few years. A variety of sociological variables, including high and low social status, age, race, marital status, urban–rural residence, and ecological distribution were related to the suicide and homicide rates. Of specific relevance to the present work was their finding that homicide and aggravated assault correlated positively with the business cycle, in contrast to suicide. In other words, the authors stated that: "While suicide increases during economic depression, homicide decreases. While suicide drops during prosperity, homicide increases" (p. 45).

Henry and Short's work presents several problems. Their data were suicide and homicide rates for specific locations (e.g., cities) and for relatively short time spans, crimes against property and people, social status, strength of the relational system, and measures of the business cycle. Their use of specific locations (e.g., cities) may add accuracy but cost them the larger perspective of national mortality (i.e., data for an entire population). Second, Henry and Short conceptualized the suicide–homicide problem from the perspective of aggression: The subtitle of their book is *Some Economic, Sociological and Psychological Aspects of Aggression.* Freud's intrapsychic understanding of aggression may have influenced Henry and Short's hypothesis that suicide and homicide are inversely related. Freud (1917) suggested that, as a result of frustration, aggression could be directed either externally (possibly resulting in homicide) or turned back on the self (possibly resulting in suicide). Consistent with this, Henry and Short state that suicide and homicide "are alike in the sense that they are both aggressive reactions to frustrations . . . [but] become sharply differentiated aggressive acts when we consider the object of the aggression rather than its source" (p. 15). However, Henry and Short may have misapplied Freud's intrapsychic model as they made the shift to population levels. The transition from individuals (from which the hypothesis derives) to populations is complicated by the often-overlooked fact that homicide data refer specifically to those killed (the objects of the aggression), not to the killers (those who, when frustrated, direct their aggression outward). In other words, homicide data say nothing, strictly speaking, about the aggressors or the nature or amount of aggression. It seems unwarranted to assume anything about aggression in a population or characteristics of killers based on data that describe only characteristics of people who are killed. Data on suicide and homicide in populations might best be conceptualized as similar in that both measure the object of the aggression, not the source.

Porterfield's (1960) less well-known but important work involved studies of metropolitan areas and found that their combined suicide–homicide rates correlated positively with their traffic fatality rates; that is, he demonstrated that cities with a high suicide–homicide rate tended to have high traffic fatality rates. Porterfield suggested that persons involved in suicide, homicide, and traffic fatalities were similar in having "little regard for their own lives or the lives of others, or both" (p. 897). While Porterfield did not separate the suicide, homicide, and motor-vehicle accident rates, his assumptions, type of data, and conclusions clearly differed from those of Henry and Short.

Brenner's (1971, 1979) work on the relationship between economic cycles and mortality rates is also relevant in this respect. Brenner demonstrated that indicators of economic instability and insecurity, such as unemployment, were associated over time with higher mortality rates. The explanation for this association was that the lack of economic security is stressful—social and family structures break down, and habits that are harmful to health are adopted. The effect may manifest acutely as a psychopathological event (e.g., suicide and homicide) or, after a time lag of a few years, as a chronic disease (e.g., cancer or heart disease). Brenner's conclusions thus differ from Henry and Short's findings. Specifically, data for the entire United States showed that indices of acute pathological disturbances, including suicide and homicide, rose within a year of increased unemployment rates.

Holinger and Klemen (1982) also presented data and conclusions that differed from those of Henry and Short. Holinger and Klemen studied the relationship between suicide, homicide, and accidents in the United States, 1900–1975. The data suggested that national mortality rates for suicide, homicide, and motor-vehicle accidents tend to be parallel over time; non-motor-vehicle accidents, while showing some fluctuations similar to suicide, homicide, and motor-vehicle accidents, manifested a more general decrease throughout the century (see Figure 1-2, and Figures 9-1 through 9-5).

Examples of other studies that related mortality data of one type of violent death to those of another are Lester's (1979) and Jenkins and Sainsbury's (1980) research. Lester examined temporal variations in suicide and homicide in the United States over 2 years and found clear differences: Suicide peaked in the spring and fall and was more common on Mondays, while homicide peaked in July and December and was more common on Saturdays and Sundays. Jenkins and Sainsbury compared the age and seasonal distribution of suicide with 528 single-occupant auto accidents. They found the following differences: Suicide rates peaked in April and increased with age, while the auto accidents peaked in November and were highest in the young age groups. The authors of these studies do not address the issue that unconscious self-destructive tendencies in accidents and homicides (as opposed to deliberate, conscious suicidal behavior) might result in age and seasonal distribution that would differ from overt suicide.

Some studies compared different types of violent deaths without utilizing national mortality data. For example, Wolfgang's (1968) study of homicide should be recalled here, although he did not directly relate homicide rates to other forms of violent deaths. Similarly, Tabachnick (1973) studied automobile accidents in relation to suicidal tendencies. Using psychoanalytically oriented interviews, Tabachnick's study did not support the hypotheses that auto accidents were disguised suicides or represented strong self-destructive tendencies.

VIOLENT DEATHS AS REFLECTING SELF-DESTRUCTIVE TENDENCIES

There is a large body of literature and various levels of data that address whether or not accidents and homicides, in addition to suicide, represent self-destructive tendencies. Regarding accidents, Freud, in *The Psychopathology of Everyday Life* (1901), emphasized the role of psychic determinism in human behavior and stressed that accidents are unconsciously precipitated by the victim. Freud (1920) later added the concept of the death instinct to his understanding of man's self-destructive tendencies. Menninger (1938) and Farberow (1979) have been particularly effective in using clinical and small-group data to document the ubiquitous nature of self-destructive tendencies. Several studies using small-group data have been conducted to address the issue of accident-proneness, that is, that certain people are more likely than others to have accidents. In 1919, Greenwood and Woods wrote a historically important paper in this area and reported that in a British munitions factory a relatively small number of workers had most of the accidents. The authors cautiously suggested that some people were inherently more likely than other people to have accidents. A number of studies testing this hypothesis were conducted, and, while there has been some support of the hypothesis, serious methodologic problems exist. Tabachnick (1973) has carefully summarized these studies and the controversy surrounding them. Other studies, some involving motor vehicles, have shown that deaths due to accidents may be due to accident-proneness and risk taking that reflect depression and suicidal tendencies (e.g., Selzer & Payne, 1962; Kaplan & Pokorny, 1976). However, Tabachnick's (1973) study did not support the hypothesis that suicidal tendencies were predominant among those involved in auto accidents, and Schmidt, Shaffer, Zlotowitz, and Fisher (1977) found that only a small percentage of deaths from motor-vehicle accidents could be classified as intentional suicide. To summarize, both clinical data and studies of small groups seem to suggest that the concepts of accident-proneness and excessive risk taking have therapeutic and predictive value and that accidents and accidental deaths may be psychologically determined by underlying self-destructive tendencies; however, testing the hypothesis that accidents reflect unconscious self-destructive tendencies is extremely difficult and fraught with methodologic problems, and several studies do not confirm the hypothesis.

The most important work specifically relating homicide to self-destructive tendencies has been done by Wolfgang (1959, 1968). As mentioned briefly above, Wolfgang examined homicide data from the perspective of those killed. He studied the records of several hundred persons who were murdered in Philadelphia and found that more than 25% of them could be said to have provoked their own deaths. He spoke of this group as having committed "suicide by means of victim-precipitated homicide." Wolfgang's study supported clinical notions that some patients could bring trouble upon themselves by not taking care of themselves and by being "in the wrong place at the wrong time."

Holinger and Klemen (1982) studied homicides and accidents as well as suicides, using national mortality data. Suicide rates showed significant positive correlations over time with homicide, motor-vehicle- and non-motor-vehicle-accident death rates for most race and sex combinations, United States, 1900–1975. They suggested that these data did not support the idea that there was no relationship between suicide, homicide, and accidents, and that the epidemiologic data did lend support to the concept that self-destructive tendencies may underlie all forms of violent death.

THE PREDICTION OF VIOLENT DEATHS

In Section IV violent death rates are related to population changes in an attempt to predict the patterns of violent deaths. The general idea that changes in population may be related to suicide rates has some, but not complete, support in the literature. For example, Wechsler (1961) found that rapidly growing communities tended to produce significantly higher rates of suicide. Gordon and Gordon's (1960) earlier results tended to be consistent with Wechler's data. Klebba (1975), discussing the increase of homicide among the young, suggested but did not systematically pursue an etiologic connection between the rising rates of homicide and increases in the adolescent population over the past two decades. On the other hand, Levy and Herzog (1974, 1978) and Herzog, Levy, and Verdonk (1977) found negative or insignificant correlations between both population density and crowding and suicide rates.

Two investigators have made important contributions to the potential prediction of violent death rates by studying separate aspects of the problem. Easterlin (1980) has examined in some detail the relationship between population changes and a variety of variables, although with little mention of violent deaths. Brenner (1971, 1979) has demonstrated the negative correlations between economic changes and various causes of mortality, including suicide and homicide (i.e., the better the economy, as measured by unemployment rates, the lower the mortality rates). Colledge (1982), focusing particularly on Brenner's work, has recently summarized the data relating economic fluctuations to changes in mortality, noting that the evidence suggests a causal relationship between the economy and mortality rates. However, Colledge cautions about the explanatory use of macroanalysis and the problems of utilizing concepts on the micro level to understand data gathered on the macro level. With respect to prediction, the economic variable may not be as capable of prediction of violent deaths as is the population variable: while the economy is in itself difficult to predict, population changes for teenagers and older are known far in advance on the basis of the number of children and preadolescents. Holinger and Offer (1982) found significant positive correlations among adolescent suicide rates, changes in the adolescent population, and changes in the proportion in the population of United States, 1933–1976. In other words, increases or decreases in the suicide rates of 15- to 19-year-olds were temporally related to corresponding increases and decreases in adolescent population (and in the proportion of 15- to 19-year-olds in the total population); in contrast, the suicide rate of an older age group (65- to 69-year-olds) was inversely, but not significantly, related to shifts in that older adult population. More recently, Holinger and Offer (1984) found significant positive correlations among suicide, homicide, and non-motor-vehicle-accident mortality rates of 15- to 24-year-olds, and the changes in the proportion of 15- to 24-year-olds in the population of the United States, 1933–1976; significant negative correlations were found between motor-vehicle-accident mortality rates and the change in the proportion of adolescents and young adults in the U.S. population. The results suggested that the violent death rates for the adolescent and young adult age group could be predicted.

In summary, although the relationship between the economy and mortality rates is well documented (bad economic conditions are related to higher mortality rates (Brenner, 1971), one cannot predict future mortality rates from this relationship because without considering population variables one does not know what economic conditions will be like in the future. On the other hand, the population model suggested in this book may allow future predictions not only of violent death rates (Holinger & Offer, 1982, 1984) but also of economic conditions (Easterlin, 1980) for certain age groups because the population shifts for certain age groups are known years ahead. Finally, this predictive cycle becomes perhaps even more complete when one considers that the birth rate in the United States (which is responsible for most of the relevant population changes) tends to be inversely related to economic changes in the United States (i.e., high and low birth rates correspond to good and bad economic conditions, respectively) (Turner, Fenn, & Cole, 1981).

Thus the interrelationship of these variables becomes clearer: From the birth rate comes relevant population changes; these population changes appear to influence economic conditions (i.e., unemployment); economic conditions (and the population changes) tend to influence not only changes in violent death rates, but also changes in the birth rates, thus completing the cycle. The potential for prediction of violent death rates seems to exist by breaking into the cycle and extracting the data on population changes.

CHAPTER THREE

METHODOLOGY

National mortality rates (number of deaths per population) are the major data source for this study. It should be noted that beginning in 1933, the data used are for the total U.S. population, not samples (prior to 1933 not all states were included in the national mortality data, an issue discussed more fully below). However, a variety of methodologic problems exist in utilizing national mortality data to study violent deaths. While specific methodologic issues will be addressed in the relevant chapters, this chapter is aimed at addressing some general problems related to the kind of data used in this study.* Since the data are primarily in the form of mortality rates (i.e., number of deaths per population), this chapter will be divided into sections investigating problems calculating the number of deaths; problems assessing the population; and the issue of age-adjusted mortality rates. The specific sources of national mortality data are indicated on the individual graphs or tables. It should be mentioned that in addressing the major questions raised in this book (see Chapter 1), the dates of the cutoff of the data on the graphs and tables occasionally vary (e.g., some correlations may utilize data from 1900–1975, and others from 1900–1980), usually with a cutoff date from 1975–1980. These discrepancies in the cutoff date relate to the final year for which data were available when a particular aspect of the study was being conducted, inasmuch as a consistent attempt was made to keep the data as current as possible. This varying of cutoff dates is distinct from the issue noted above regarding use of data before and after 1933.

---

*Readers interested in a more detailed description of the history and specifics of collecting and analyzing national mortality data are urged to consult *Vital Statistics—Special Reports* (1944, 1956); Klebba and Dolman (1975); Faust and Dolman (1963a, 1963b, 1965); Dunn and Shackley (1944); and Klebba (1979).

NUMBER OF DEATHS

The major problem in obtaining an accurate count of the numbers of death by suicide, homicide, and accidents can be divided into two groups: misclassification (errors on the local level) and national changes in classification over time (errors on the national level).

Misclassification

Misclassification refers to errors made by physicians, coroners, and the like, on the death certificates of those who die by suicide, homicide, or accidents. In other words, misclassification involves problems of data gathering at the most basic, local level—the cause of individual deaths before such data get to the federal government for national compilations. Difficulties arise because individual coroners and physicians or agencies may have biases or rules that distort the data. For example, a situation existed in one state for some time that a death could be listed as a suicide only if a suicide note were left—hence only the literate could be listed as dying by suicide! Such rules could both decrease numbers and bias the results with respect to age, sex, and racial groups. Insurance benefits or religious beliefs (e.g., for Roman Catholics, suicide may prevent a church funeral and burial) may lead a physician to label a suicide an accident. These kinds of errors in gathering data result in either underreporting or overreporting.

Underreporting may be intentional or unintentional. Intentional coverup of suicide by the family or the doctor may occur for a variety of reasons: insurance benefits, religious reasons, social stigma, guilt, malpractice problems, and so on. Unintentional underreporting may result when actual suicides are classified as accidents simply because there is not enough evidence to support a final determination of suicide. For example, mortality from some single-car crashes, overdoses, and poisoning that are actually suicides may be labeled "accidents" because they are unverifiable as suicides. Of the three forms of violent deaths, suicide and homicide rates are probably more susceptible to underreporting than are accident rates. Published rates of suicide may be at least two or three times lower than the actual number (Seiden, 1969; Toolan, 1962, 1975; Kramer et al., 1972).

Overreporting is probably most likely to occur with accidents: There would seem to be more intentional and unintentional motivation to classify actual suicides and homicides as accidents rather than vice versa. Overreporting of accidents may be intentional (covered-up suicides classified as accidents) or unintentional (suicides classified as accidents for lack of evidence or deaths of severely "accident-prone" individuals that represent suicide; this latter group, of course, begs the major question of the possible existence of self-destructive tendencies in accident-prone people and those who die in accidents.

Working with younger age groups poses special problems of misclassification. It may be easier to cover up suicides among the young and call them accidental deaths. Poisoning and other methods of suicide are more easily conceived of as accidents in those age groups than in older age groups. Second, parents' investment in children and adolescents often creates pressure to make diagnoses other than suicide in younger groups, there is great social stigma and guilt surrounding suicide among the young because of such issues as parents being seen as having been "bad parents." While one loses the patterns of the specific type of death with the violent death rate (i.e., the aggregate of suicide, homicide, and accident rates), one gains some advantages with this measure. First, there is no loss of any deaths through misclassification, since a suicide incorrectly classified as an accident is still accounted for in the aggregate. Second, the aggregate violent death rate gives an overall sense of the violent death patterns over time, a particularly important consideration if one conceptualizes violent death rates as reflecting self-destructive tendencies in populations and wants to compare violent death rates to other forms of mortality or variables such as the economy or population changes.

National Changes in Classification over Time

The International Lists of Diseases and Causes of Death (International Classification of Diseases [ICD]), used in this country since 1900, have been revised every 10 years so that the disease classification might be consistent with advances in medical science and changes in diagnostic practice. As shown in Table 3-1, there have now been nine revisions of the ICD (Klebba & Dolman, 1975;

Table 3-1. Years of Revision and Use of the International Classification of Diseases

Revision of the International Classification of Diseases	Year of conference by which adopted	Years in use in United States
1st	1900	1900–1909
2nd	1909	1910–1920
3rd	1920	1921–1929
4th	1929	1930–1938
5th	1938	1939–1948
6th	1948	1949–1957
7th	1955	1958–1967
8th	1965	1968–1978
9th	1975	1979 to date

National Center for Health Statistics, 1980). Each decennial revision has produced some break in the comparability of cause-of-death statistics. For example, say a man tries to kill himself by jumping out a window and survives but dies 2 weeks later of pneumonia, resulting from the internal injuries associated with the fall. One classification might list the death as a suicide, while a revision might list the death as due to pneumonia. Overall, the comparability of violent deaths from one revision to the next has been fairly good. Throughout the first 4 editions of the International Lists, suicide, homicide, and accidents are comparable, with the following exceptions: motor-vehicle accidents did not include auto collisions with trains and streetcars before 1926 (these collisions represented about one-third of all railroad and streetcar accidents), and the "accident" category (which later evolved into non-motor-vehicle- and motor-vehicle-accident categories) included food poisoning, executions, and motor-vehicle accidents before 1906 (when the motor-vehicle-accident category was started).

Quantitative evaluation of these changes was not possible. However, the changes created by the revision from the 4th to the 5th edition were quantified by the percent (%) change, and all revisions since then have been quantified by the comparability ratios. Comparability ratios are derived by coding the mortality data of the new revision by the criteria of the old revision. A comparability ratio of 1.00 indicates that the same number of deaths was assigned to a particular cause or combination of causes whether an earlier or later revision was used. A ratio of 1.00 does not necessarily mean that no changes were made, however, as the changes may have compensated for one another. A comparability ratio of less than 1.00 usually results from a decrease in the assignments of deaths to a cause in the later revision as compared to the earlier revision. A comparability ratio of more than 1.00 usually results from an increase in assignments of deaths to a cause in the later revision as compared to the earlier one (Klebba & Dolman, 1975). There are also separate comparability ratios for each 10-year age group (e.g., 15–24 years, 35–44 years); thus the total comparability ratio may be 1.00 for a specific cause of death with the 15- to 24-year-olds having a ratio of 1.03, the 35- to 44-year-olds 0.97, and so on. The changes in the various causes of violent death for the 4th revision and after are summarized in Table 3-2 (Dunn & Shackley, 1944; Faust & Dolman, 1963a, 1963b, 1965; Klebba & Dolman, 1975; National Center for Health Statistics, 1980).

As can be seen, for suicide, homicide, and motor-vehicle accidents the changes have been small. Non-motor-vehicle-accident categories show greater changes. These changes will be dealt with in more detail in the individual chapters on each kind of violent death.

Table 3-2. Changes in Causes of Violent Death since the 4th Revision of the International Classification of Diseases

Revision of the International Classification of Diseases	Suicide	Homicide	Motor-vehicle accidents	Non-motor-vehicle accidents	Accidents (total)
4th–5th[a]	0%	−1.8%	−0.1%	[c]	−0.3%
5th–6th[b]	1.00	1.00	1.00	0.93	0.95
6th–7th[b]	1.03	1.00	1.00	0.95	0.97
7th–8th[b]	0.9472	0.9969	0.9921	0.9250	0.9570
8th–9th[b]	1.0032	1.0057	1.0117	0.9841	0.9970

[a]Percentage change.

[b]Comparability ratio.

[c]Percentage change not available; non-motor-vehicle-accident category not used in these revisions.

Finally, mention should be made of a category begun in 1968 in the United States: (deaths due to) Injuries Undetermined Whether Accidentally or Purposely Inflicted (E980–E989). The initiation of the category may account to some extent for the comparability ratios for suicide, homicide, and accidents for the 7th–8th revision all being less than 1.00. For example, in 1975, 4,838 deaths were listed in E980–E989 (in the same year, it listed, 27,063 suicides; 21,310 homicides; 103,030 accidents). This category will also need to be considered in the aggregate violent death rate.

POPULATION

The population statistics used for the derivation of national mortality rates are based on the U.S. Census of the population conducted every ten years, and on the estimates of the population (for the years when no census is taken) which are based on the Census. Two specific issues regarding the population are noteworthy: First, beginning in 1933 the entire population in the United States was included in the mortality rates, whereas prior to 1933 only some states and cities were included; and second, that during World Wars I and II there were shifts of younger people overseas.

Prior to 1933, the population figures used by the federal government to derive national mortality statistics included only some of the states in the United States, as well as certain cities and metropolitan areas. This population aggregate, termed Death Registration States, was increased by additional reporting states until 1933 when all the states were included (with Alaska added in 1959 and Hawaii in 1960). The composition and admission order of the Death Registration States can be found in *Vital Statistics—Special Reports* (1956). Thus, prior to 1933 the data represent only a sample of the U.S. patterns, whereas from 1933 on the entire population is utilized. Therefore, in examining patterns of violent deaths in the United States, the data from 1933 to the present are emphasized rather than the more limited samples prior to 1933. In addition, from 1933 on any changes in mortality rates (as described in Section II) are statistically "significant" inasmuch as the data involve the entire population and not just samples.

The second population issue involves the location of the population used to derive rates. In this study, the focus is on deaths occurring within the United States—it seemed advisable to limit the study to a specific country and location, and usually the population overseas is relatively small. However, during World Wars I and II there were large population shifts overseas, particularly of young people, and those data need to be examined because of the large numbers involved.

Regarding the definitions of race, the category "white" includes, in addition to those reported as white, persons reported to be Mexican and Puerto Rican (Klebba, 1979). The categories "races other than white" and "all other" (combined as "nonwhite") consist of persons reported as Negro, American Indian, Chinese, Japanese; other numerically small racial groups; and persons of mixed white and other races (Klebba, 1979). The Bureau of Census reported that in 1976 about 28,424,000 of the 214,649,000 people in the United States (or 13.2%) belonged to "races other than white." Of these 28,424,000 people, about 24,763,000 (or 87.1%) were black (Klebba, 1979).

AGE-ADJUSTED RATES

The data in this book are frequently age-adjusted, which is a method of comparing mortality rates over time (or across cultures) while keeping the age structure of the population constant. For example, suppose one is interested in cancer rates and finds rather low cancer rates in the early years of the century and much higher rates near the end of the century. How can one determine whether or not this rise is "real" or due to an artifact, such as age? Inasmuch as cancer is known to manifest much higher rates in the older rather than younger age groups, it would be necessary to determine the age structure and shifts of the population under study. It is possible that the rise in cancer rates near the end of the century is based merely on the fact that there were relatively more old people in the population later in the century and relatively more young people earlier. The way out of this dilemma is to "age-adjust" mathematically, that is, to adjust the age structures of the populations being compared to a standard population. Only then can one tell whether or not a rise in mortality is "real" or due to a population shift that has simply increased the numbers of people who are at high risk of dying of the disease in question. Most of the national mortality data used in this book is in the age-adjusted form, and the graphs utilizing age-adjusted rates are so labeled. The national age-adjusted rates are almost invariably, by convention, adjusted to the standard of the 1940 U.S. population.

EPIDEMIOLOGY

with
Jay Sandlow

This section presents the epidemiology of violent deaths. From 1900 to 1980, non-motor-vehicle accidents have tended to have the highest mortality rates, followed by motor-vehicle accidents, suicide, and homicide, respectively. With respect to trends across time, most forms of violent deaths demonstrate increases in rates during the economic depressions of both the early 1930s and the late 1960s to mid-1970s, with decreases occurring around 1917–1920 (World War I) and during the early 1940s (World War II). Males have higher mortality rates than females for nearly every age group in every type of violent death. Nonwhites have tended to have higher rates than whites for homicide and non-motor-vehicle-accident rates; suicide rates have been higher for whites than nonwhites; and white and nonwhite rates have been similar for motor-vehicle-accident mortalities. Age patterns vary with the type of violent death: For suicide, rates for males increase with age, whereas women aged 34–65 are at highest risk; for homicide, 15- to 44-year-olds (especially 25–34 years) are at most risk; for motor-vehicle accidents, rates among 15- to 34-year-olds have recently been higher than for other age groups; and the youngest and oldest age groups have been at highest risk of dying by non-motor-vehicle accidents.

Ultimately, three major patterns emerge from the epidemiologic data. First, the data would seem to suggest that a certain proportion of the population is at risk of dying a violent death, but that the type of violent death is dependent on one's age, race, and sex (the "typological factor"). For example, whites are at much greater risk of dying by suicide, whereas nonwhites are much more likely to die by homicide; young people are more at risk of dying by

39

homicide, and older people by suicide, motor-vehicle accidents, and non-motor-vehicle accidents. In addition, race and age appear to determine the type of violent death from which one is most likely to die; sex seems to determine the degree of risk of dying from a particular type of violent death (e.g., females have lower rates than males for virtually every type of violent death at every age).

Second, neither age, race, or sex protects against the marked increases and decreases seen in the time trends for suicides, homicides, and accidents. The term "societal factor" will be used to account for these remarkably consistent peaks and valley in rates. The societal factor is probably a mixture of variables, the most prominent of which are the economy, war, and population shifts.

Third, within each specific type of violent death, the age patterns are usually similar, regardless of sex and race considerations (the "generation factor"). One exception to this is suicide: Male rates tend to increase with age, whereas female rates increase to a peak at 35–64 years and then decrease.

For each chapter in Section II, the graphed data are presented as follows: The 1st graph shows the time trends 1900–1980 for total rates and by race and sex; the 2nd presents the age-adjusted patterns; the 3rd demonstrates the age patterns; the 4th and 5th demonstrate the rates for males and females by age; the 6th and 7th graphs present white and nonwhite patterns by age; and the 8th through 11th show the rates for white males, white females, nonwhite males, and nonwhite females, respectively.

CHAPTER FOUR

SUICIDE

The trends and patterns in suicide are perhaps more familiar than those of any other cause of violent death. Many books and articles which describe the suicide trends from descriptive as well as etiologic perspectives (e.g., Durkheim, 1897; Dublin, 1963; etc.). However, one rarely finds time trends for the age, race, and sex variables of suicide rates in a single source, and rarer still are these data graphed, a method of presentation that seems more effectively to highlight well-known as well as obscure patterns.

Figures 4-1 and 4-2 show the mortality rates and age-adjusted mortality rates, respectively, for suicide throughout the 20th century in the United States. Several important patterns are apparent. Male rates are higher than female rates, with white males having by far the highest rates. Whites have higher suicide rates than nonwhites for both males and females. With respect to trends over time, suicide rates have shown two marked peaks: one in the early 1900s and one around 1930 corresponding to the Great Depression. There have been two marked decreases in rates: one around 1917–1920 and one about 1940–1945, corresponding to World War I and World War II, respectively. The suicide rates for both race and sex groups have been increasing since 1955 with a slight decrease in the late 1970s. Male rates increased slightly and then plateaued following the drop during World War II, whereas female rates did not show that increase and plateau prior to the recent increase.

Figure 4-3 presents the age patterns for suicide by sex and race. The rates have been averaged from 1900–1980 and plotted by 10-year age intervals. The rates for white males increase with age, while the 35- to 64-year-olds have the highest rates among white females; the nonwhite rates show patterns somewhat different from the white rates, peaking around 25–34 years and then tending to level off. The changes in age patterns over the century are seen in the figures below.

41

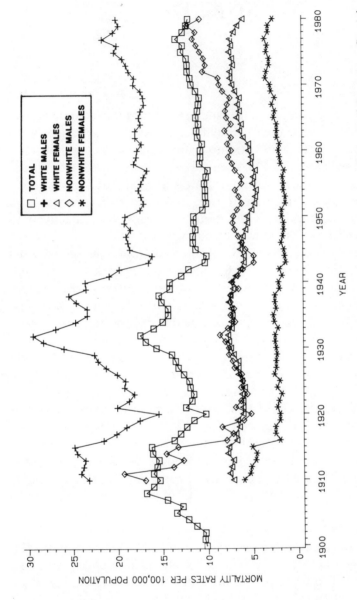

Figure 4-1. Suicide rates, by sex and race, United States, 1900–1980. *Sources of data: Vital Statistics—Special Reports* (1956) (for 1900–1953); *Grove and Hetzel* (1968) (for 1954–1960); *Vital Statistics of the United States* (1961–1978) (for 1961–1978); unpublished data, National Center for Health Statistics (for 1979 and 1980).

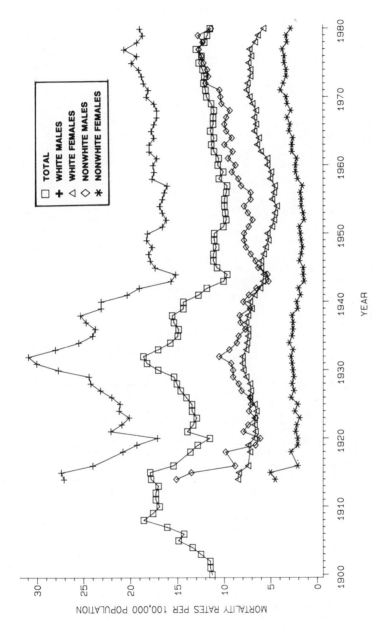

Figure 4-2. Age-adjusted suicide rates, by sex and race, United States, 1900–1980. *Sources of data: Vital Statistics— Special Reports* (1956) (for 1900–1953); Grove and Hetzel (1968) (for 1954–1960); unpublished data, National Center for Health Statistics (for 1961–1980).

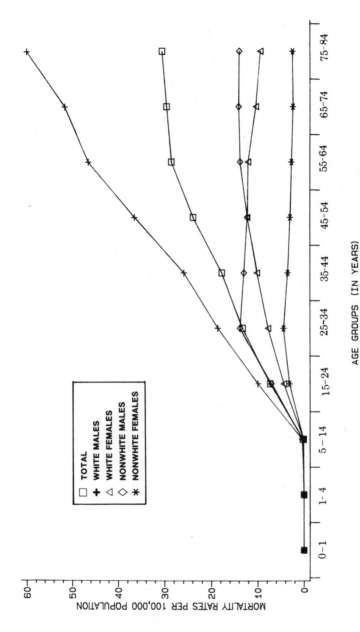

Figure 4-3. Age patterns of suicide rates, by sex and race, United States, 1900–1980. *Sources of data:* Same as Figure 4-1, and calculated as described in text of Chapter 4.

Figures 4-4 and 4-5 present the male and female suicide rates by age. The suicide rates for males are greater than females for all ages. In addition, the age patterns are different. For males, the suicide rates almost invariably increase with age, with children, preadolescents, and adolescents having the lowest rates and the oldest males the highest rates. While the younger females also have the lowest rates, it is women in the 35- to 64-year-old age group who have been consistently at highest risk for suicide. Interestingly, the male age pattern may be changing over the past 15–20 years: Rates for the older males have tended to decrease, whereas rates for young males have increased. It is possible that over the next few decades the rates for some of the younger groups will exceed those of the older ages, and for the first time in this century the pattern of male suicide rates invariably increasing with age will be altered. The female age pattern has remained rather constant across the century. Both male and female rates tend to show the major changes over time noted above for Figures 4-1 and 4-2: the peaks in the early 1900s and Depression, the decreases during World Wars I and II, and the recent increases. However, there are some differences between males and females in these changes across the century. First, the shifts in male rates were often of greater magnitude than female rates. And, second, the age patterns for females have remained more consistent over the past 20 years than for males: The recent increase in male rates has occurred because of the increase among the younger males and despite the decrease among older males. Females, on the other hand, show an increase from the mid-1950s to the mid-1970s in all age groups. It is interesting to note, as one studies the time trends by age, how (with the recent exception among males) the shifts in rates occur in virtually all age groups together. That is, age seems to make a difference with respect to the degree of risk of suicide, but age does not seem to be able to counteract the major shifts that occur, for example, in conjunction with World Wars I and II and the Depression of the 1930s.

Figures 4-6 and 4-7 show the suicide patterns by race and age. Two features in addition to the general patterns mentioned above are noteworthy. First, the suicide rates for whites can readily be seen to be greater than nonwhites for virtually all age groups with the exception of children and preadolescents. Second, the suicide rates for whites tend to increase with age (consistent with the patterns for males), whereas the younger nonwhite age groups (15–44

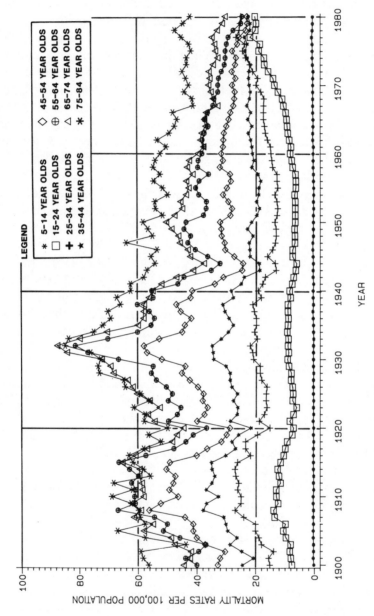

Figure 4-4. Suicide rates for males, by age, United States, 1900–1980. *Sources of data*: Same as Figure 4-1.

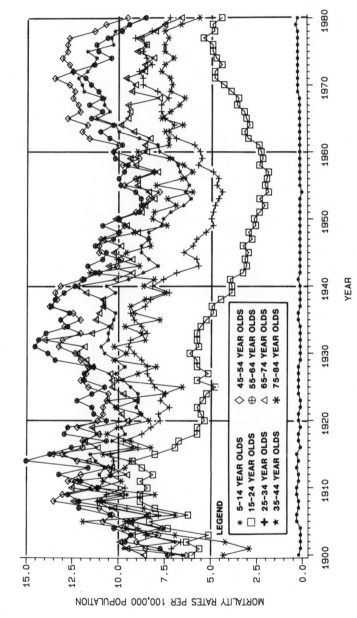

Figure 4-5. Suicide rates for females, by age, United States, 1900–1980. *Sources of data:* Same as Figure 4-1.

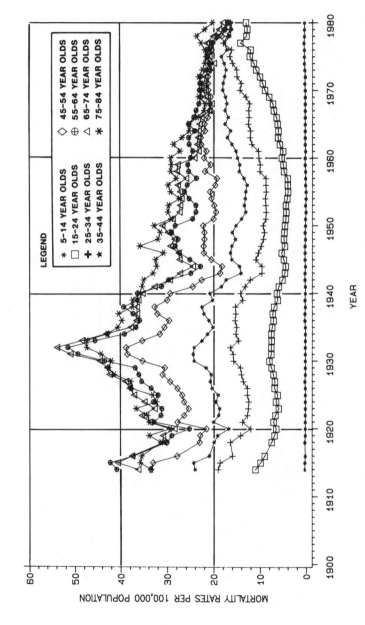

Figure 4-6. Suicide rates for whites, by age, United States, 1914–1980. *Sources of data*: Same as Figure 4-1.

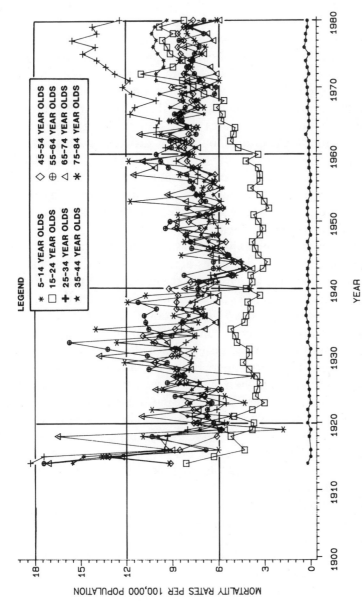

Figure 4-7. Suicide rates for nonwhites, by age, United States, 1914–1980. *Sources of data:* Same as Figure 4-1.

years) have recently increased and are currently higher than the older age groups.

Figures 4-8, 4-9, 4-10, and 4-11 provide a breakdown of suicide patterns across the century by age, race, and sex. The rates for white males show most markedly the characteristic increases and decreases found in suicide rates throughout the century. The almost invariable increase of rates with age is striking as well, although, as noted above, this may soon change as the older groups are recently showing a decrease and the younger age groups an increase. The white female rates show similar changes throughout the century for all age groups, but have a different age distribution, in which the 35- to 64-year-olds have the highest rates. Unlike the white males, however, the age distribution of the white females shows little sign of changing from the pattern of youngest and oldest age groups having the lower rates and the 35- to 64-year-olds being at greatest risk of suicide.

Suicide rates for nonwhite males (Figure 4-10) show the characteristic increases and decreases across the century, but they do not show age patterns as clearly as those for white males. Suicide risk seems much less based on age for nonwhite males than it is for other race and sex groups. Until recently, there has been some tendency toward lower rates among the young and highest rates among the old, but over the past two decades the rates among 15- to 34-year-olds have been increasing so that currently the 25- to 34-year-olds have the highest suicide rates among nonwhite males. It is also difficult to generalize the age patterns of nonwhite females (Figure 4-11). The very young (5–14 years) have consistently been at lowest risk, but the 15- to 54-year-olds (especially 25–34 years) have tended to be at highest risk. Thus the age groups at highest risk among nonwhite females tend to be somewhat younger than for white females.

Other variables associated with high risk of suicide have been dealt with in detail elsewhere and will not be repeated here. For example, seasonal and daily variation (suicides being most frequent in the spring and on Mondays), marital status (divorced and widowed persons are at greater risk than married persons), method (firearms are the commonest cause), and location (western states have the highest rates) have been discussed by many authors (Dublin, 1963; Massey, 1976; Seiden, 1969; Holinger, 1978; Klebba, 1979).

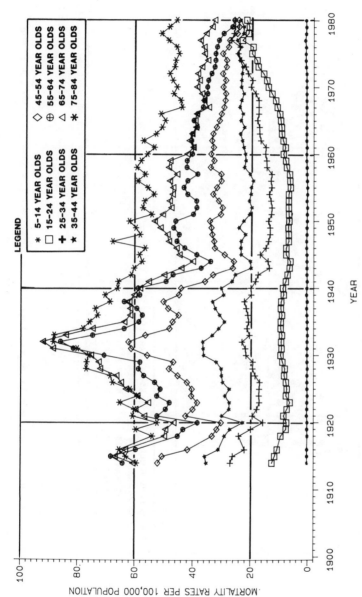

Figure 4-8. Suicide rates for white males, by age, United States, 1914–1980. *Sources of data*: Same as Figure 4-1.

51

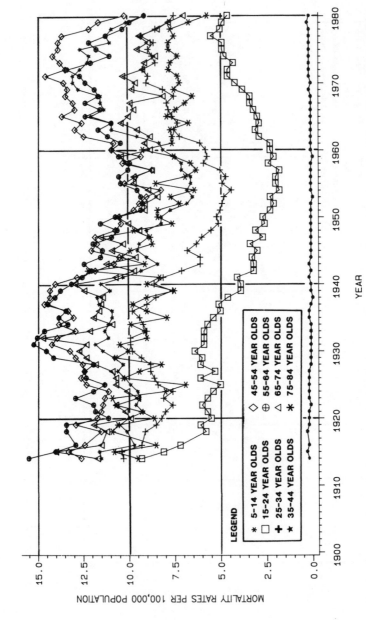

Figure 4-9. Suicide rates for white females, by age, United States, 1914–1980. *Sources of data:* Same as Figure 4-1.

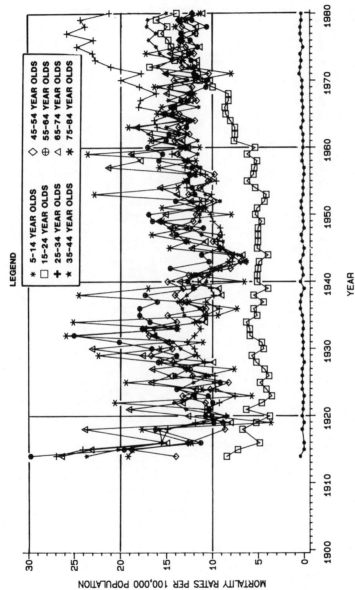

Figure 4-10. Suicide rates for nonwhite males, by age, United States, 1914–1980. *Sources of data:* Same as Figure 4-1.

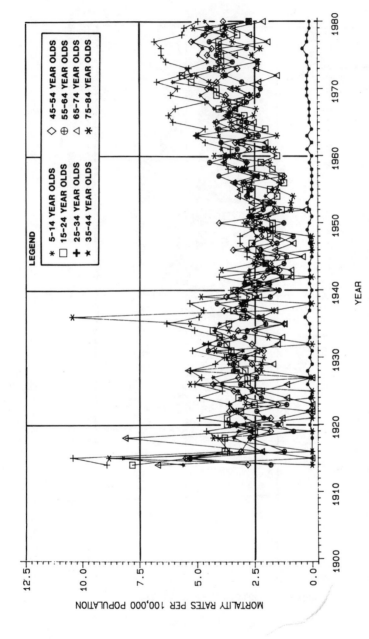

Figure 4-11. Suicide rates for nonwhite females, by age, United States, 1914–1980. *Sources of data:* Same as Figure 4-1.

54

Comparability

As noted in Chapter 3, on methodology, the comparability ratio for suicide was 1.03 for the 6th–7th revision of the ICD (1957–1958), 0.9472 for the 7th–8th (1967–1968) revision, and 1.0032 for the 8th–9th (1978–1979) revision. Thus it should be noted that a very slight increase in rates would have occurred in 1958 compared to 1957 on the basis of classification changes alone (comparability ratio 1.03). However, the continuing increase in suicide rates since 1968 is even more likely to be real rather than artifact inasmuch as there were slightly fewer deaths classified as suicides strictly on the basis of category changes (comparability ratio 0.9472 for the 7th–8th [1967–1968] revision, and 1.0032 for the 8th–9th [1978–1979] revision).

CHAPTER FIVE

HOMICIDE

Patterns of homicide rates tend to be less familiar than those of suicide, and one gets the impression from studying published bibliographies that less scientific attention is paid to homicide than to suicide. Homicide does account for fewer deaths than other types of violent deaths. Interestingly, though, in 1980, while there were more suicides than homicides, the difference was perhaps not as great as one might think: 26,869 suicides and 23,920 homicides, or approximately a 10% difference (Rosenberg, Gelles, Holinger, Zahn, Conn, Fajman, & Karlson, 1984). Regardless of how one perceives the numerical differences between suicide and homicide, homicide certainly occurs in numbers that make it a serious public health and psychiatric problem in this country.

The main issue to be kept in mind when examining homicide data is that the homicide rates refer only to those killed. These rates imply nothing, strictly speaking, about the killers. To go a step further, the homicide rates cannot be said to tell us much about the externally directed aggression in a population, because these rates give only the numbers killed per population. It thus seems an unwarranted jump in logic to begin making assumptions about the killers and degree of aggression in a population on the basis of national mortality rates for homicide.

The general time trends for homicide are shown in Figures 5-1 and 5-2 as well as in Chapter 9. After low rates early in the century, the homicide rates tended to peak during the Depression of the 1930s. There was a decrease during World War II, with a slight rise following it in the late 1940s and early 1950s. Somewhat lower rates prevailed during the end of the 1950s, and with the 1960s a steady increase began which has persisted to the present. This recent, long-term increase has resulted in homicide rates being higher than ever recorded in this country. Furthermore, this increase does not seem to be artifact based on federal classification changes: the only change of note, between the 7th and 8th revisions of the ICD

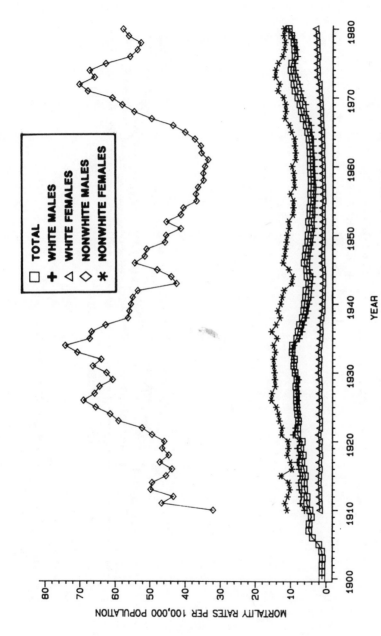

Figure 5-1. Homicide rates, by sex and race, United States, 1900–1980. *Sources of data: Vital Statistics—Special Reports* (1956) (for 1900–1953); Grove and Hetzel (1968) (for 1954–1960); *Vital Statistics of the United States* (1961–1978) (for 1961–1978); unpublished data, National Center for Health Statistics (for 1979 and 1980).

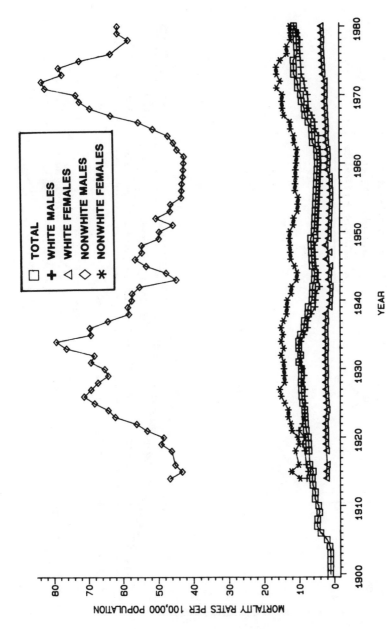

Figure 5-2. Age-adjusted homicide rates, by sex and race, United States, 1900–1980. *Sources of data: Vital Statistics— Special Reports* (1956) (for 1900–1953); Grove and Hetzel (1968) (for 1954–1960); unpublished data, National Center for Health Statistics (for 1961–1980).

(1967–1968), led to a very slight decrease in deaths classified as homicides (see below; comparability ratio of 0.9969). Therefore this increase in homicide rates over the past 20–25 years has occurred in spite of a classification change that would have led to slightly decreased homicide rates.

Thus the patterns for homicide tend to be similar to those of suicide over time. However, the race and sex patterns are somewhat different. As Figures 5-1 and 5-2 show, the rates for males of each racial category are higher than for females of the corresponding racial category, and the rates for nonwhites are greater than for whites. The nonwhite factor is apparently so great in increasing the risk of homicide that, unlike suicide, the nonwhite female homicide rates are greater than those for white males. Most striking, however, is the finding that homicide rates for nonwhite males are 5 to 10 times higher than for any other group.

Figure 5-3 demonstrates the age patterns for homicide in the United States, 1900–1980. The highest rates are found between the ages of 15 and 44 years, and particularly among 25- to 34-year-olds. These age patterns are seen in all sex and race groups, and have stayed constant throughout the century.

Figures 5-4 and 5-5 show homicide rates over time for males and females, respectively, by age. The general time trends noted above (e.g., the peaks in the early 1930s, the decreases during the early 1940s, and the recent increase) tend to prevail for both males and females for most age groups. Male rates are 2 to 5 times higher than female rates for all ages except infancy through young adolescence (0–14 years). In these younger groups, the male and female rates are rather similar. The large difference of male and female rates occurs from midadolescence through older adulthood. Both male and female homicide rates demonstrate similar age patterns: relatively high rates in infancy which decrease until they reach the lowest rates of the 5- to 14-year-olds. The highest homicide rates occur at ages 15–44, with decreasing rates into older adulthood. Homicide rates for males and females have been consistently highest for the 25- to 34-year-olds throughout the century (with the exception of the high female infant rates early in the century).

Figures 5-6 and 5-7 demonstrate the white and nonwhite homicide rates over time. The fluctuations over time noted for homicide in general are apparent in this data breakdown by race. The nonwhite rates are higher than white rates for every age group.

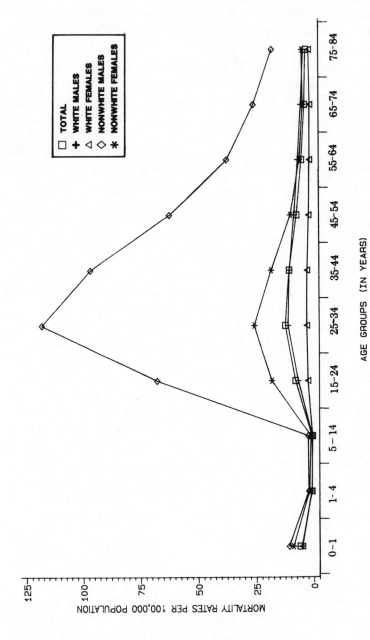

Figure 5-3. Age patterns of homicide rates, by sex and race, United States, 1900–1980. *Sources of data:* Same as Figure 5-1, and calculated as described in text of Chapter 4.

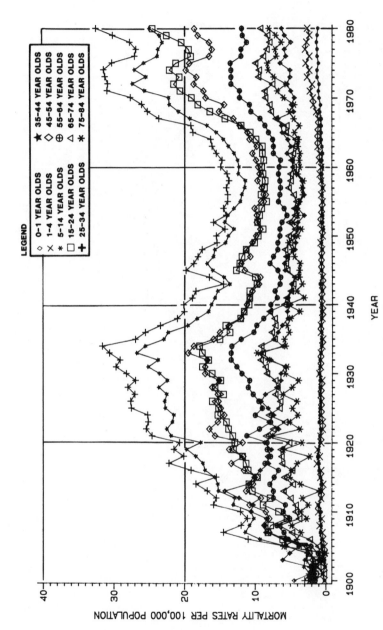

Figure 5-4. Homicide rates for males, by age, United States, 1900–1980. *Sources of data:* Same as Figure 5-1.

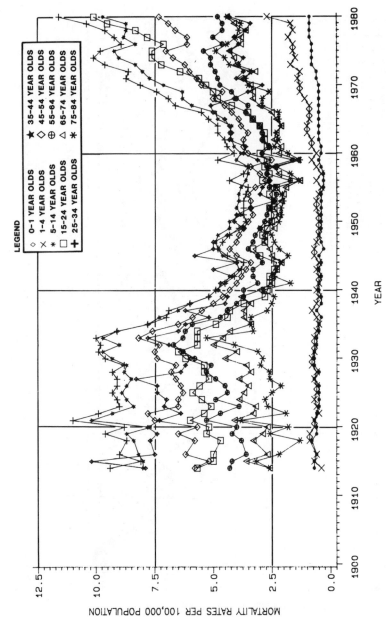

Figure 5-5. Homicide rates for females, by age, United States, 1900–1980. *Sources of data*: Same as Figure 5-1.

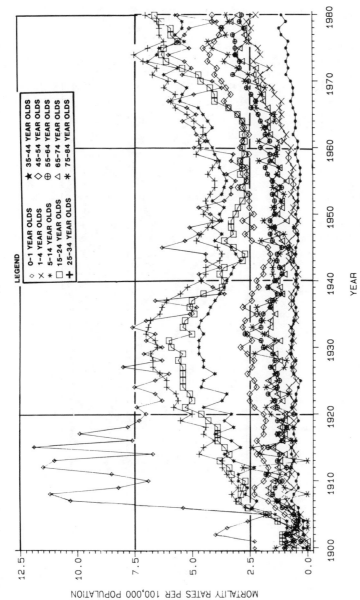

Figure 5-6. Homicide rates for whites, by age, United States, 1914–1980. *Sources of data:* Same as Figure 5-1.

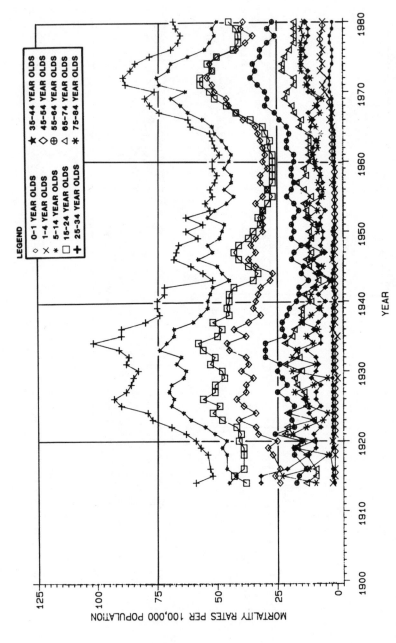

Figure 5-7. Homicide rates for nonwhites, by age, United States, 1914–1980. *Sources of data:* Same as Figure 5-1.

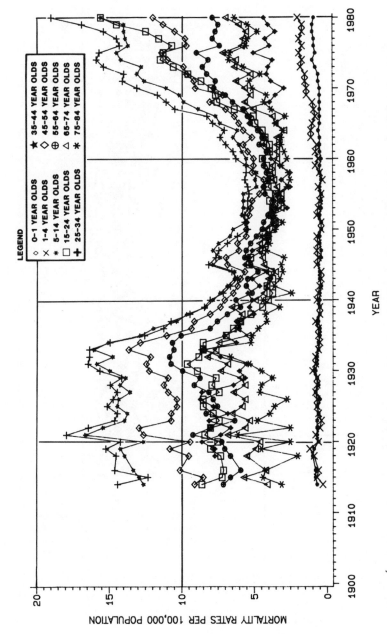

Figure 5-8. Homicide rates for white males, by age, United States, 1914–1980. *Sources of data:* Same as Figure 5-1.

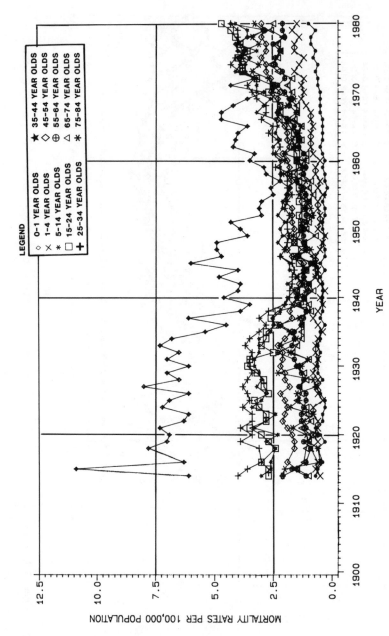

Figure 5-9. Homicide rates for white females, by age, United States, 1914–1980. *Sources of data:* Same as Figure 5-1.

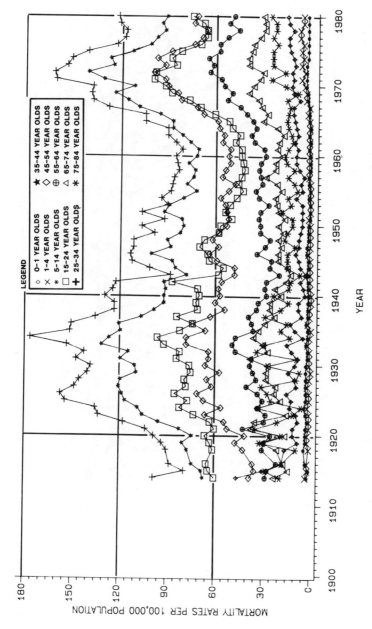

Figure 5-10. Homicide rates for nonwhite males, by age, United States, 1914–1980. *Sources of data:* Same as Figure 5-1.

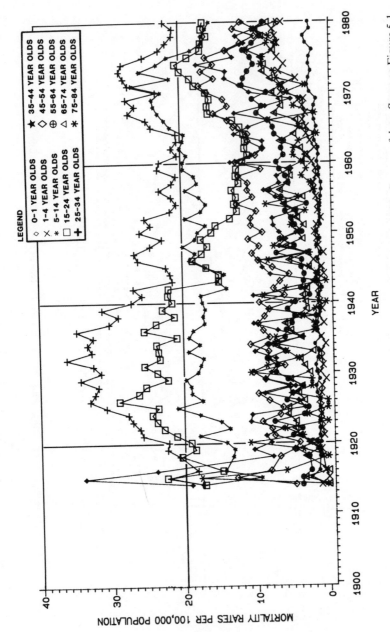

Figure 5-11. Homicide rates for nonwhite females, by age, United States, 1914–1980. *Sources of data:* Same as Figure 5-1.

·The nonwhite homicide rates range up to about 10 times higher than the white rates, with the degree of disparity dependent on the age group studied. The age patterns for whites and nonwhites are similar: relatively high rates in infancy with decreases until early adolescence; the highest homicide rates are found among 15- to 44-year-olds (with peaks at 25–34 years); and the rates then decrease with age.

Figures 5-8, 5-9, 5-10, and 5-11 present the white male, white female, nonwhite male, and nonwhite female homicide rates by age. Two points are particularly noteworthy. First, the general fluctuations for homicide rates (peaks in the early 1930s, decreases during the early 1940s, and recent increases) are apparent for virtually all ages of each race and sex combination. That is, the social forces operating to produce the fluctuations over time are able to make their pressure felt regardless of the age, race, or sex of the group being studied. Certain groups may be at greater risk of homicide on the basis of age, race, and sex variables, but those variables do not protect any groups from the social forces that create the fluctuations in homicide rates over time. Second, the age patterns for homicide tend to be similar regardless of sex or race variables. This finding contrasts with suicide rates, which show distinct differences between males and females in age patterns. A notable exception to the similar age patterns is found in the consistently high homicide rates among white female infants, who have been at greatest risk among white females of dying by homicide throughout most of this century.

Comparability

There are no major comparability problems for homicide rates over the century (see Chapter 3). The comparability ratios for the 7th–8th (1967–1968) and 8th–9th (1978–1979) revisions of the ICD were 0.9969 and 1.0057, respectively. Thus the recent rise in homicide rates is probably real and not artifact based on changes in federal classification. The 8th and 9th revision changes led only to very slight alterations: The 8th revision changes led to a slight decrease in the number of deaths classified as homicides (with the recent rise in homicide occurring despite this decrease by classification), and the 9th revision changes (involving only years 1979 and 1980 in this study) led to a very slight increase in the number of deaths classified as homicides.

CHAPTER SIX

MOTOR-VEHICLE ACCIDENTS

Recording of mortality rates for motor-vehicle accidents in the United States began in 1906. Figures 6-1 and 6-2 show the motor-vehicle-accident mortality rates and age-adjusted rates over time by race and sex. The fluctuations over time are rather clear and tend to be consistent for the different race and sex combinations. Motor-vehicle-accident rates increased to peaks during the Depression of the early 1930s, with another brief rise in the late 1930s. Motor-vehicle-accident rates then decreased during the early 1940s (World War II). They increased again throughout the late 1940s and 1950s, though not reaching the peaks of the 1930s. Finally, the rates show increases in the late 1960s which are nearly as high as those of the 1930s. These fluctuations over time occur· for all races and sexes, although they are not as prominent for females as they are for males. Male rates are consistently higher than female rates, by a ratio of about 3–4 : 1. White and nonwhite rates have been relatively similar, at least when compared with the large difference seen in suicide and homicide rates. For males, the· white rates tended to be a bit higher until the 1940s; since then, nonwhite male rates have been slightly but consistently higher until very recently when the rates have been more equal. For women, white female rates are slightly but consistently higher than nonwhite female rates. The age-adjusted and non-age-adjusted rates tend to be similar for the total rates and various race and sex combinations.

Figure 6-3 presents the age patterns of motor-vehicle-accidents for the United States averaged over 1900–1980. Unlike suicide and homicide, there have been shifts in the age patterns over the century. In particular, the rates of motor-vehicle-accident deaths tended to increase with age earlier in the century, whereas more recently, for most race and sex groups the rates among 15- to 34-year-olds have increased to levels as high or higher than the older ages.

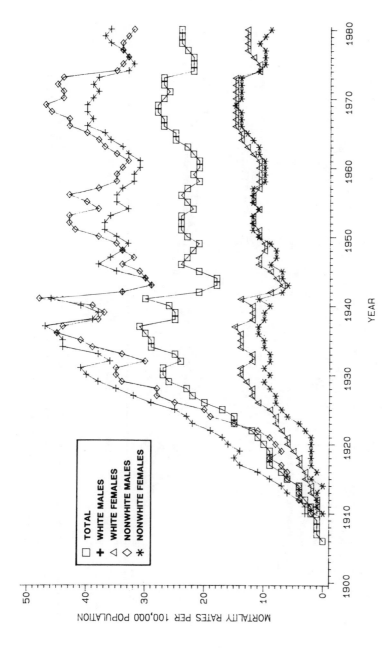

Figure 6-1. Motor-vehicle-accident mortality rates, by sex and race, United States, 1906–1980. *Sources of data: Vital Statistics—Special Reports* (1956) (for 1900–1953); Grove and Hetzel (1968) (for 1954–1960); *Vital Statistics of the United States* (1961–1978) (for 1961–1978); unpublished data, National Center for Health Statistics (for 1979 and 1980).

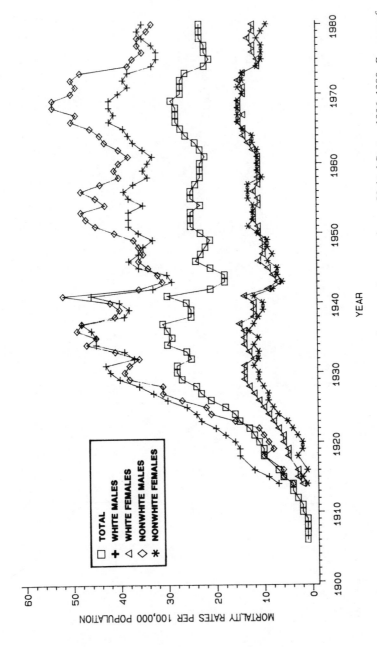

Figure 6-2. Age-adjusted motor-vehicle-accident mortality rates, by sex and race, United States, 1906–1980. *Sources of data: Vital Statistics—Special Reports* (1956) (for 1900–1953); Grove and Hetzel (1968) (for 1954–1960); unpublished data, National Center for Health Statistics (for 1961–1980).

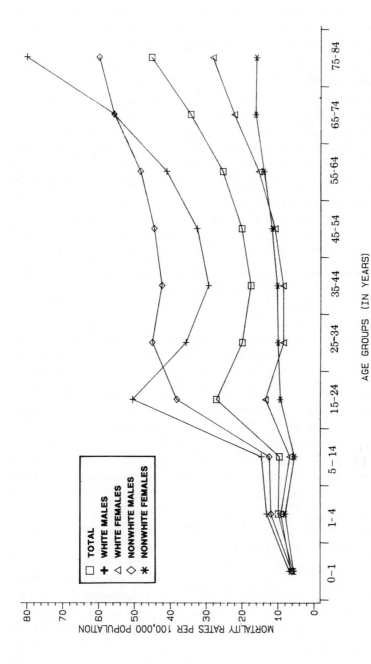

Figure 6-3. Age patterns of motor-vehicle-accident mortality rates, by sex and race, United States, 1906–1980. *Sources of data*: Same as Figure 6-1, and calculated as described in text of Chapter 4.

Figures 6-4 and 6-5 present the motor-vehicle-accident time trends by age for males and females, respectively. For males, initially the motor-vehicle-accident rates tended to increase with age, with the older age groups at greatest risk of dying from a motor-vehicle accident. However, gradually the rates for 15- to 24- and 25- to 34-year-olds increased relative to the other age groups. This increase has been particularly important among 15- to 24-year-old males: Motor-vehicle-accident rates are now higher for 15- to 24-year-olds than for any other age group. Female rates show similarities as well as differences with respect to the age patterns of males. Female rates are similar in that the oldest age groups are at greatest risk, the rates tend to increase with age (except for 15- to 24-year-olds), and the 15- to 24-year-old rates have increased relatively more over the past several decades so that they are nearly as high as the rates for the oldest age groups. The female rates differ from male rates in that, first, the 15- to 24-year-old rates only very recently surpassed the rates for the oldest age groups, and, second, the rates for the younger age groups (0–14 years) are more comparable to the rate of the middle age groups (e.g., 25–64) than is the case for males.

Figures 6-6 and 6-7 present the motor-vehicle-accident rates for whites and nonwhites, respectively. Early in the century, the rates for whites tended to increase with age. More recently, the rates for 15- to 24-year-olds, and, to a lesser extent, 25- to 34-year-olds have increased to assume greater prominence. Nonwhite rates are somewhat different. They tended to increase with age during the first part of the century, but later in the century the relative rise of the 15- to 34-year-olds is not so great as it is for whites. In addition, the recent rates for the several age groups between 15 and 84 years are rather similar, and they fluctuate in concert over time.

Figures 6-8, 6-9, 6-10, and 6-11 show the motor-vehicle-accident trends for white males, white females, nonwhite males, and nonwhite females, respectively. White males show time trends over the century similar to the total rates discussed earlier, with peaks in the early 1930s, late 1940s, and early 1950s and 1960s. Early in the century, rates tended to increase with age, but quickly the rates of the 15- to 24-year-old group began to increase relatively more than the other groups so that since the mid-1960s, 15- to 24-year-olds have had the highest rates. The rates for the oldest age groups have tended to decrease during the century, but recently the

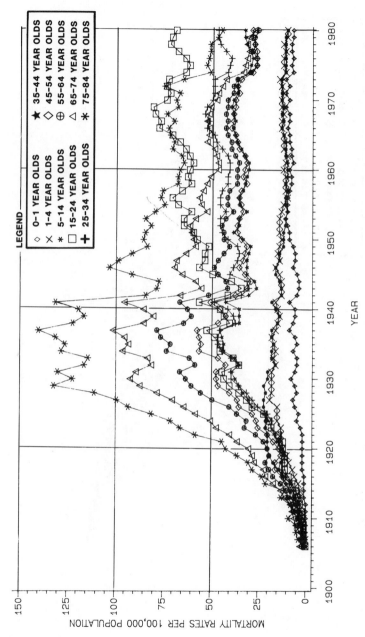

Figure 6-4. Motor-vehicle-accident mortality rates for males, by age, United States, 1906–1980. *Sources of data:* Same as Figure 6-1.

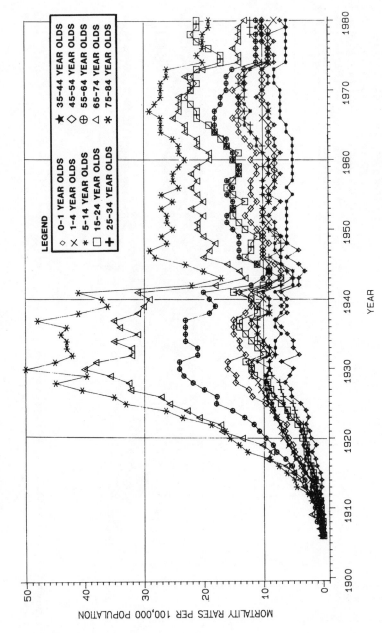

Figure 6-5. Motor-vehicle-accident mortality rates for females, by age, United States, 1906–1980. *Sources of data:* Same as Figure 6-1.

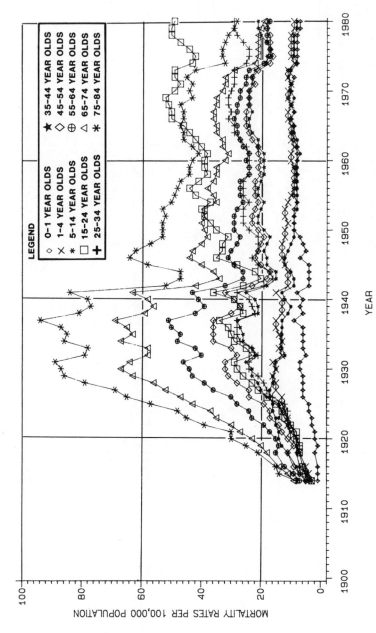

Figure 6-6. Motor-vehicle-accident mortality rates for whites, by age, United States, 1914–1980. *Sources of data:* Same as Figure 6-1.

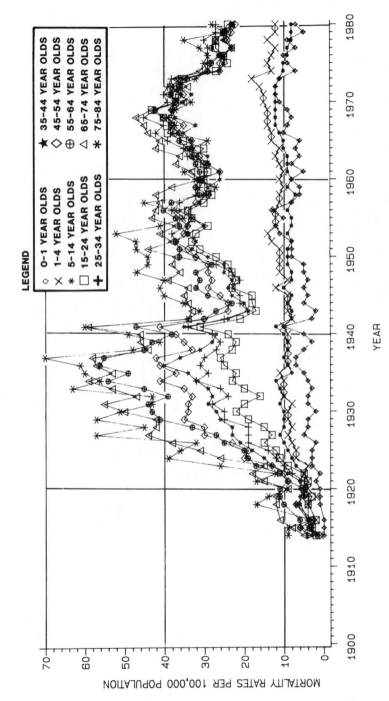

Figure 6-7. Motor-vehicle-accident mortality rates for nonwhites, by age, United States, 1914–1980. *Sources of data:* Same as Figure 6-1.

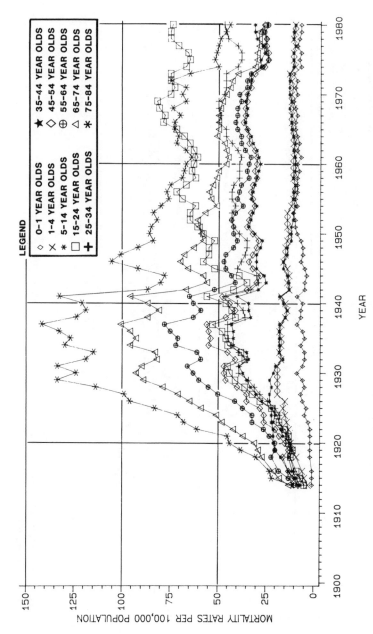

Figure 6-8. Motor-vehicle-accident mortality rates for white males, by age, United States, 1914–1980. *Sources of data:* Same as Figure 6-1.

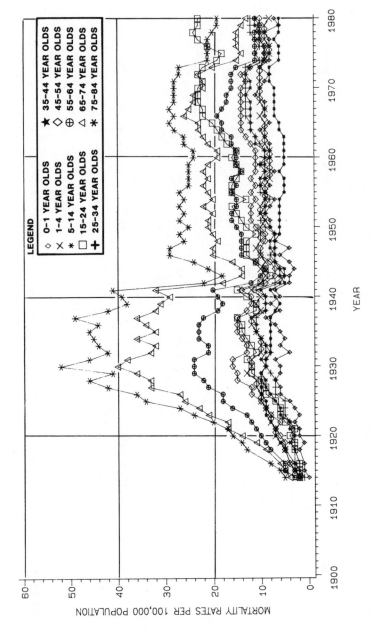

Figure 6-9. Motor-vehicle-accident mortality rates for white females, by age, United States, 1914–1980. *Sources of data:* Same as Figure 6-1.

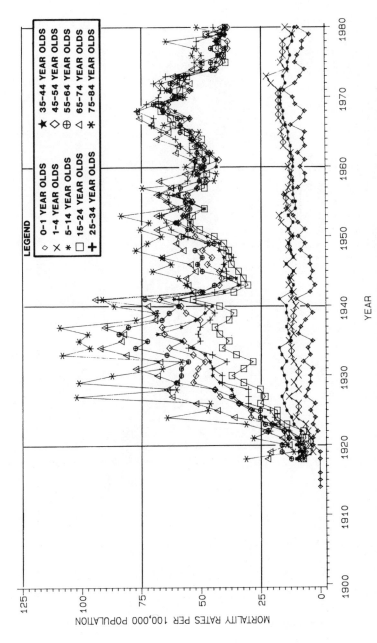

Figure 6-10. Motor-vehicle-accident mortality rates for nonwhite males, by age, United States, 1914–1980. *Sources of data:* Same as Figure 6-1.

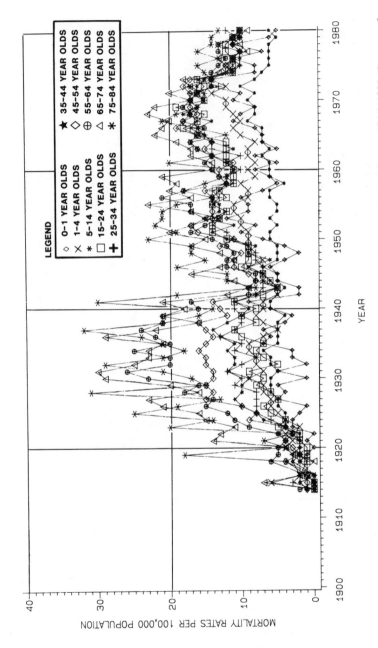

Figure 6-11. Motor-vehicle-accident mortality rates for nonwhite females, by age, United States, 1914–1980. *Sources of data*: Same as Figure 6-1.

75- to 84-year-olds have had the second highest rates. The 25- to 34-year-olds also increased relatively more than the other groups (excepting the 15- to 24-year-olds) and recently have had the third highest rates. The rates for white females follow patterns similar to those of white males, with two interesting differences: First, the relatively greater increase of the rates for the 15- to 24-year-old white females tended to occur later in the century; and, second, the rise of the rates for the 25- to 34-year-old white females has not been as great. Nonwhite male and female motor-vehicle-accident rates have had fluctuations similar to white males and females over the century, but the age patterns are somewhat different. As mentioned above, nonwhite rates for 15- to 84-year age groups are rather similar, unlike the corresponding rates for whites. For nonwhite males, the rates tended to increase with age except for the rates of 24- to 34-year-olds, which have increased most rapidly and now tend to have the highest rates; the nonwhite 15- to 24-year-old males do not show the rise characteristic of whites. Nonwhite female rates have tended to increase with age, except that the rates of 5- to 14-year-olds have been low.

Comparability

The comparability between revisions of the ICD for motor-vehicle-accidents has been excellent over the century (see Chapter 3). The comparability ratios of the 5th–6th (1948–1949), 6th–7th (1957–1958), 7th–8th (1967–1968), and 8th–9th (1978–1979) revisions were 1.00, 1.00, 0.9921, and 1.0117, respectively. Thus the fluctuations in motor-vehicle-accident rates due to changes in federal classification are virtually negligible.

CHAPTER SEVEN

ACCIDENTS EXCLUDING MOTOR-VEHICLE ACCIDENTS
(Non-Motor-Vehicle Accidents)

Accidents excluding motor-vehicle accidents, or non-motor-vehicle accidents, present somewhat different problems and patterns than the other forms of violent death. There has been a rather gradual decline of non-motor-vehicle accidents over the century, a pattern somewhat different from suicides, homicides, and motor-vehicle accidents which are characterized by more fluctuations. In addition, while non-motor-vehicle accidents have some shifts in common with the other forms of violent deaths, they show other changes that are quite different. Finally, the comparability for non-motor-vehicle accidents has not been as good over the past 30 years as it has been for suicides, homicides, and motor-vehicle accidents. The comparability ratios for the 5th–6th (1948–1949), 6th–7th (1957–1958), 7th–8th (1967–1968), and 8th–9th (1978–1979) revisions of the ICD have been 0.93, 0.95, 0.9250, and 0.9841, respectively. Thus, at least over the past 30 years, some of the gradual decline in non-motor-vehicle-accident rates is due to changes in federal classification.

Figures 7-1 and 7-2 present the non-age-adjusted and age-adjusted mortality rates, respectively, for non-motor-vehicle accidents. Non-motor-vehicle accidents have tended to decrease over the century, with some leveling off over the past 15–20 years. Non-motor-vehicle accidents have three fluctuations characteristic of the other forms of violent death: first, decreases during World War I; second, increases during the early 1930s; and, third, a recent leveling-off of rates, which is in reality an increase in rates (this "real" increase has been reduced by the artifact of federal classification changes and shows up graphically as a "leveling-off" consistent with the increases, beginning about 1960, in the other forms of violent death). In addition, non-motor-vehicle-accident rates show

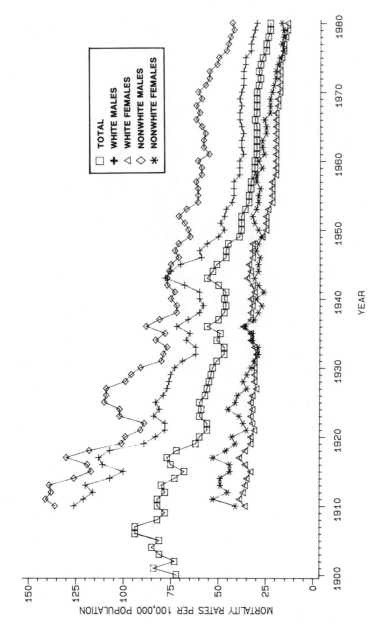

Figure 7-1. Non-motor-vehicle-accident mortality rates, by sex and race, United States, 1900–1980. *Sources of data: Vital Statistics—Special Reports* (1956) (for 1900–1953); Grove and Hetzel (1968) (for 1954–1960); *Vital Statistics of the United States* (1961–1978) (for 1961–1978); unpublished data, National Center for Health Statistics (for 1979 and 1980).

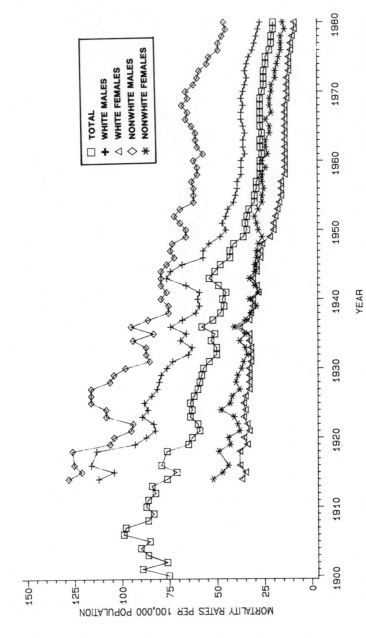

Figure 7-2. Age-adjusted non-motor-vehicle-accident mortality rates, by sex and race, United States, 1900–1980. *Sources of data: Vital Statistics—Special Reports* (1956) (for 1900–1953); Grove and Hetzel (1968) (for 1954–1960); unpublished data, National Center for Health Statistics (for 1961–1980).

increases around 1910 similar to those of suicide. However, the increase in non-motor-vehicle accidents in the early 1940s during World War II is opposite to the pattern found in the other forms of violent death. (The increase in non-motor-vehicle accidents occurring during the early 1940s was due primarily to an increase in air transport deaths within U.S. borders; *Vital Statistics—Special Reports*, 1946.) As Figures 7-1 and 7-2 demonstrate, male rates are higher than female rates, and nonwhite rates tend to be higher than white rates. Nonwhite males have the highest non-motor-vehicle-accident rates, and white females have the lowest.

Figure 7-3 shows the age patterns for non-motor-vehicle accidents from 1900–1980. The rates tend to be highest among the youngest and oldest age groups. This pattern has been consistent throughout the century and is seen in all race and sex groups.

Figures 7-4 and 7-5 present the non-motor-vehicle-accident patterns for males and females, respectively. Male and female rates both tend to follow the general time trends described above for accidents excluding motor-vehicle accidents, and male rates have been roughly 2 to 6 times higher than female rates throughout the century. One major exception to the latter statement is the finding that females aged 75–84 have had rates as high or higher than any other age groups, male or female, throughout most of the century. The age patterns for males and females are similar: The oldest and youngest are at greatest risk of dying in a non-motor-vehicle accident. The rates tend to increase with age beginning with the 5- to 14-year age group. Both male and female infants (0–1 year old) have had relatively high rates, with only the oldest age groups being at greater risk.

The non-motor-vehicle-accident rates for whites and non-whites are presented in Figures 7-6 and 7-7, respectively. The rates for both whites and nonwhites tend to follow the general time trends presented above. The age pattern is consistent with that of males and females (oldest and youngest at greatest risk), with one interesting exception: For much of the century, infants (0–1 year) have had the highest rate among nonwhites, greater even than the oldest age groups.

Figures 7-8, 7-9, 7-10, and 7-11 present the non-motor-vehicle-accident rates for white males, white females, nonwhite males, and nonwhite females by 10-year age intervals, respectively. For white males and white females, the rates show the general time trend and

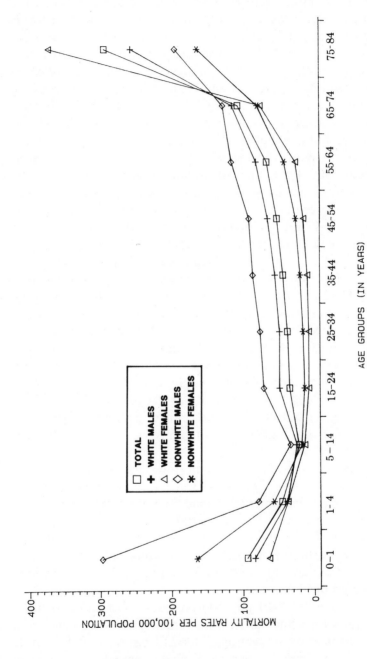

Figure 7-3. Age patterns of non-motor-vehicle-accident mortality rates, by sex and race, United States, 1900–1980. *Sources of data:* Same as Figure 7-1, and calculated as described in text of Chapter 4.

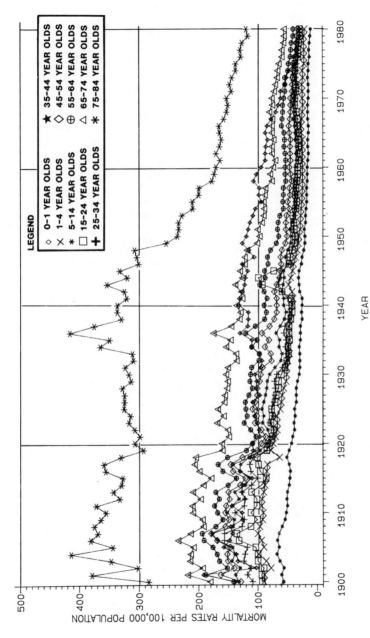

Figure 7-4a. Non-motor-vehicle-accident mortality rates for males, by age, United States, 1900–1980. *Sources of data:* Same as Figure 7-1.

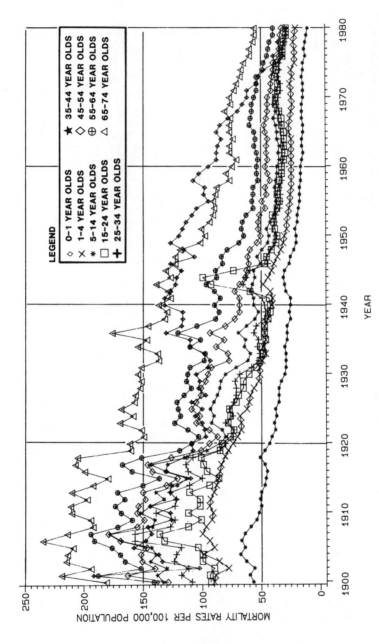

Figure 7-4b. Non-motor-vehicle-accident mortality rates for males, by age (under age 75), United States, 1900–1980. *Sources of data*: Same as Figure 7-1.

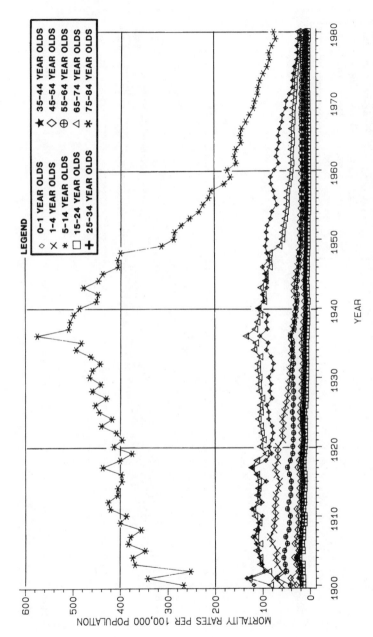

Figure 7-5a. Non-motor-vehicle-accident mortality rates for females, by age, United States, 1900–1980. *Sources of data:* Same as Figure 7-1.

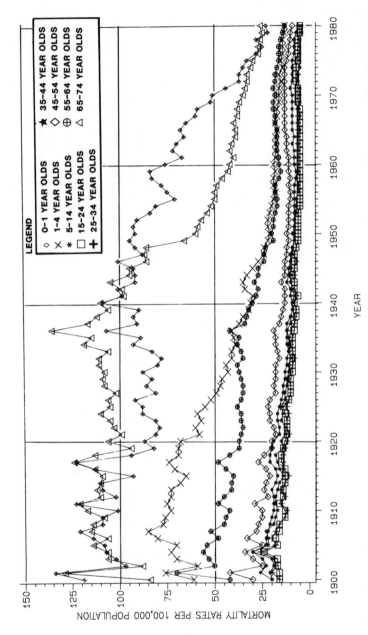

Figure 7-5b. Non-motor-vehicle-accident mortality rates for females, by age (under age 75), United States, 1900–1980. *Sources of data*: Same as Figure 7-1.

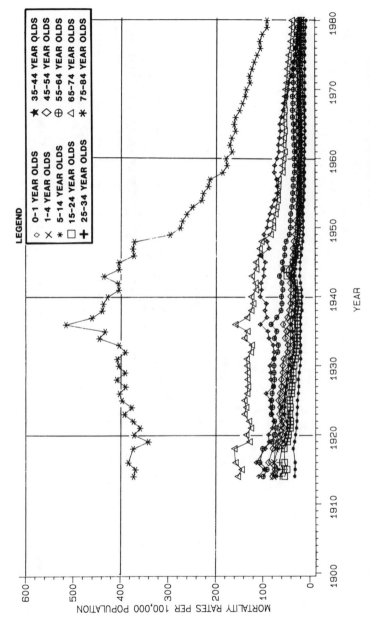

Figure 7-6a. Non-motor-vehicle-accident mortality rates for whites, by age, United States, 1914–1980. *Sources of data:* Same as Figure 7-1.

93

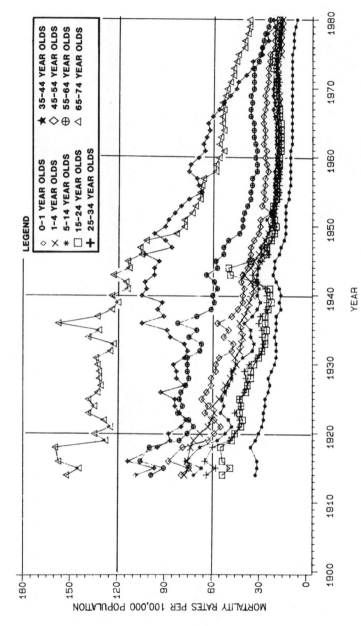

Figure 7-6b. Non-motor-vehicle-accident mortality rates for whites, by age (under age 75), United States, 1914–1980. *Sources of data:* Same as Figure 7-1.

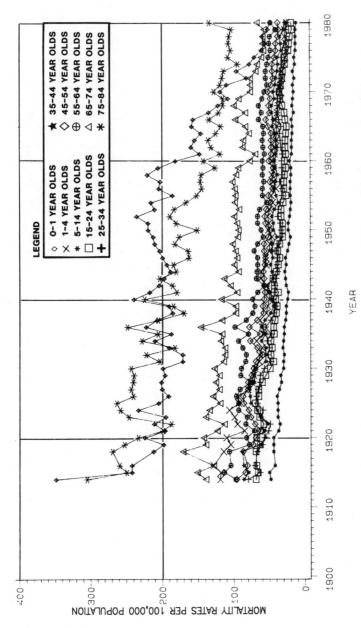

Figure 7-7. Non-motor-vehicle-accident mortality rates for nonwhites, by age, United States, 1914–1980. *Sources of data:* Same as Figure 7-1.

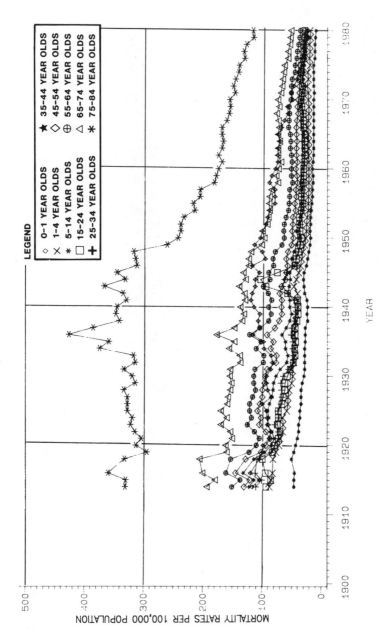

Figure 7-8a. Non-motor-vehicle-accident mortality rates for white males, by age, United States, 1914–1980. *Sources of data:* Same as Figure 7-1.

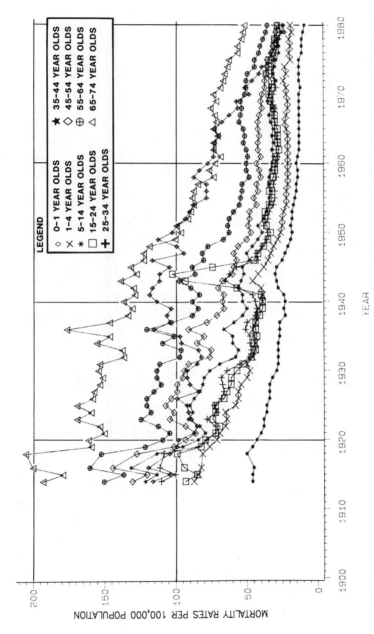

Figure 7-8b. Non-motor-vehicle-accident mortality rates for white males, by age (under age 75), United States, 1914–1980. *Sources of data*: Same as Figure 7-1.

97

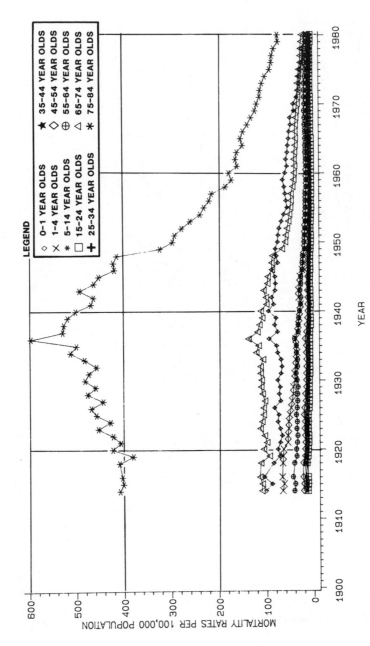

Figure 7-9a. Non-motor-vehicle-accident mortality rates for white females, by age, United States, 1914–1980. *Sources of data*: Same as Figure 7-1.

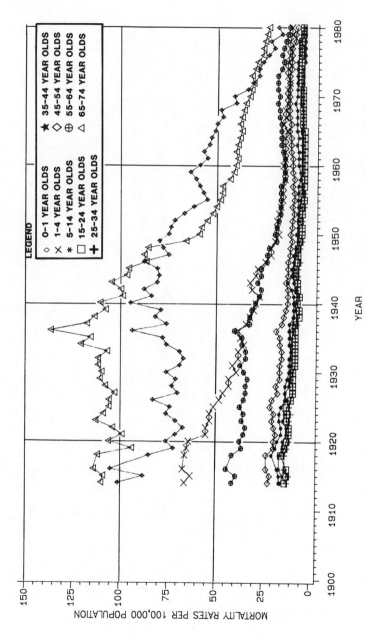

Figure 7-9b. Non-motor-vehicle-accident mortality rates for white females, by age (under age 75), United States, 1914–1980. *Sources of data:* Same as Figure 7-1.

99

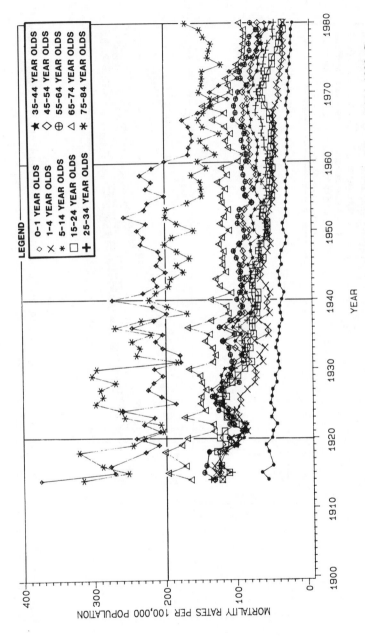

Figure 7-10. Non-motor-vehicle-accident mortality rates for nonwhite males, by age, United States, 1914–1980. *Sources of data*: Same as Figure 7-1.

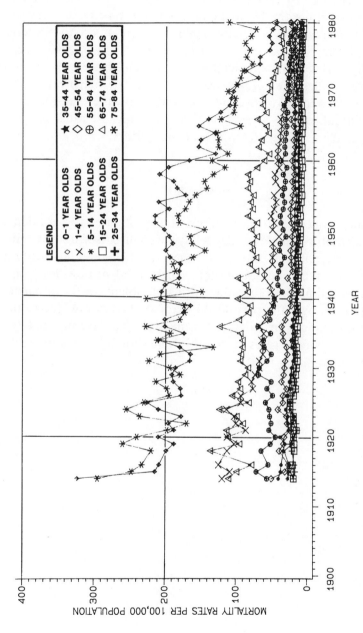

Figure 7-11. Non-motor-vehicle-accident mortality rates for nonwhite females, by age, United States, 1914–1980. *Sources of data:* Same as Figure 7-1.

age patterns described above, with one small exception: For white females, the 5- to 14-year-olds have had higher non-motor-vehicle-accident rates than the 15- to 24-year-olds for most of the century. Nonwhite males and nonwhite females also manifest the general time trends and age patterns described above, but with two exceptions: First, as seen in white females, for most of the century among nonwhite females, the 5- to 14-year-olds have had higher rates than the 15- to 24-year-olds. Second, for both nonwhite males and females, the infants (0–1 year) have had the highest rates of non-motor-vehicle accidents for much of the century.

Comparability

The major issues regarding comparability of rates for accidents excluding motor-vehicle accidents have been discussed at the beginning of this chapter and in Chapter 3. Federal classification changes have rendered non-motor-vehicle-accident rates less comparable over time than the other forms of violent death. In particular, the rates over the past 30–40 years are falsely low due to the artifact of changes in federal classification. This means that the "leveling-off" of the rates during this time should be seen in reality as an increase.

CHAPTER EIGHT

TOTAL ACCIDENTS

Total accidents will be discussed only briefly inasmuch as their components (motor-vehicle accidents and non-motor-vehicle accidents) have already been dealt with in detail. The patterns for total accidents are somewhat more difficult to describe than the other causes of violent death. Figures 8-1 and 8-2 show the mortality rates and age-adjusted rates, respectively, for accidents (total) by race and sex. Rates for males are 2 to 3 times higher than for females, and nonwhite rates tend to be slightly higher than white rates. The time trends across the century show a general decrease, although marked fluctuations exist. The total mortality rates for accidents (total) show increases prior to 1910, a decrease around World War I (from about 1918–1922), a gradual increase (except for a 2-year decrease in 1932 and 1933) during the Depression in the late 1920s and early 1930s, and a general decrease until the increases of the 1960s. The time trends by race and sex tend to be similar for those noted above for the total mortality rates for accidents (total), but there are some exceptions. For example, the rates for white males show some increase in accident rates during the early 1940s. Also, nonwhite rates, both male and female, show a greater increase in accident rates in the early 1940s than do the rates for whites.

Figure 8-3 presents the age patterns for accidents (total), averaged over the years 1900–1980. The patterns have tended to change over the century. For white males, the youngest and oldest age groups had the highest rates early in the century, whereas most recently 15- to 24-year-olds have had rates higher than any age except 75- to 84-year-olds. Age patterns for nonwhite males and white females tend to be similar to those of white males, although the recent rise in rates among 15- to 24-year-olds is less pronounced. For nonwhite females, the youngest and oldest age groups have had the highest rates rather consistently throughout the century. Thus, for accidents (total), the age patterns not

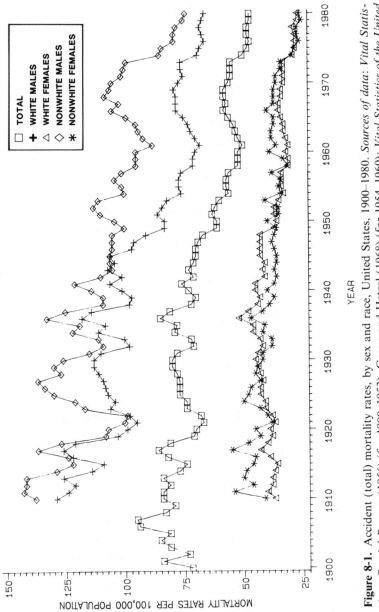

Figure 8-1. Accident (total) mortality rates, by sex and race, United States, 1900–1980. *Sources of data: Vital Statistics—Special Reports* (1956) (for 1900–1953); Grove and Hetzel (1968) (for 1954–1960); *Vital Statistics of the United States* (1961–1978) (for 1961–1978); unpublished data, National Center for Health Statistics (for 1979 and 1980). Accident (total) mortality rates calculated by using motor-vehicle-accident mortality rates and non-motor-vehicle-accident mortality rates from the above sources.

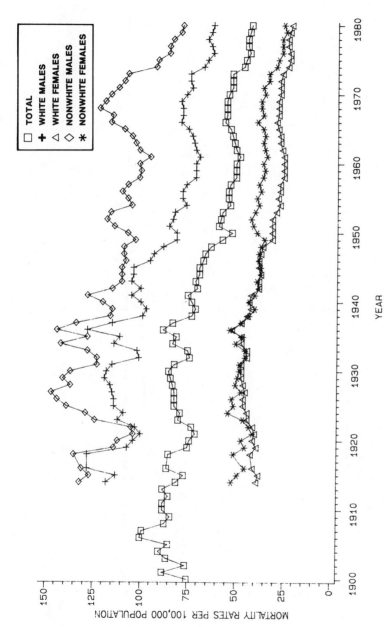

Figure 8-2. Age-adjusted accident (total) mortality rates, by sex and race, United States, 1900–1980. *Sources of data: Vital Statistics—Special Reports* (1956) (for 1900–1953); Grove and Hetzel (1968) (for 1954–1960); unpublished data, National Center for Health Statistics (for 1961–1980). Age-adjusted accident (total) mortality rates calculated by using age-adjusted motor-vehicle-accident mortality rates and age-adjusted non-motor-vehicle-accident mortality rates from the above sources.

105

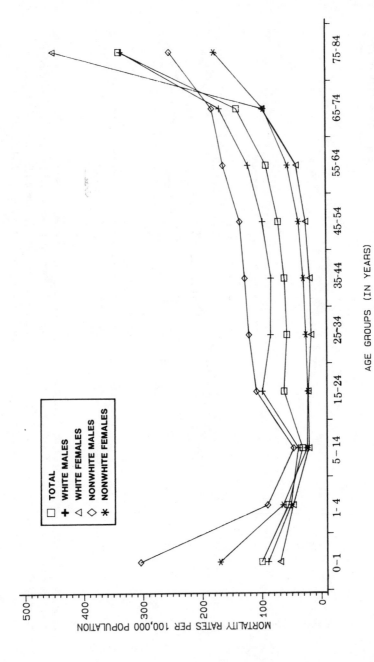

Figure 8-3. Age patterns of accident (total) mortality rates, by sex and race, United States, 1900–1980. *Sources of data:* Same as Figure 8-1, and calculated as described in text of Chapter 4.

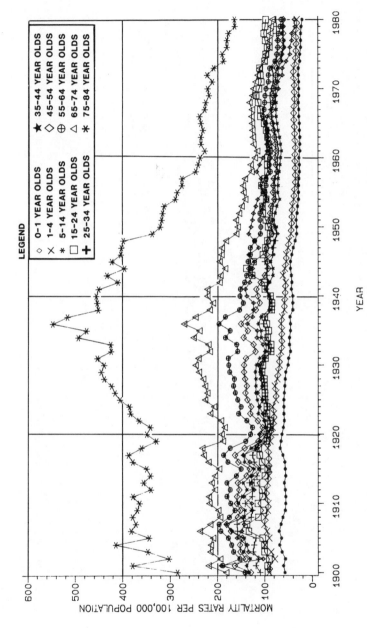

Figure 8-4a. Accident (total) mortality rates for males, by age, United States, 1900–1980. *Sources of data:* Same as Figure 8-1.

107

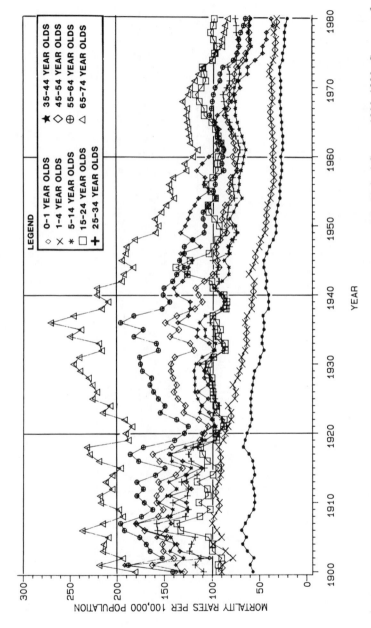

Figure 8-4b. Accident (total) mortality rates for males, by age (under age 75), United States, 1900–1980. *Sources of data*: Same as Figure 8-1.

108

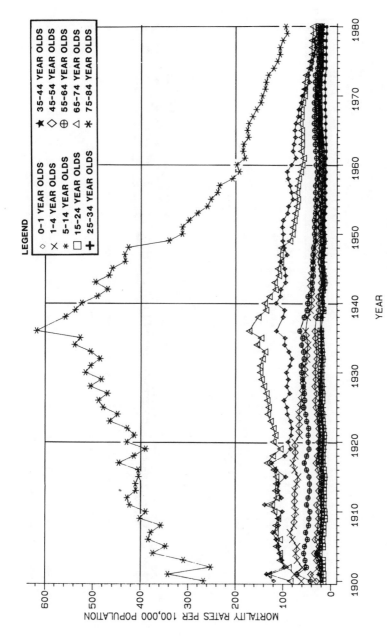

Figure 8-5a. Accident (total) mortality rates for females, by age, United States, 1900–1980. *Sources of data:* Same as Figure 8-1.

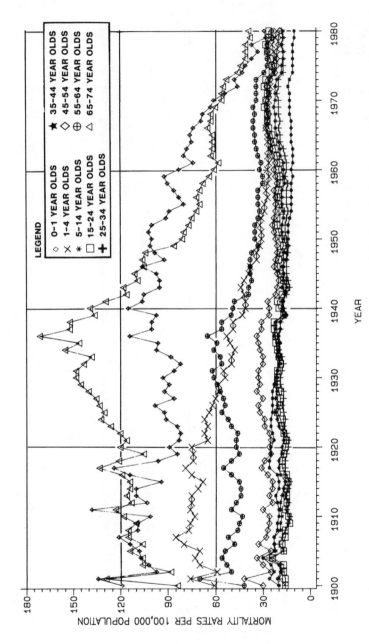

Figure 8-5b. Accident (total) mortality rates for females, by age (under age 75), United States, 1900–1980. *Sources of data*: Same as Figure 8-1.

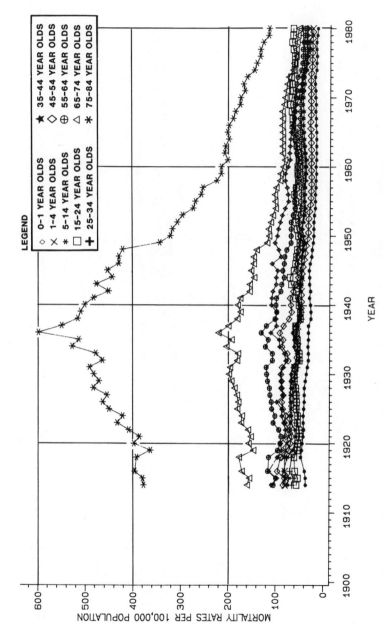

Figure 8-6a. Accident (total) mortality rates for whites, by age, United States, 1914–1980. *Sources of data:* Same as Figure 8-1.

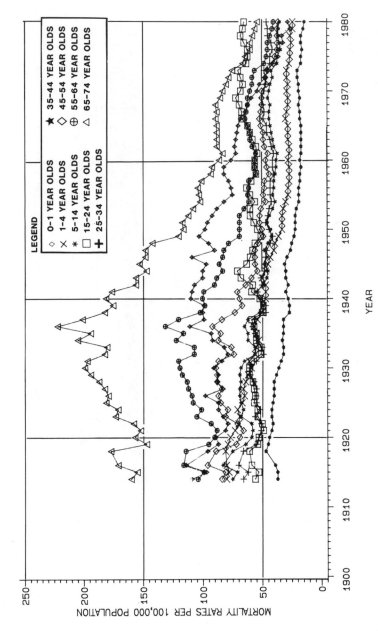

Figure 8-6b. Accident (total) mortality rates for whites, by age (under age 75). United States, 1914–1980. *Sources of data:* Same as Figure 8-1.

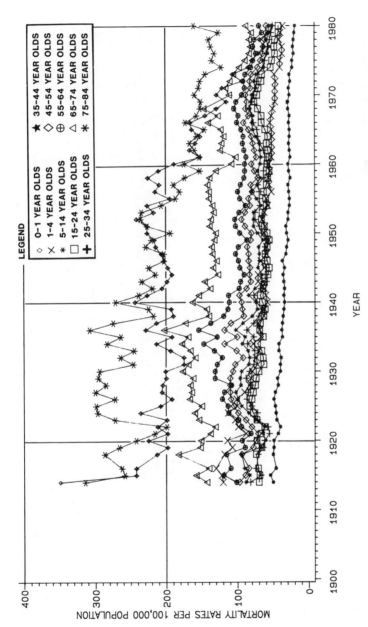

Figure 8-7. Accident (total) mortality rates for nonwhites, by age, United States, 1914–1980. *Sources of data:* Same as Figure 8-1.

113

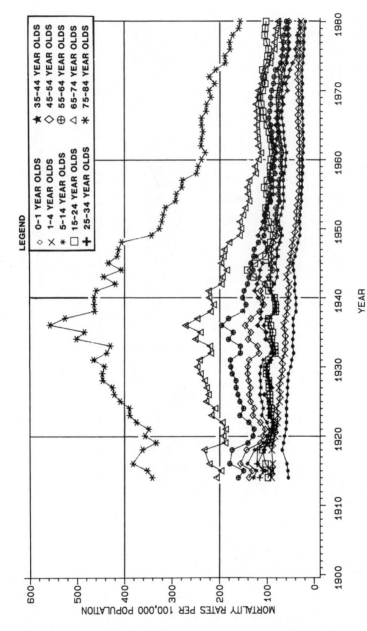

Figure 8-8a. Accident (total) mortality rates for white males, by age, United States, 1914–1980. *Sources of data:* Same as Figure 8-1.

114

116

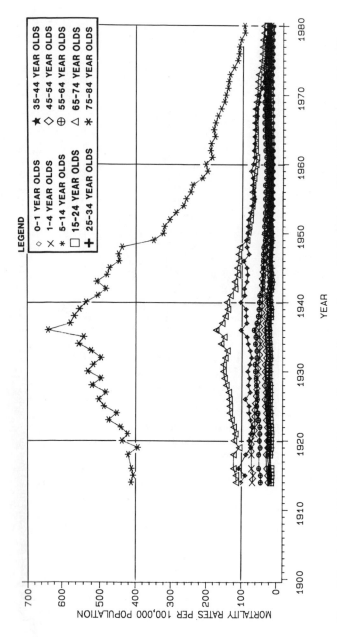

Figure 8-9a. Accident (total) mortality rates for white females, by age, United States, 1914–1980. *Sources of data:* Same as Figure 8-1.

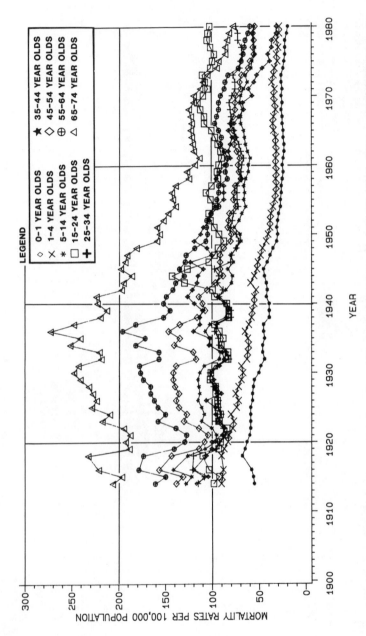

Figure 8-8b. Accident (total) mortality rates for white males, by age (under age 75), United States, 1914–1980. *Sources*

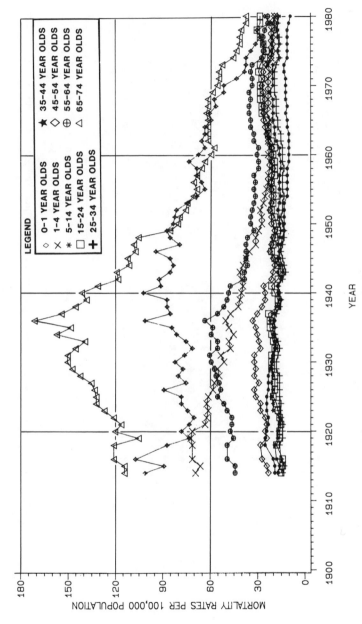

Figure 8-9b. Accident (total) mortality rates for white females, by age (under age 75), United States, 1914–1980. *Sources of data*: Same as Figure 8-1.

117

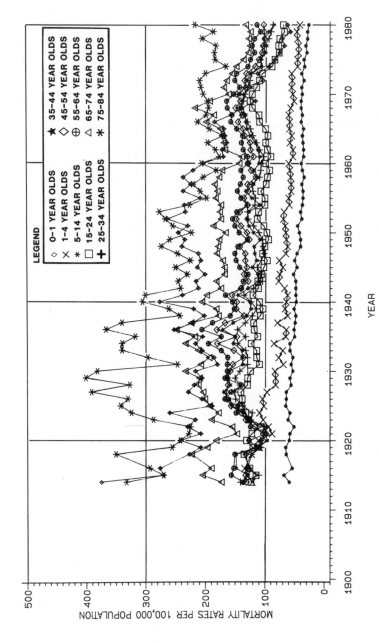

Figure 8-10. Accident (total) mortality rates for nonwhite males, by age, United States, 1914–1980. *Sources of data: Same as Figure 8-1.*

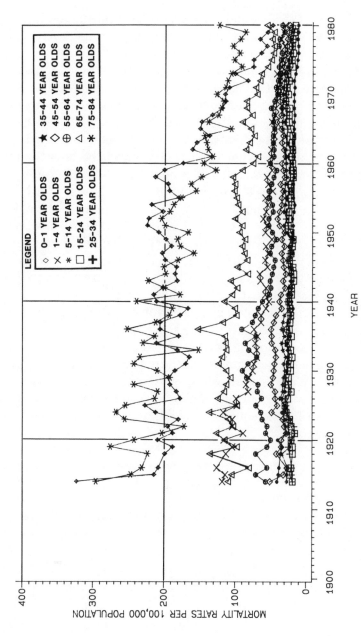

Figure 8-11. Accident (total) mortality rates for nonwhite females, by age, United States, 1914–1980. *Sources of data:* Same as Figure 8-1.

only shift throughout the century but differ depending on race and sex.

Figures 8-4, 8-5, 8-6, and 8-7 present the accident (total) rates by age for males, females, whites, and nonwhites, respectively. Figures 8-8, 8-9, 8-10, and 8-11 present the accident (total) rates by age for white males, white females, nonwhite males, and nonwhite females, respectively. The age patterns take two somewhat similar forms, as shown by the male and female rates. Figure 8-4 shows the age patterns for males: Throughout the early part of the century, the older and youngest (infants, i.e., 0–1 year) age groups had the highest rates; however, as the century continued, the rates for 15- to 24-year-olds increased relatively more than other age groups so that currently the older age groups and the 15- to 24-year-olds have the highest rates. The female rates were also highest for the older and youngest age groups at the beginning of the century; however, while the 15- to 24-year-old rates do increase relative to other age groups across the century, they do not increase as much for females as for males, so that currently the older and youngest age groups retain the highest rates. Rates for whites tend to follow the age patterns described for males, and rates for nonwhites tend to follow the patterns described for females. White males show age patterns described above for males (except that early in the century the youngest age groups were not as relatively high as seen in rates for males alone). White females show patterns more like those of females alone, as do nonwhite males. Nonwhite female accident rates are highest for the youngest and oldest ages with little change through the century.

Comparability

As noted in Chapter 3, the comparability ratios for accidents (total) were 0.95, 0.97, 0.9570, and 0.9970 for the 5th–6th (1948–1949), 6th–7th (1957–1958), 7th–8th (1967–1968), and 8th–9th (1978–1979) revisions of the ICD, respectively. Thus a small part of the gradual decrease in accidents (total) across the century is due to classification changes. As noted previously, this artifactual decrease is due almost entirely to classification changes in non-motor-vehicle accidents.

VIOLENT DEATHS AND SELF-DESTRUCTIVENESS

In Section III, the relationships among suicide, homicide, and accidental deaths are examined. The data suggests that national mortality rates for suicide, homicide, and motor-vehicle accidents tend to be parallel over time. Non-motor-vehicle accidents, while showing some fluctuations similar to those of other forms of violent deaths, manifest a more general decrease throughout the century. In addition, suicide rates tend to show significant positive correlations over time with homicide, motor-vehicle and non-motor-vehicle-accident death rates for most race and sex combinations. These results need to be viewed with caution due to the methodologic problems inherent in using national mortality data. However, the findings raise serious questions about the traditional understanding of the relationships among the various forms of violent death in populations, in particular, about the popular view that suicide and homicide are inversely related in populations. The explanatory usefulness of conceptualizing violent deaths as reflecting self-destructive tendencies is discussed.

The mortality rates for suicide, homicide, and accidental deaths are also combined into an aggregate "violent death rate" and evaluated by age, sex, and race variables. Three findings are particularly noteworthy: First, contrary to popular opinion, the violent death rate has tended to decrease throughout the 20th century in the United States and is currently near the lowest rate ever recorded; second, nonwhite males have the highest violent death rate; and, third, the violent death rate, peaking in infancy and older age groups, stays remarkably constant throughout adulthood.

CHAPTER NINE

VIOLENT DEATHS AS REFLECTING SELF-DESTRUCTIVE TENDENCIES

with
Elaine H. Klemen

Controversy exists regarding the nature of the relationships among suicide, homicide, and accidental deaths on both individual and population bases. Similarly, it is not firmly established whether homicide and accidental deaths, along with suicide, reflect self-destructive tendencies. Many studies have addressed these issues from varying perspectives and using several different kinds of data—psychoanalytic, sociologic, and epidemiologic (see Chapter 2). This chapter utilizes population data (national mortality data from the United States, 1900–1975) to examine these questions. The purpose of this chapter is twofold. First, the time patterns of suicide, homicide, motor-vehicle accidents, and non-motor-vehicle accidents will be compared in order to understand better the relationships of these forms of death in large populations. Second, these data will be used to address the question of whether homicides and accidental deaths, along with suicide, may reflect self-destructive tendencies on a population level: The strategy employed is to compare the epidemiologic patterns of overt self-destructiveness (i.e., suicide) with homicides and accidental deaths. Theoretically, this work attempts to bridge intrapsychic disciplines involving individuals, that is, clinical psychiatry and psychoanalysis (from which the hypotheses are derived), and fields that deal with populations, that is, sociology and epidemiology (in which the hypotheses are tested).

This chapter is focused in two specific ways. First, the epidemiologic rather than intrapsychic motivational aspects of self-destructive behaviors will be examined; the intrapsychic models regarding the motivations underlying such self-destructiveness (e.g., masochism, narcissism, grandiosity, etc.) will be the subject of other communications. Second, this chapter is focused on self-destructive rather than aggressive behaviors; that is, it is victim-oriented rather than perpetrator-oriented. Clinically, the victim-oriented approach is optimistic in that it implies that people can, by recognizing and controlling unconscious self-destructive tendencies (whatever the origins), take greater control over their lives and more actively avoid misfortunes that have previously been perceived as unavoidable, externally-occurring events.

The literature on the two issues under consideration (first, the relationships among suicide, homicide, and accidents; and, second, the question of whether suicides, homicides, and accidents may represent self-destructive tendencies) has been presented in Chapter 2. The relevant methodology has been outlined in Chapter 3.

RESULTS

Figure 1-2 (see Chapter 1) presents the age-adjusted mortality rates for suicide, homicide, motor-vehicle accidents, non-motor-vehicle accidents and total accidents, 1900–1975, United States. Of particular interest in examining the relationships among the various forms of violent deaths are: the increases in suicide, homicide, motor-vehicle accidents, and non-motor-vehicle accidents during the economic depression of the early 1930s; the decreases in suicide, homicide, and motor-vehicle accidents during World War II, in the early 1940s; the slight increases in suicide, homicide, and motor-vehicle accidents in the late 1940s and early 1950s; and the increases in suicide, homicide, and motor-vehicle accidents throughout the 1960s. Non-motor-vehicle accidents have tended to decrease throughout the century with some of this decrease over the past 30 years being artifact due to classifications changes (see Chapter 3); they show the increase during the first decade of the 1900s and the decreases during World War I which characterize suicide, as well as the increase during the early 1930s that characterizes all forms of violent deaths, but they increase in the early 1940s unlike the other causes of mortality.*

---

*The increase in non-motor-vehicle accidents among 15- to 24-year olds occurring in the early 1940s was due to an increase in air transport deaths within U.S. borders (*Vital Statistics—Special Reports*, 1946).

The relationship between suicide and homicide can be seen most clearly in Figure 9-1, which presents their age-adjusted time trends, 1900–1975, in greater detail. Before 1933 (i.e., before data were compiled from all states in the United States), the major difference was that the suicide rate was biphasic (peaking around 1910 and 1930 and decreasing during World War I), whereas the homicide rate tended to be monophasic (increasing to a peak during the economic depression of the early 1930s). After 1933, the rates are rather parallel: peaks in the early 1930s, decreases in the early 1940s, slight increases in the late 1940s and early 1950s, and larger increases in the 1960s and 1970s.

Figures 9-2, 9-3, 9-4, and 9-5 present the age-adjusted violent death trends by race and sex for 1914–1975 (data for both race and sex are available only from 1914 on). The generally parallel nature of the fluctuations in mortality rates is especially noticeable for suicide, homicide, and motor-vehicle accidents.

Correlations are also presented for the age-adjusted mortality time trends and they are separated into the years 1900 (or 1914 if race and sex are used) to 1975 (Table 9-1) and 1933 to 1975 (Table 9-2). Of particular concern in addressing the second purpose of this chapter (regarding the self-destructive nature of violent deaths) are the correlation coefficients of suicide with the other forms of violent death. For example, for 1900–1975, suicide, when correlated with homicide, motor-vehicle accidents, non-motor-vehicle accidents, and total accidents, showed coefficients of $+.22$ ($p < .05$), $-.46$ ($p < .001$), $+.63$ ($p < .001$), and $.71$ ($p < .001$), respectively. For 1933–1975, suicide correlated $+.58$ ($p < .001$), $+.53$ ($p < .001$), $+.54$ ($p < .001$), and $+.66$ ($p < .001$) with homicide, motor-vehicle accidents, non-motor-vehicle accidents, and total accidents, respectively. The inverse correlation between suicide and motor-vehicle accidents from 1900 to 1975 appears to result from the continuous increase in motor-vehicle deaths from 1900 to 1975 when cars were just beginning to appear in the population and assume prominence as a cause of mortality. Once the use of automobiles had become widespread, the time trends showed a significantly positive correlation between suicide and motor-vehicle accidents, 1933–1975. When the data are broken down into race and sex differences (1914–1975 and 1933–1975), the correlation patterns between suicide and the other forms of violent death are maintained with the following major exceptions: For all groups

Figure 9-1. Age-adjusted suicide and homicide rates, United States, 1900–1975. *Sources of data: Vital Statistics—Special Reports* (1956) (for 1900–1953); Grove and Hetzel (1968) (for 1954–1960); *Vital Statistics of the United States* (1961–1975); unpublished data, National Center for Health Statistics (for 1961–1975).

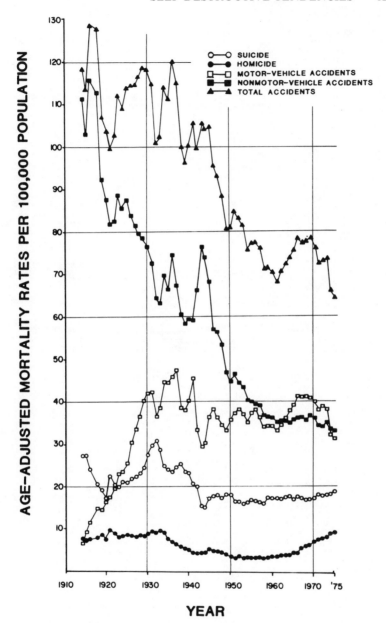

Figure 9-2. Age-adjusted violent death rates, white males, United States, 1914–1975. *Sources of data*: Same as Figure 9-1.

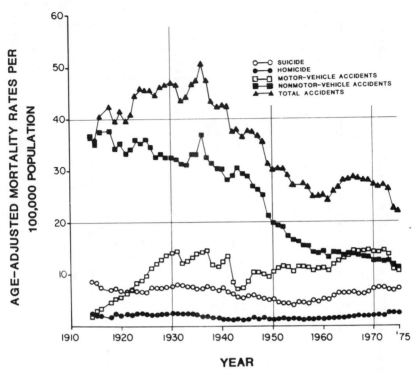

Figure 9-3. Age-adjusted violent death rates, white females, United States, 1914–1975. *Sources of data*: Same as Figure 9-1.

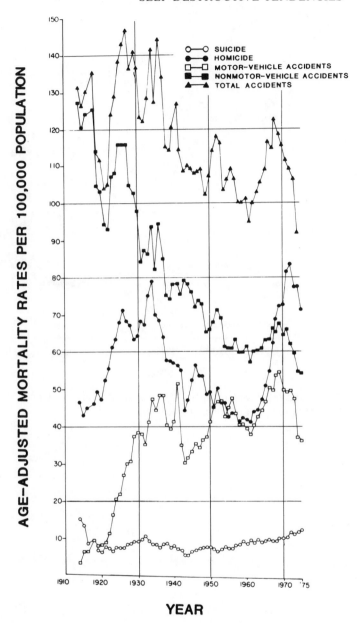

Figure 9-4. Age-adjusted violent death rates, nonwhite males, United States, 1914–1975. *Sources of data*: Same as Figure 9-1.

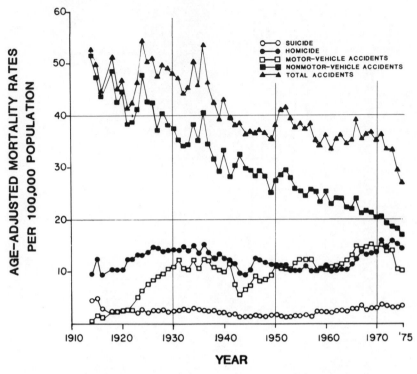

Figure 9-5. Age-adjusted violent death rates, nonwhite females, United States, 1914–1975. *Sources of data*: Same as Figure 9-1.

Table 9-1. Correlation Coefficients for Violent Death Rates (Age-Adjusted), United States, 1900–1975

Total violent deaths, 1900–1975

	H	MVA	NMVA	TA
S	+.22*	−.46***	+.63***	+.71***
H		+.39***	+.38***	NS
MVA			+.81***	−.55***
NMVA				+.93***

Violent deaths, white males, 1914–1975

	H	MVA	NMVA	TA
S	+.67***	NS	+.56***	+.66***
H		−.26*	+.49***	+.49***
MVA			−.66***	−.33**
NMVA				+.92***

Violent deaths, white females, 1914–1975

	H	MVA	NMVA	TA
S	+.72***	NS	+.49***	+.55***
H		NS	NS	NS
MVA			−.47***	NS
NMVA				+.94***

Violent deaths, nonwhite males, 1914–1975

	H	MVA	NMVA	TA
S	.28*	NS	NS	NS
H		+.27*	NS	+.38***
MVA			−.75***	NS
NMVA				+.76***

Violent deaths, nonwhite females, 1914–1975

	H	MVA	NMVA	TA
S	+.33**	+.05	+.04	+.10
H		+.29*	−.06	+.08
MVA			−.75***	−.43***
NMVA				+.91***

Sources of data: Same as Figure 9-1.

Abbreviations: S = suicide; H = homicide; MVA = motor-vehicle accidents; NMVA = non-motor-vehicle accidents; TA = total accidents; NS = not significant.

*p < .05; **p < .01; ***p < .001.

Table 9-2. Correlation Coefficients for Violent Death Rates (Age-Adjusted), United States, 1933–1975

Total violent deaths, 1933–1975

	H	MVA	NMVA	TA
S	+.58***	+.53***	+.54****	+.66***
H		+.43***	NS	NS
MVA			NS	+.32*
NMVA				+.96***

Violent deaths, white males, 1933–1975

	H	MVA	NMVA	TA
S	+.58***	+.52***	+.49***	+.59****
H		+.32*	NS	NS
MVA			NS	+.42**
NMVA				+.96***

Violent deaths, nonwhite males, 1933–1975

	H	MVA	NMVA	TA
S	+.58***	+.42**	−.51***	NS
H		+.39**	NS	+.40**
MVA			NS	+.48***
NMVA				+.85***

Violent deaths, white females, 1933–1975

	H	MVA	NMVA	TA
S	+.68***	+.56***	+.27*	+.42**
H		+.55***	−.29*	NS
MVA			NS	NS
NMVA				+.96***

Violent deaths, nonwhite females, 1933–1975

	H	MVA	NMVA	TA
S	+.53***	+.61***	−.44***	NS
H		NS	NS	NS
MVA			−.42**	NS
NMVA				+.90***

Source of data: Same as Figure 9-1.
Abbreviations: Same as Table 9-1.
*$p < .05$; **$p < .01$; ***$p < .001$.

there is no significant inverse correlation between suicide and motor-vehicle accidents, 1914–1975, probably because much of the initial increase in motor-vehicle-accident mortality is excluded; and the nonwhite male and nonwhite female suicide rates for 1914–1975 show no significant correlation with non-motor-vehicle accidents and, for 1933–1975, show a significant inverse correlation with non-motor-vehicle accidents.

In examining the data by race and sex variables, the following relative comparisons should be noted: Male rates for all forms of violent deaths are higher than female rates; for whites, non-motor-vehicle accidents show the highest mortality rates, followed by motor-vehicle accidents, suicide, and homicide, respectively; however, for nonwhites, non-motor-vehicle accidents are followed by homicide, motor-vehicle accidents, and suicide rates, respectively. Age patterns have been presented elsewhere (Section II) and will be mentioned only briefly: Suicide rates tend to increase with age for males, while female rates are highest between the ages of 35 and 64; homicide rates are highest among young adults for males and among infants and young adults for females; the highest rates of motor-vehicle-accident deaths for both sexes are found in teenagers and young adults and in the oldest age groups; and the oldest and youngest (infancy) ages are at greater risk of dying by non-motor-vehicle accidents for both males and females.

DISCUSSION

Time trends have been presented for suicide, homicide, and accident mortality rates in the United States. The focus has been on the years 1933–1975 inasmuch as the data include the entire U.S. population only during those years and, at approximately the same time, motor vehicles reached levels they were to maintain as a prominent cause of mortality. These data suggest that mortality rates for suicide, homicide, motor-vehicle accidents, and, to a lesser extent, non-motor-vehicle accidents tend to be parallel over time. In particular, homicide, motor-vehicle-, and non-motor-vehicle-accident death rates tend to demonstrate significant positive correlations with suicide rates over time for most race and sex combinations.

At least two specific methodologic artifacts might cause the reported mortality rates for suicide, homicide, and accidents to increase or decrease simultaneously. First, federal classification changes must be considered as a possible cause of parallel fluctuations. For example, a man shoots himself (or is shot), but not fatally, and then dies 2 weeks later of pneumonia, which indirectly results from the shooting. A classification change that shifted the cause of such deaths from pneumonia to suicide (or homicide) would lead to simultaneous increases in the suicide and homicide rates. However, the comparability ratios indicate that no such simultaneous classification shifts have occurred that were large enough to account for the parallel fluctuations. A second possible artifact that might cause simultaneous fluctuations in the various forms of violent deaths involves increases or decreases in the number of reported deaths based on local or national budget or political issues. For example, if budgeting were low for health officials, more deaths of "undetermined etiology" might be reported, with a general decrease in the specific forms of violent deaths. Although in this instance the actual trend is opposite (i.e., in times of great economic depression the violent death rates have increased), the example illustrates a potential problem that could lead to simultaneous fluctuations of violent deaths.

Due to methodologic problems inherent in using national data, these results must be viewed with caution. However, the data seem to raise serious questions about the traditional understanding of the relationships among the various forms of violent death in populations, particularly with respect to suicide and homicide. The classic view that suicide and homicide rates are inversely related in populations (e.g., Henry & Short, 1954) is not supported by these data; rather, the data seem to support the opposite tendency, that suicide and homicide rates fluctuate in parallel over time. Brenner's (1971, 1979) and Klebba's (1975) work also supports the parallel fluctuation of suicide and homicide rates. One must ask how the traditional view of an inverse relationship between suicide and homicide came to have such wide acceptance in light of the contradictory evidence presented in this chapter and elsewhere (Brenner, 1971, 1979; Klebba, 1975). First, and perhaps most important, the data used by Henry and Short (1954) were very different from those utilized in this chapter and by Brenner (1979) and Klebba (1975). Henry and Short's data were suicide and homicide rates for specific locations (e.g., cities) and for relatively short time spans, crimes against property and people, social status, strength of the relational system, and measures of the business cycle. Our data, as well as in those of Brenner (1979) and Klebba (1975), differ in two important ways: They are national mortality data (i.e., not a sample but an entire population), and they focus on longer time trends. Such differences in data could account for the contradictory findings. Second, Henry and Short (1954) conceptualized the suicide–homicide problem from the perspective of aggression, subtitling their book *Some Economic, Sociological and Psychological Aspects of Aggression*. The difficulties created by this approach were detailed in Chapter 2.

Having addressed the first purpose of this study (the comparison of the time trends and relationships between the various forms of violent deaths in the population) the second question must be dealt with: whether or not homicides and accidents, in addition to suicide, can be said to reflect self-destructive tendencies. The initial strategy was to compare suicide rates (overt self-destructiveness) with homicide and accident rates. Examination of the hypothesis that violent deaths reflect self-destructive tendencies is made especially difficult due to the different levels of abstraction involved. The findings that suicide, homicide, and motor-vehicle-accident rates tend to be parallel over time and that homicides, motor-vehicle accidents, and non-motor-vehicle accidents correlate significantly with overt self-destructiveness—that is, with suicide—can perhaps at best be said to suggest that self-destructiveness is an important variable associated with various forms of violent death on a population level. Within this hypothesis, the differences between non-motor-vehicle accidents and the other forms of violent death would be explained as follows:

1. Non-motor-vehicle accidents have enough major fluctuations to correlate positively with suicide (the increases around 1910; the decreases during World War I; the increases in the early 1930s; and the recent "leveling-off," which is in reality an increase that manifests as a leveling-off because of the comparability ratio).
2. The tendency of non-motor-vehicle accidents and motor-vehicle accidents toward an inverse relationship (with the exceptions of the marked fluctuations both have with suicide) would suggest that for persons who were at risk of

dying an accidental death throughout the century, all that may have changed was the form of the accidental death, with a relatively increased number of motor-vehicle-accident deaths occurring as motor vehicles became more prominent.

It should be noted that a number of intrapsychic explanations underlie the hypothesis that conscious and unconscious self-destructive tendencies may account for the correlation between suicide, homicide, and accidents on a population level. For example, on an intrapsychic level of abstraction, grandiosity, needs for admiration and appreciation, masochism, and inwardly directed aggression may all result in any form of violent death and be intrapsychic etiologic factors leading to the deaths and the parallelism seen on the population level.

This hypothesis regarding self-destructiveness seems to be supported by Brenner's (1971, 1979) work on the relationship between national mortality rates and economic cycles, as detailed in Chapter 2. Brenner demonstrated that indicators of economic instability and insecurity, such as unemployment, are associated over time with higher suicide and homicide rates. His explanation for this association is that the lack of economic security is psychologically stressful, with increased mortality rates as one consequence. Brenner's model suggests a reason why suicide, homicide, and accident rates are parallel over time: economic cycles. In addition, his explanation of why the economy is related to mortality rates (i.e., immoderate and unstable life habits) seems consistent with the idea that to some extent self-destructive tendencies may underlie all forms of violent deaths.

Porterfield (1960) found a positive correlation of suicide–homicide, other crimes, and accident death rates, and he tended toward an explanation of aggression rather than underlying self-destructiveness in motor-vehicle accidents and homicide data: "There is no reason to doubt that aggressive, hazardous driving is likely to be characteristic of persons similar to those who have suicidal or homicidal or both tendencies—and *vice-versa*" (p. 900). However, in an interesting footnote, Porterfield addressed the issue of self-destructiveness in violent deaths quite clearly: "What would lead the investigator to begin with the prediction that 'the same conditions that generate the suicide prone and the homicide prone' would 'also generate the accident prone.' Such a rationale would have to make room for a milieu which produces a *positive* correlation between different types of behavior and, at the same time, the 'different sorts of persons' who 'react respectively in one way or the other' to yield these positively correlated 'different' types of response" (pp. 900–901). The data presented in this chapter seem to support this kind of rationale: There are positive correlations between suicide, homicide, and accidents but the specific type of violent death involved and the degree of risk is based on the age, race, and sex of the individual. For example, suicide and homicide rates are positively correlated over time, but older white males are at greatest risk of dying by suicide and younger nonwhite males are at greatest risk of dying by homicide.

CHAPTER TEN

SYNTHESIS
Violent Deaths in Aggregate

with
Kevin W. Luke
Paul Montes II
Sonia Perez
Jay Sandlow

Sociologic and epidemiologic perspectives allow, and force, one to look beyond individual patterns and study the influence of variables on entire populations. The population itself can take on a significance different from that of the individual. Lewis Thomas in *The Lives of a Cell* (1974) has discussed this idea eloquently. Thomas drew upon insect models to suggest that human beings can be viewed in two perspectives: as individuals, and as component parts, "cellular elements," of a larger organism. He writes:

> What makes us most uncomfortable is that [ants], and the bees and termites and social wasps, seem to live two kinds of lives: they are individuals, going about the day's business without much evidence of thought for tomorrow, and they are at the same time component parts, cellular elements, in the huge, writhing, ruminating organism, of the Hill, the nest, the hive. It is because of this aspect, I think, that we most wish for them to be something foreign. We do not like the notion that there can be collective societies with the capacity to behave like organisms. . . . Termites are even more extraordinary in the way they seem to accumulate intelligence as they gather together. Two or three termites in a chamber will begin to pick up pellets and move them from place to place, but nothing comes of it; nothing is built. As more join in, they seem to reach a critical mass, a quorum, and the thinking begins. They place pellets atop pellets, then throw up columns and beautiful, curving, symmetrical arches, and the crystalline architecture of vaulted chambers is created. It is not known how they communicate with each other, how the chains of termites

building one column know when to turn toward the crew on the adjacent column, or how, when the time comes, they manage the flawless joining of the arches. The stimuli that set them off at the outset, building collectively instead of shifting things about, may be pheromones released when they reach committee size. . . . They become agitated, excited, and when they begin working, like artists. (pp. 12–13)

This quote, conveying the idea that the whole may be greater than the sum of its parts, leads us to the task of the present chapter, that is, to an examination of the epidemiology of all types of violent death in aggregate. As described in the preceding chapters, it may be useful to conceptualize suicide, homicide, and accidents as all reflecting self-destructive tendencies to some extent. Hence, it may also be valuable to examine these causes of mortality in aggregate. By combining suicide, homicide, and accident rates, one can obtain an aggregate rate that presents the epidemiologic trends for violent deaths over the century and by age, race, and sex patterns. This aggregate rate will be called the "violent death rate."* The question being raised is: Having examined suicide, homicide, and accidents separately, what patterns emerge when these data are combined?

Figures 10-1 and 10-2 show the mortality rates and age-adjusted mortality rates, respectively, for violent deaths throughout the 20th century in the United States. Contrary to popular opinion, the violent death rate has tended to decrease over the century and is currently near the lowest rate ever recorded. In particular, as demonstrated by Figures 10-4 and 10-5 there have been marked decreases in the violent death rates among infants (0–1 year) and the very elderly (75–84 years) across the century. There is a tendency toward an increase during the economic depression of the early 1930s and a decrease during World War II.

Nonwhite males have the highest violent death rates. They are followed by white males, nonwhite females, and white females, respectively. Male rates are higher than female, and nonwhite higher than white. The race and sex patterns over the century are similar to those described for the total rate. The age-adjusted rates are quite

*The violent death rate consists of the aggregate of the following causes of mortality: suicide, homicide, and accident mortality rates; and (deaths due to) injuries undetermined whether accidentally or purposely inflicted (a category begun in 1968—see Chapter 3).

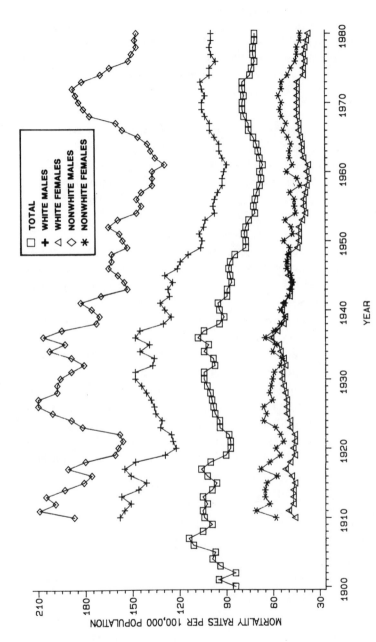

Figure 10-1. Violent death rates, by sex and race, United States, 1900–1980. *Sources of data*: Same as Figures 4-1, 5-1, and 8-1, for suicide, homicide, and accident rates, respectively; unpublished data, National Center for Health Statistics for (deaths due to) injuries undetermined whether accidentally or purposely inflicted (for 1968–1980).

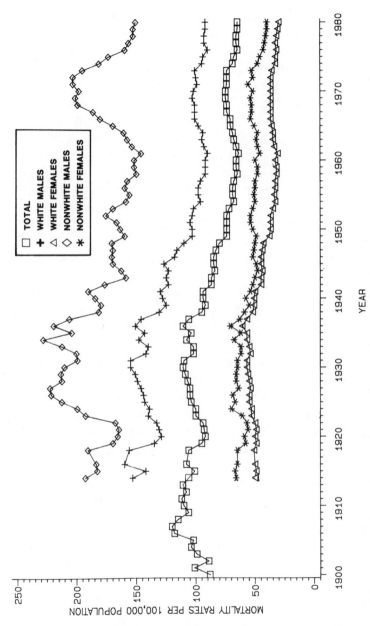

Figure 10-2. Age-adjusted violent death rates, by sex and race, United States, 1900–1980. *Sources of data:* Same as Figures 4-2, 5-2, and 8-2, for suicide, homicide, and accident rates, respectively. (Age-adjusted data for injuries undetermined whether accidentally or purposely inflicted are not included in Figure 10-2 inasmuch as these data were not available at the time of this report.)

similar to the non-age-adjusted rates. In light of the currently low violent death rate, one might ask why public opinion appears to support the idea that the present era is marked by a high violent death rate. It has been suggested that any given generation for some reason "needs" to focus on violence and to see itself as living in a particularly violent time. However, there may be more than this notion to account for the current feeling. For instance, although the rate of violent death is currently low, inasmuch as the population has increased, the actual numbers of violent deaths are higher than previously recorded. In addition, homicide rates (as well as actual number of homicides) may be perceived as particularly indicative of violence in a society, and homicide rates are currently very high in comparison to previous years. Thus there may be reason for the popular view that the current era is especially violent, despite data that indicate the violent death rate itself to be at an all-time low.

Figure 10-3 presents the age patterns for the violent death rate by race and sex. The rates have been averaged from 1900–1980 and plotted by 10-year intervals. The total violent death rate is high at infancy and then decreases to a low for 5- to 14-year-olds. The rates begin to increase with adolescence, hold fairly steady with some slight increase throughout adulthood, and increase markedly for the oldest age groups. As noted above, nonwhite males tend to have the highest rates, followed by white males, nonwhite females, and white females, respectively.

Rates for whites tend to follow the pattern seen in the total: high rates in infancy, decreasing until adolescence, increasing at adolescence, leveling off with only slight increases in adulthood, and increasing markedly in older age. Nonwhite rates differ in that they manifest increases among the 25- to 44-year-olds. Mention should also be made of another exception to the usual pattern, namely, that the highest violent death rate is found in white females aged 75- to 84-year-olds.

Figures 10-4 through 10-7 present the violent death rates for males, females, whites and nonwhites, respectively. As noted, male rates tend to be higher than female and nonwhite higher than white, with exceptions in the oldest age groups. For males (Figure 10-4), the highest rates are found among oldest age groups, with 15- to 24-year-olds recently having rates as high or higher than most adult age groups. Violent death rates are high during infancy, decrease into adolescence, and begin increasing in early

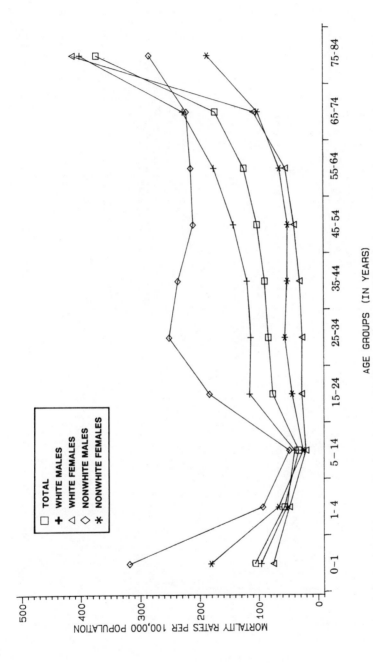

Figure 10-3. Age patterns of violent death rates, by sex and race, United States, 1900–1980. *Sources of data*: Same as Figure 10-1, and calculated as described in text of Chapter 4.

143

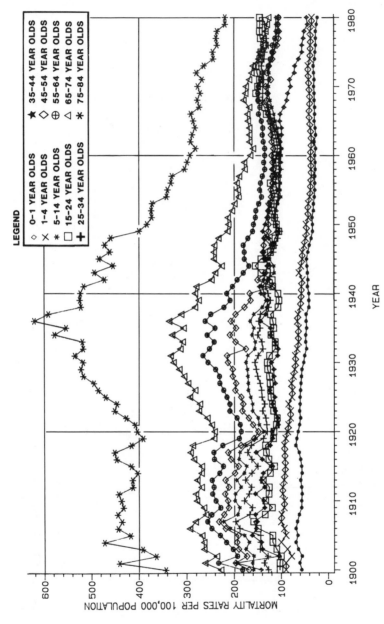

Figure 10-4a. Violent death rates for males, by age, United States, 1900–1980. *Sources of data:* Same as Figure 10-1.

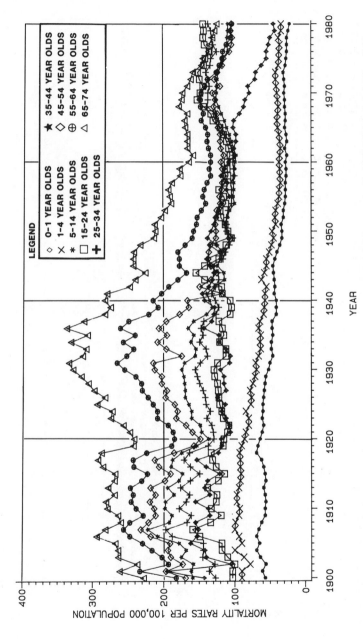

Figure 10-4b. Violent death rates for males, by age (under age 75), United States, 1900–1980. *Sources of data:* Same as Figure 10-1.

145

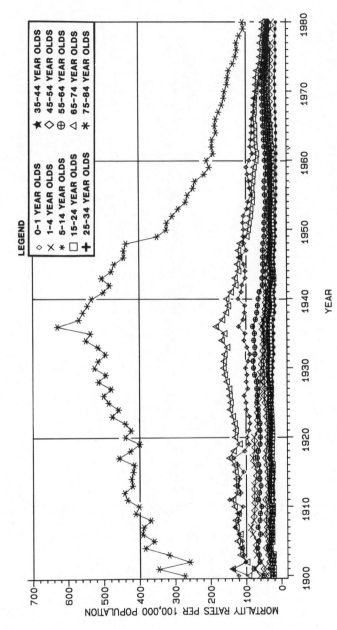

Figure 10-5a. Violent death rates for females, by age, United States, 1900–1980. *Sources of data:* Same as Figure 10-1.

146

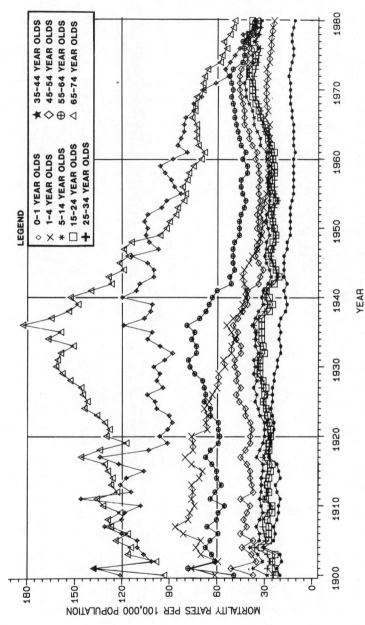

Figure 10-5b. Violent death rates for females, by age (under age 75), United States, 1900–1980. *Sources of data:* Same as Figure 10-1.

147

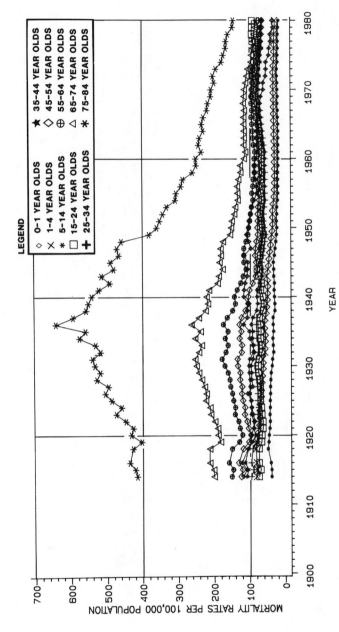

Figure 10-6a. Violent death rates for whites, by age, United States, 1914–1980. *Sources of data*: Same as Figure 10-1.

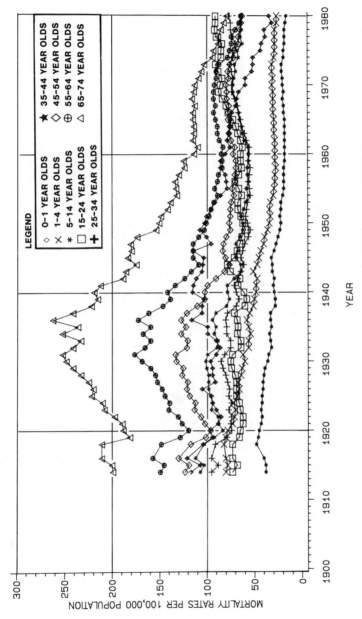

Figure 10-6b. Violent death rates for whites, by age (under age 75), United States, 1914-1980. *Sources of data:* Same as Figure 10-1.

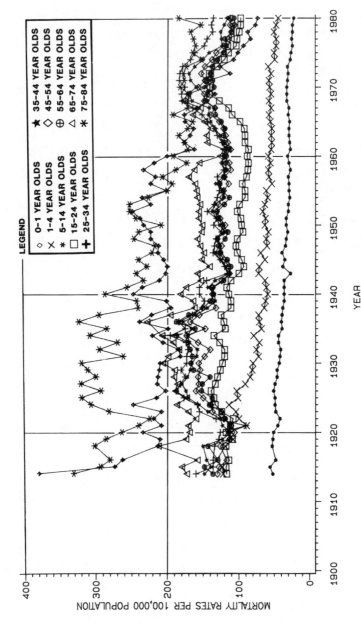

Figure 10-7. Violent death rates for nonwhites, by age, United States, 1914–1980. *Sources of data:* Same as Figure 10-1.

150

adolescence throughout adulthood. This pattern has been maintained throughout the century, with the exception of the past 30 years or so when the rates for 15- to 24-year-olds have become higher than many of the other age groups. Figure 10-5 shows similar patterns for females, with two important differences: First, infant females have had rates higher than all but the oldest age groups until very recently; and, second, the recent increase of rates for 15- to 24-year-olds has not been as marked. The rates for whites, given in Figure 10-6, also show patterns similar to those described for males. The patterns for nonwhites (Figure 10-7) are somewhat different from the other groups. First, the highest rates tend to be found among infants as well as the oldest age groups, until very recently when the rates for infants have decreased. Second, throughout much of the century the 25- to 34- and 35- to 44-year-olds have had rates as high or higher than the rates for the other adult age groups, except the oldest. This pattern is strikingly different from the other groups.

Figures 10-8, 10-9, 10-10, and 10-11 show the epidemiologic patterns of violent deaths for white males, white females, nonwhite males, and nonwhite females, respectively. For white males (Figure 10-8), while there is a tendency toward the characteristic increase during the economic depressions and decreases during the world wars, the violent death rates for all age groups have decreased throughout the century with the exception of 15- to 24-year-olds. The older age groups have the highest rates and the 1- to 4- and 5- to 14-year-olds have increased throughout the century so that they are currently higher than any other group except for 75- to 84-year-olds.

The patterns for white females (Figure 10-9) are similar to those of white males (with the general decrease in rates throughout the century and the oldest groups having the highest rates), except that rates for white female infants have tended to be higher than all but the oldest age groups. The increase in rates of 15- to 24-year-olds has occurred somewhat more recently for white females than for white males.

The violent death rates for nonwhite males (Figure 10-10) have somewhat different patterns from those of white males and females. First, for nonwhite males there is a more marked increase in rates during the mid-1960s to mid-1970s. In addition, while there are similarities in that the highest rates among nonwhite males tend

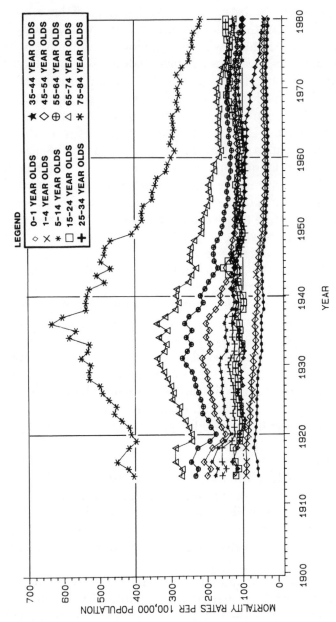

Figure 10-8a. Violent death rates for white males, by age, United States, 1914–1980. *Sources of data:* Same as Figure 10-1.

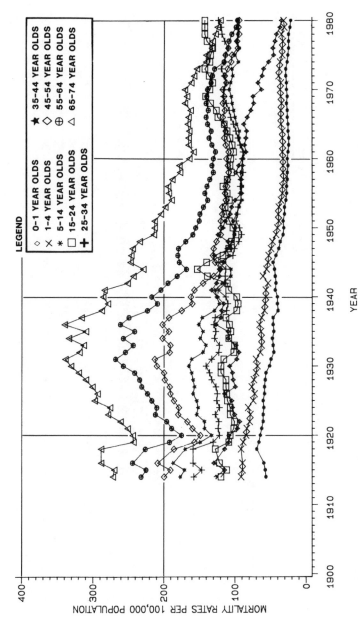

Figure 10-8b. Violent death rates for white males, by age (under age 75), United States, 1914–1980. *Sources of data: Same as Figure 10-1.*

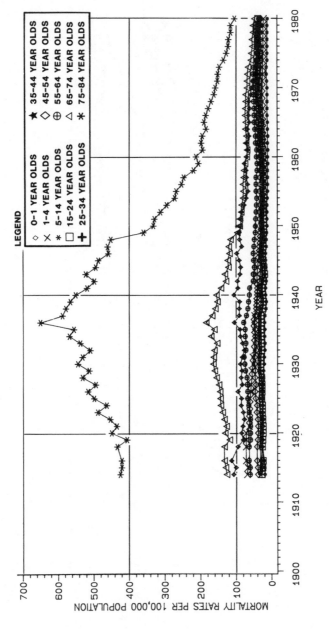

Figure 10-9a. Violent death rates for white females, by age, United States, 1914–1980. *Sources of data:* Same as Figure 10-1.

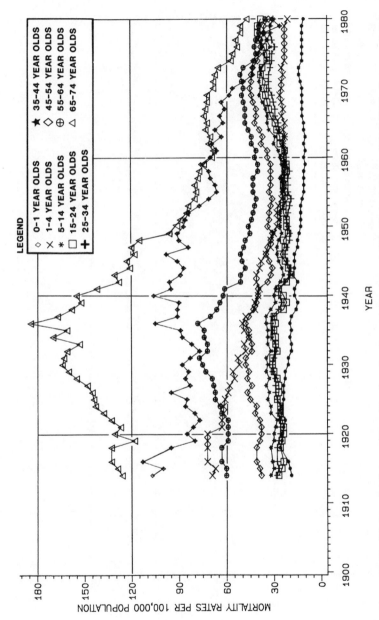

Figure 10-9b. Violent death rates for white females, by age (under age 75), United States, 1914–1980. *Sources of data: Same as Figure 10-1.*

155

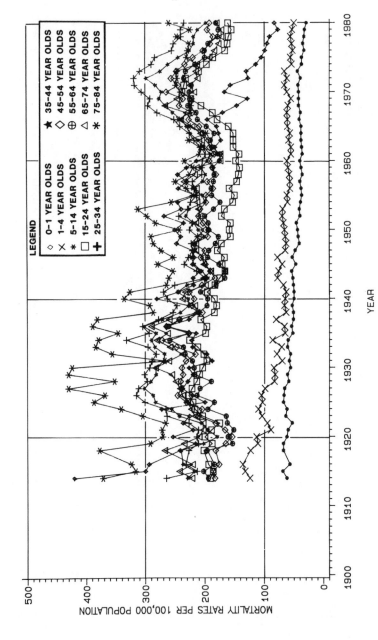

Figure 10-10. Violent death rates for nonwhite males, by age, United States, 1914–1980. *Sources of data*: Same as Figure 10-1.

156

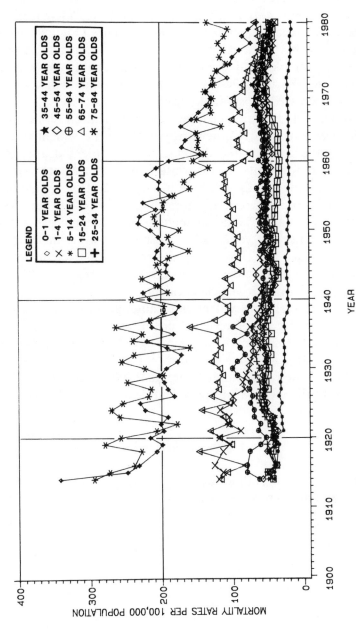

Figure 10-11. Violent death rates for nonwhite females, by age, United States, 1914–1980. *Sources of data:* Same as Figure 10-1.

to be found in the oldest age groups, there are differences in that the violent death rates for 24- to 34- and 35- to 44-year-olds have actually been higher at times than those of the 75- to 84-year-olds.

The violent death rates for nonwhite females (Figure 10-11) are different in that for much of the century the nonwhite female infants (0–1 year old) had the highest violent death rate, higher even than rates for the oldest age groups. This high rate among infants has decreased substantially in recent years.

Before concluding this chapter, specific mention should be made of three particularly noteworthy shifts in the violent death rates across the century: the decrease in the violent death rate among infants (for white males, white females, nonwhite males, and nonwhite females); the decrease in violent death rates among the oldest age groups (especially for white males, white females, and nonwhite females); and the increase in violent death rates among adolescents and young adults (especially white males and white females aged 15–24 years). The decreases in violent death rates for infants and the oldest age groups is primarily the result of decreases in non-motor-vehicle-accident rates; substantial decreases in motor-vehicle-accident rates among older white males have also helped decrease the violent death rate in that group. The increase in the violent death rates among white adolescents has been due to increases in suicide and motor-vehicle-accident rates; increased homicide rates among white male adolescents have also contributed to the increase of the violent death rate in that group.

Comparability

Chapters 4, 5, and 8 outline the comparability effect for suicide, homicide, and accident rates, respectively.

TOWARD PREDICTION AND ETIOLOGY

with
Daniel Offer

Section IV explores the potential for the prediction of patterns of violent death rates based on an understanding of population shifts in the United States. Relationships are examined between suicide and other forms of violent death (homicide, motor-vehicle accidents, and non-motor-vehicle accidents) and population changes for all age groups in the United States, 1933–1982. Significant positive correlations exist between adolescent and young adult (15- to 24-year-olds) suicide and homicide rates, and the changes in the proportion of this age group in the U.S. population from 1933 to 1982 (i.e., an increase in the proportion of 15- to 24-year-olds in the United States is associated with an increase in suicide and homicide rates among 15- to 24-year-olds). Opposite trends exist for adults: significant negative correlations between suicide and homicide rates for most adult age groups (35–64 years) and the changes in the proportion of these adult age groups in the U.S. population (i.e., an increase in the proportion of 35- to 64-year-olds is associated with a decrease in suicide and homicide rates among 35- to 64-year-olds). Motor-vehicle accident mortality rates tend to be inversely related, and non-motor-vehicle accident mortality rates tend to be positively related, to shifts in the population for most age groups.

Chapter 11 focuses on the younger age groups, beginning with suicide and then including homicide and accidents. Chapter 12 presents an expansion of this model to include all forms of violent deaths in adult as well as younger age groups.

Inasmuch as the future number of adolescents and adults can

159

be estimated years ahead based on current population data for children and preadolescents, these results suggest that the epidemiologic patterns for suicide and other forms of violent death may be predictable for certain age groups.

CHAPTER ELEVEN

VIOLENT DEATHS AMONG THE YOUNG

THE PREDICTION OF ADOLESCENT SUICIDE

Increasing evidence seems to justify the notion that suicide among the young is a serious public health problem in our country. Suicide is the third leading cause of death among adolescents, following accidents and homicide, respectively (*Vital Statistics of the United States*, 1980). Adolescent suicide rates doubled between 1961 and 1975 and tripled between 1956 and 1975 (Holinger & Offer, 1981; Holinger, 1978). Central to most scientific problems, and particularly so in the medical sciences, are the ideas of prediction and effective intervention. Would it be possible to predict the trends in suicide rates among adolescents, and could such a predictive model logically imply effective intervention?

A recent examination of the increase in suicide rates among 15- to 19-year-olds (middle adolescence or, essentially, high-school age) (Holinger & Offer, 1981) reported that simultaneous with an increase in suicide rates was a steady increase in the population of 15- to 19-year-olds, from just over 11 million in 1956 to nearly 21 million in 1975. The purpose of this chapter is to expand these observations and relate the changes in the adolescent population and changes in the proportion of adolescents in the total population to the adolescent suicide rates during the 20th century in the United States. One possible consequence of this work is the formation of a model for the prediction of suicide rates for certain ages, which would allow for intervention at the population as well as the individual level. Such a model would have an important impact on public health.

It should be noted that the general idea that changes in population may be related to suicide rates has some, although not complete, support in the literature. In Chapter 2, the conflicting

161

 dings by researchers such as Wechsler (1961), Gordon and Gordon (1960), Klebba (1975), Levy and Herzog (1974, 1978), and Herzog *et al.* (1977) were discussed. However, none of these reports addressed systematically the relationship between population changes and suicide rates among the young.

It should be stressed that this part of the chapter is specifically focused in two ways. First, it focuses on one age group, 15- to 19-year-olds. It was felt to be most helpful for explaining and testing this model to concentrate on a single age group. An older age group (65- to 69-year-olds) is used primarily to provide a contrast and to demonstrate the importance of focusing on specific age groups in attempting to develop a predictive model. In examining the positive relationship between adolescent suicide rates and population changes, we had found that suicide among older adults tended to move in the opposite direction, and we decided to test the hypothesis that the larger the population of 65- to 69-year-olds, the lower would be the suicide rates for that age group. Second, we focus on only one variable—population changes—in relation to adolescent suicide. Suicide is probably most properly viewed as a multidetermined phenomenon involving a variety of elements: heredity, individual psychopathology, socioeconomic forces, and so on. These various aspects of adolescent suicide have been explored in detail elsewhere (Holinger & Offer, 1981), and this chapter focuses here on the single variable of population because of its potential for the prediction of rates for the entire age group.

Figure 11-1 shows the changes over time in suicide rates for 15- to 19-year-olds, the population of 15- to 19-year-olds, and the proportion of adolescents aged 15–19 in the population from 1933 to 1978 in the United States. The suicide rates, population changes, and changes in the proportion of adolescents in the population can be seen to be rather parallel. It should be recalled that while one might assume that the *number of deaths* from a particular cause will increase with increases in the population, the *mortality rates* do not necessarily increase with an increase in population because the denominator is constant (i.e., deaths per 100,000 population). The changes in adolescent suicide rates might be real; they might be artifact (i.e., resulting from changes in reporting and classification over time); or they might be both. However, the changes in adolescent suicide rates do not appear to be the result of changes in the federal classification system (*Vital Statistics—Special Reports*,

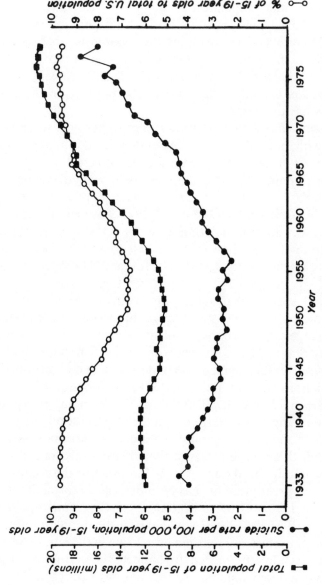

Figure 11-1. Suicide rate per 100,000 population, population (in millions) of adolescents 15–19 years old, and percentage of adolescents 15–19 years old in the total population, United States, 1933–1978. *Sources of data:* See Holinger and Offer (1982, Figure 1).

163

1956; Holinger, 1978; for a detailed description of the methodologic issues, see Chapter 3 and Holinger & Offer, 1982).

Figure 11-2 shows the changes over time in suicide rates for 65- to 69-year-olds, the population of 65- to 69-year-olds, and the proportion of 65- to 69-year-olds in the total population during 1933–1978. Figure 11-2 show an inverse relationship between the suicide rates and the population changes in this age group (and their proportion of the total population): The suicide rate of 65- to 69-year-olds has tended to decrease as the population of 65- to 69-year-olds has increased.

Adolescent suicide rates as well as older adult suicide rates were correlated with both the adolescent and older adult population changes and changes in the proportion of adolescents and older adults in the population. Adolescent suicide rates had a significant positive correlation with both the adolescent population and the proportion of adolescents in the population. The negative correlations in the older adult population were not statistically significant although although they showed the inverse trend (the specific correlations and methodology used can be found in Holinger & Offer, 1982).

The data suggest that significant positive correlations exist between adolescent suicide rates, changes in the adolescent population, and changes in the proportion of adolescents in the population of the United States. That is, increases or decreases in the population of 15- to 19-year-olds (and increases or decreases in their proportion in the population) are temporally related to corresponding increases and decreases in adolescent suicide rates. Although one always has to keep in mind the multidetermined nature of suicide and question whether or not such single-variable relationships are spurious, the importance of these findings lies in the potential for prediction of suicide rates among specific age groups. Inasmuch as the population of children and preadolescents has been decreasing throughout the late 1960s and 1970s (Grove & Hetzel, 1968; *Vital Statistics of the United States*, 1961–1978), we would expect the population of 15- to 19-year-olds to shift and to begin decreasing in the late 1970s and 1980s (this has already started to happen; U.S. Bureau of the Census, 1984) and we would predict that the adolescent suicide rates would decrease simultaneously.

An important implication of the suggested relationship between adolescent suicide rates and changes in the adolescent

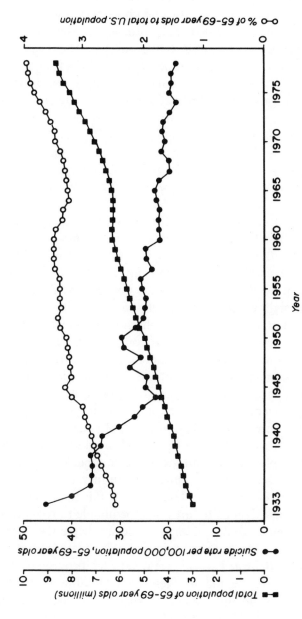

Figure 11-2. Suicide rate per 100,000 population, population (in millions) of older adults 65–69 years old, and percentage of older adults 65–69 years old in the total population, United States, 1933–1978. *Sources of data:* See Holinger and Offer (1982, Figure 2).

population may be in the public health area and involves the possi-
blility of effective intervention. Intervention is possible with a population model such as this because the changes in the adolescent
population can be determined years ahead by the population
figures for children and preadolescents. Society often evidences a
time lag in adjusting to changes in population: Time is needed, for
example, to establish more jobs, to increase college enrollment by
building dormitories and adding faculty, to build more high
schools, and to add more psychiatric services and school counselors. Thus the task of prevention of increased rates of adolescent
suicide seems possible by addressing the need for more services
(psychiatric) and positions (jobs, high schools, college enrollment)
sooner and by cutting the time lag between the adolescent population increase and society's response to it.

Although it is necessary to avoid mere speculation about these
results until further hypotheses can be tested at various levels of
data, it seems worthwhile to try to explain these relationships on a
clinical basis and justify suggestions for interventions. There are at
least two psychodynamic explanations, not necessarily mutually
exclusive, that might enhance the understanding of the relationship
between adolescent suicide rates and changes in the population of
adolescents. The first involves issues of competition and failure. As
the number of adolescents initially increases, there are more com-
petitors for the same number of positions: jobs, positions on sports
teams, places in the freshman classes of good colleges, access to
various social services (e.g., school counselors to help adolescents
with problems, probation officers, vocational counselors), and so
on. With the increased adolescent population and increased competition for such places come an increased number of adolescents
who fail to get these positions. Thus with an increased adolescent
population, relatively more adolescents will fail to achieve their
goals, will see themselves as failures, will be unable to reestablish a
balance in their self-esteem equilibrium, and will begin the downhill
slide resulting in suicide. Second, Teicher (1970) demonstrated that
adolescents who attempted suicide went through progressive isolation from important people in their lives, leading to a chain-
reaction dissolution of any remaining meaningful social relationships. The increase in the adolescent population may intensify the
sense of isolation and tendency to suicide: It may be more difficult
for an adolescent to gain a sense of self-worth and to find friends

in the large, impersonal high schools of today than in the smaller schools of the past. The lonely, emotionally depleted, depressed adolescent may see most of his peers as functioning relatively well, sharpening his awareness of his personal problems and increasing his loneliness and isolation. Seeing so many seemingly well-functioning peers may also lower his already low and excessively vulnerable self-esteem with a consequent sense of hopelessness, resulting in a suicide attempt or a successful suicide.

The suicide rates for older age groups do not show significant inverse correlations with the population changes in the older ages, although the trend exists. This tendency may be due to less neglect and greater economic benefits occurring as the population of older people increases. That is, as this minority group grows, the government will pay it more attention. The psychology of older adults is such that they would obtain strength from seeing others live longer, even if their lives were besieged with illness (emotional and/or physical), and that they would gain socioeconomic benefits as their numbers grew. The greater number of older people would not lead to increased competitiveness and failure, as with the adolescents, but rather to greater attention and benefits. In addition, the loneliness that often accompanies old age might decrease with the increased numbers, resulting in a decrease in suicide rates.

It should be noted that any attempt to apply these hypotheses (i.e., the potential prediction of suicide rates for specific age groups by the population changes in those age groups) to countries other than the United States needs to be done with the full understanding of the socioeconomic structure of the other countries. The psychological tasks at 15–19 years of age (end of high school, separation from parents, "going out into the world") and at 65–69 years of age (retirement issues, loss of loved ones) in the United States will not necessarily occur at the same ages in other countries.

THE PREDICTION OF SUICIDE, HOMICIDE, AND ACCIDENTS AMONG THE YOUNG

Attempting to understand self-destructive tendencies by studying only suicide may be a limited approach. The purpose of this subsection is to relate adolescent and young adult homicide and accident rates, as well as suicide rates, to changes in the adolescent and young adult population and changes in the proportion of adolescents and young adults in the total population in the United States during the 20th century.

The general idea that changes in the population may be related to suicide, homicide, and accident rates has some support in the literature, described above. Two other investigators, whose work was also discussed in more detail in Chapter 2, have made important contributions to the potential prediction of violent death rates: Easterlin (1980), with his studies of population shifts, and Brenner (1971, 1979), with research on the economy. Others have more directly begun to relate population changes, economic changes, and violent death rates and suggest the potential for prediction (Seiden & Frietas, 1980; Peck & Litman, 1973). However, there is a lack of systematic research focusing on the potential for a population model to predict the patterns of violent deaths and the relationship of this predictive model to economic changes.

The major methodologic issues have been presented elsewhere (Holinger & Offer, 1984). It should be noted that the data are for the complete population, not samples. They include all reported suicides, homicides, and accidental deaths among 15- to 24-year-olds that occurred in the United States between 1933 and 1976 (1933–1976 for correlations; 1933–1978 for Figures 11-1, 11-2, 11-4, and 11-5; and 1933–1979 for Figure 11-3).* Sources of population, suicide, homicide, and accident data are the same as the sources for population and suicide data in our earlier report (Holinger & Offer, 1982).

Figure 11-3 shows the changes over time in mortality rates for suicide, homicide, motor-vehicle accidents, and non-motor-vehicle accidents, for 15- to 24-year-olds, and the population and the proportion of 15- to 24-year-olds from 1933 to 1979 in the United States. The mortality rates, population changes, and proportion of this age group in the population can be seen to be rather parallel, except for the opposing trends seen for motor-vehicle-accident rates. The changes in the mortality rates might be real, they might

---

*Figures 11-1 through 11-5 use national mortality data from 1933 to 1978 (except for Figure 11-3, which uses data from 1933–1979), while the correlations utilize data from 1933 to 1976; these differences are due to the fact that the data for 1977 through 1979 were not available when the correlations were calculated but were available to be included in some of the graphs.

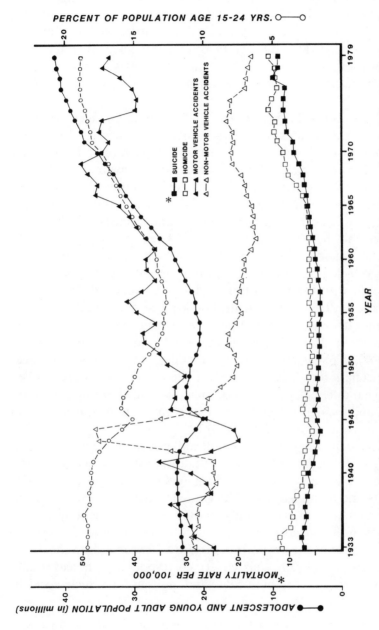

Figure 11-3. Violent death rates and population changes, 15- to 24-year-olds, United States, 1933–1979. *Sources of data:* Grove and Hetzel (1968) (for 1933–1960); *Vital Statistics of the United States* (1961–1976) (for 1961–1976); unpublished data, National Center for Health Statistics (for 1977 and 1979).

be artifact (i.e., resulting from changes in reporting and classification over time), or they might be both. However, the changes in the suicide, homicide, and motor-vehicle-accident rates do not appear to be due to changes in federal classification; the non-motor-vehicle-accident rates are slightly lower due to an artifact in federal classification, and the recent leveling-off of rates is in actuality a slight increase (Holinger & Klemen, 1982; Klebba & Dolman, 1975).

Figures 11-4, 11-5, 11-6, and 11-7 show the changes over time in violent death rates, population, and proportion of 15- to 24-year-olds in the United States, 1933–1978, by race and sex: white males, nonwhite males, white females, and nonwhite females, respectively. The general trends for suicide, homicide, and non-motor-vehicle-accident mortality rates tend to increase and decrease with corresponding increases and decreases in both the number and the proportion of 15- to 24-year-olds.*

The suicide, homicide, motor-vehicle-accident, and non-motor-vehicle-accident mortality rates for 15- to 24-year-olds were correlated with the proportion of 15- to 24-year-olds in the U.S. population, 1933–1976. Suicide, homicide, and non-motor-vehicle-accident rates had significant positive correlations with the proportion of 15- to 24-year-olds ($+.46$, $+.49$, and $+.52$, respectively; $p < .001$), whereas motor-vehicle accidents had a significant negative correlation ($-.60$; $p < .001$). (The correlations were derived somewhat differently than in our previous study [Holinger & Offer, 1982], and the derivation of the present correlations is described in detail in Holinger & Offer, 1984.)

The data suggest that significant positive correlations exist between adolescent and young adult rates of suicide, homicide, and non-motor-vehicle accidents and changes in the proportion of adolescents and young adults in the United States. A significant negative correlation exists between motor-vehicle-accident rates and changes in the proportion of 15- to 24-year-olds; that is, increases and decreases in the proportion of 15- to 24-year-olds in the population are temporally related to corresponding increases and decreases in suicide, homicide, and non-motor-vehicle-accident

---

*The sharp increase in non-motor-vehicle accidents among 15- to 24-year-olds occurring during the early 1940s was due to an increase in air transport deaths within the United States borders (*Vital Statistics—Special Reports*, 1946).

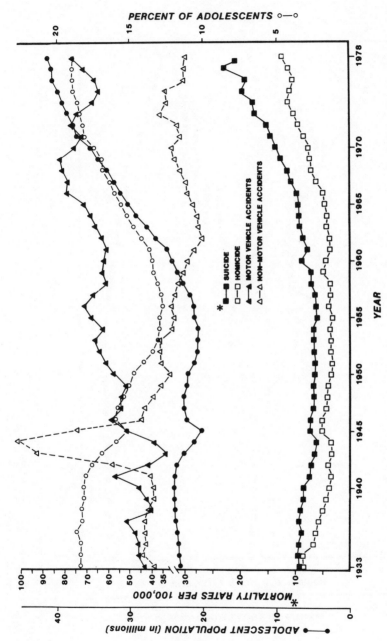

Figure 11-4. Violent death rates and population changes, 15- to 24-year-old white males, United States, 1933–1978. *Sources of data:* See text of Chapter 11.

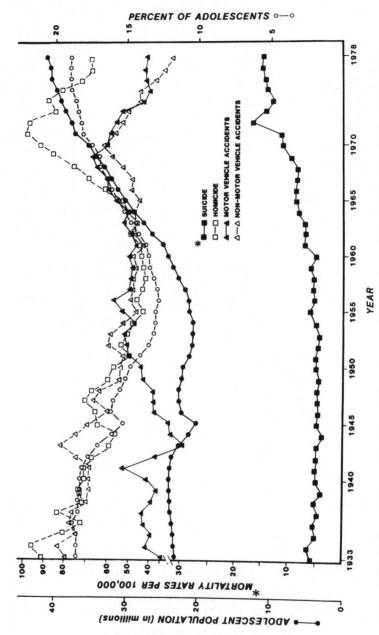

Figure 11-5. Violent death rates and population changes, 15- to 24-year-old nonwhite males, United States, 1933–1978. *Sources of data:* See text of Chapter 11.

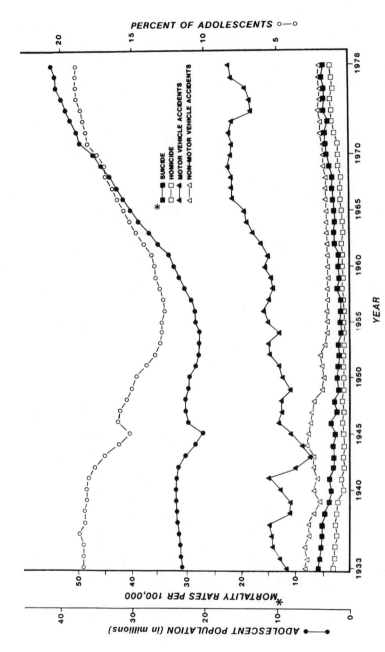

Figure 11-6. Violent death rates and population changes, 15- to 24-year-old white females, United States, 1933–1978. *Sources of data:* See text of Chapter 11.

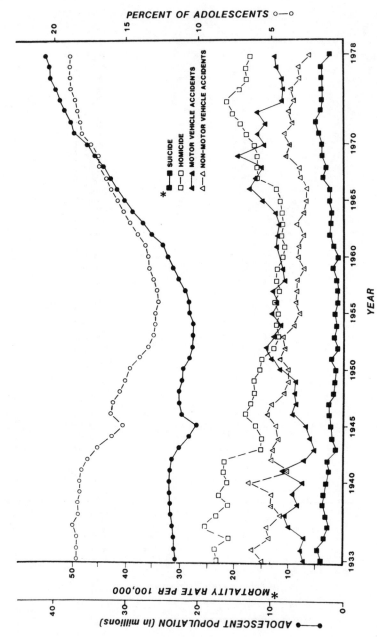

Figure 11-7. Violent death rates and population changes, 15- to 24-year-old nonwhite females, United States, 1933–1978. *Sources of data:* See text of Chapter 11.

mortality rates for those ages, with motor-vehicle-accident rates being inversely related to the proportion of 15- to 24-year-olds. These findings enlarge the results above in two important ways. First, homicide, motor-vehicle-accidents, and non-motor-vehicle-accidents, in addition to suicide rates, are shown to be significantly correlated with the population changes in the younger ages. Second, there is evidence that these relationships exist in most race and sex breakdowns and in the 15- to 24-year-old age group in addition to the 15- to 19-year-olds.

One must always keep in mind the multidetermined nature of the various forms of violent death and question whether or not such single-variable relationships are spurious. The importance of the above findings lies in the potential for prediction of suicide, homicide, and accident rates among specific age groups. Inasmuch as the population of children and preadolescents decreased throughout the late 1960s and 1970s (Grove & Hetzel, 1968; *Vital Statistics of the United States*, 1961–1978), we would expect the population trends for 15- to 24-year-olds to shift and begin decreasing in the late 1970s and 1980s. We would also predict that suicide, homicide, and non-motor-vehicle-accident death rates among 15- to 24-year-olds would decrease simultaneously with the population decrease in that age group, and that the motor-vehicle-accident death rates would increase.

With respect to these relationships among violent deaths, the economy, and population changes, one must be curious about the significant negative correlation between motor-vehicle accidents and the population changes among 15- to 24-year-olds, particularly inasmuch as this finding is in opposition to the trends found in this chapter between youthful population changes and suicide, homicide, and non-motor-vehicle-accident death rates. While further research is necessary to enhance the understanding of this phenomenon, the finding regarding motor-vehicle accidents may relate to the economy and the youthful age group involved: During times of economic prosperity, there may be more opportunity for youngsters to own or use (and die in) motor vehicles, while in an economic depression such opportunity for motor-vehicle use may be less for youngsters but remain high enough for older age groups to account for their increased motor-vehicle-accident death rates.

These data appear to suggest that while the behavior of a single individual may be unpredictable, the violent death rates for populations over time are predictable. The data presented here lend themselves to potential intervention on a public health level. However, the specifics of the intervention on a social level seem discernible only when one attempts to bridge the epidemiologic–intrapsychic gap and hypothesize about what, on an intrapsychic level, could account for the epidemiologic data presented.

We made some preliminary remarks above to explain these epidemiologic relationships on a clinical basis and to justify our suggestions for interventions. Two psychodynamic explanations, not necessarily mutually exclusive, were advanced: One involved a competition, self-esteem, and failure cycle, and the other a process of progressive isolation. The intervention and prevention of increased rates of suicide, homicide, and accidents seem implied by the intrapsychic models and involve addressing the need for more focused services (psychiatric), positions (jobs, high schools, college enrollments, etc.) sooner, and cutting the time lag between the adolescent and young adult population changes and society's response to them. Such intervention is possible with this population model because the changes in the population of 15- to 24-year-olds can be predicted years in advance by the population figures for children and preadolescents.

It should also be noted that these epidemiologic data appear to be consistent with data from questionnaires and interviews with samples of normal adolescents. In studying thousands of adolescents, Offer, Ostrov, and Howard (1981) noted that the self-image of adolescents was better in the early 1960s than in the late 1970s for every category tested except the sexual sphere. These differences correspond closely to the smaller numbers of adolescents in the late 1950s and early 1960s and the larger number in the mid- to late 1970s.

In summary, although the relationship between the economy and mortality rates is well documented (bad economic conditions are related to higher mortality rates) (Brenner, 1971, 1979), one cannot predict future mortality rates from this relationship because, without considering population variables, one does not know what economic conditions will be like in the future. On the other hand, the population model suggested in this chapter may allow future predictions, not only of violent death rates (Holinger & Offer, 1982) but also of economic conditions (Easterlin, 1980) for certain age groups, because the population shifts for certain age groups are known years ahead. Finally, this predictive cycle perhaps becomes even more complete when one considers that the birth rate in the United States (which is responsible for most of the relevant population changes) tends to be inversely related to economic changes in the United states (i.e., high and low birth rates correspond to good and bad economic conditions, respectively) (Turner *et al.*, 1981).

Thus, the interrelationship of these variables becomes clearer: From the birth rate comes relevant population changes; these population changes appear to influence economic conditions (i.e., unemployment); economic conditions (and the population changes) tend to influence not only changes in violent death rates but also in the birth rate, thus completing the cycle. The potential for prediction of violent death rates seems to occur by breaking into the cycle and extracting the data on population changes.

CHAPTER TWELVE

VIOLENT DEATH PATTERNS IN THE UNITED STATES
Relationship to Population Changes and the Economy

SUMMARY, LITERATURE, AND METHODOLOGY

To summarize briefly the previous chapter: Predicting violent deaths has become an important subject of recent scientific scrutiny. The potential for the prediction of violent deaths has emerged as the relationships between violent deaths and economic and population variables have been increasingly studied by a number of investigators (Brenner, 1971, 1979; Easterlin, 1980; Shapiro & Wynne, 1982; Seiden & Freitas, 1980; Peck & Litman, 1973; Klebba, 1975; Turner, Fenn, & Cole, 1981; Holinger & Offer, 1982, 1984). Holinger and Offer (1982, 1984) suggest that the violent death rates for the adolescent and young adult age group could be predicted based on population changes (i.e., a population model). They found significant positive correlations between adolescent and young adult suicide, homicide, non-motor-vehicle-accident mortality rates, and the changes in the proportion of 15- to 24-year-olds in the population of the United States, 1933–1976. Significant negative correlations were found between motor-vehicle-accident mortality rates and the changes in the proportion of adolescents and young adults in the U.S. population. An important implication of the suggested relationship between adolescent violent death rates and changes in the adolescent population may be in the public health area and involves the possibility of effective intervention. Intervention is possible with a population model such as this because the changes in the adolescent population can be determined years ahead by the population figures for children and preadolescents.

The purpose of this chapter is to expand these results and ask the following questions: What is the relationship between violent death rates and population changes for all age groups, and might it be possible to predict fluctuations in certain violent deaths for specific age groups based on a population model?

While most of the relevant literature has been discussed above, it should also be noted that the cohort studies (Hellon & Solomon, 1980; Solomon & Hellon, 1980; Murphy & Wetzel, 1980) have supported the findings of recent upsurges in suicide rates among the young and youthful cohorts followed since about 1950; however, these studies have not systematically related such findings to population shifts in those age groups. Easterlin (1980) and Brenner (1971, 1979), with their extensive studies of population and economic variables, respectively, and other studies that relate population changes, economic changes, and violent death rates (Seiden & Freitas, 1980; Peck & Litman, 1973; Klebba, 1975; Hendin, 1982), began to suggest the potential for prediction of suicide and homicide rates. Turner *et al.* (1981) showed that the birth rate increased with good economic conditions and decreased with poor conditions.

The general methodologic problems in researching the epidemiology of violent deaths have been discussed in Chapter 3. For the study of prediction in this chapter, the sources of population, suicide, homicide, and accident data are noted in the respective tables and figures. The data used for Table 12-1 (1933–1982) and Figures 12-1 and 12-2 (1933–1982) are for the complete population, not samples. They include all suicides, homicides, and accidental deaths among the indicated age groups that occurred in the United States. Mortality data before 1933 are not included in Table 12-1 and Figures 12-1 and 12-2 because not all states were incorporated into the national mortality statistics prior to 1933 (Alaska was added in 1959 and Hawaii in 1960). The data used for Table 12-2 (1900–1979) and Figure 12-3 (1900–1979) include sample data from 1900 to 1932 (death registration areas) and data for the total U.S. population, 1933–1979. It should be reiterated that the data used in this chapter are mortality rates (deaths per 100,000 population), not simply number of deaths. Although it might be assumed that the number of deaths from a particular cause will increase with increases in the population, the mortality *rates* do not necessarily increase with an increase in population because the denominator is constant (i.e., deaths per 100,000 population).

The correlations in this chapter were derived by using the following logic: The most obvious explanation for an increase in the number of suicides, homicides, and motor-vehicle accidents in any one year in a particular age group (e.g., 15- to 24-year-olds in Table 12-1) is that there might have been more persons of that age group in that year. This obvious relationship should be linear. To remove this obvious effect, correlations were performed between the number of 15- to 24-year-olds in any one year and the number of suicides, homicides, and accidents in that year across the years 1933–1982. On the basis of these correlations, predicted suicide scores were derived that contain all the variance due to a linear association between the number of 15- to 24-year-olds in any one year and the number of suicides, homicides, and accidents in that group. Next, from suicides, homicides, and accidents in any one year the appropriate predicted scores were subtracted. The remainders were called "residual suicides," "residual homicides," "residual motor-vehicle accidents," "residual non-motor-vehicle accidents." These residual scores cannot contain any variance associated with the number of suicides, homicides, and accidents among 15- to 24-year-olds that in turn is due to a linear relationship between those numbers and the number of 15- to 24-year-olds in the general population. These residual scores were then correlated with the proportion of 15- to 24-year-olds to the general population across the years 1933–1982. There is a notable reduction in the variance in suicide, homicide, and accident rates that can be explained on the basis of the methodology presented above. It should be mentioned, however, that at issue is the potential prediction of rates for groups, not individual deaths (i.e., the purpose is not to establish a 1 : 1 correlation with individuals).

In addition to the possibility discussed below that there is a meaningful relationship between violent death rates and population shifts, one must also consider the possibility that either artifact or other variables are responsible for correlation. The possibility that the correlations are artifact due to changes in the federal classifying of suicide and homicide is unlikely, as described in earlier chapters, the comparability ratios for suicide and homicide have been rather consistent over the decades. However, the possibility that another variable is involved—specifically, period effects (Holford, 1983) due to economic trends—needs to be addressed. In the early 1930s (the starting point of these data, when the entire

U.S. population was included in the mortality figures), the mortality rates were at their peaks, probably due to the economic depression. The violent death rates decreased for several years following, reaching low points during the early 1940s (World War II). During the time of this decrease in rates, however, the population of the adults (35–64 years) in the United States increased steadily. These economic shifts could then be seen to contribute to the inverse correlations, with the population variable having coincidental rather than an etiologic relationship with the violent death rates. The time trends of violent deaths in the United States (e.g., the tendency of violent death rates to increase in times of economic depression, such as the early 1930s, and decrease during war, as in the early 1940s) have been presented in detail elsewhere (Holinger & Klemen, 1982).

RESULTS

Table 12-1 presents the correlation coefficients between violent death rates for specific age groups and the ratio of the population of that age group in the total population, United States, 1933–1982. These results focus on the findings in adolescence through

Table 12-1. Correlation Coefficients between Violent Death Rates and Population Ratios by 10-Year Age Intervals, United States, 1933–1982

	Age (years)				
	15–24	25–34	35–44	45–54	55–64
S	+.34**	NS	−.52*	NS	−.32***
H	+.41*	NS	−.68*	−.47*	−.25***
MVA	−.48*	−.55*	NS	NS	−.25***
NMVA	+.47*	+.71*	+.29***	+.32***	NS

Sources of suicide, homicide, and accident data: Vital Statistics—Special Reports (1956) (for 1933–1953); Grove and Hetzel (1968) (for 1954–1960); *Vital Statistics of the United States* (1961–1979) (for 1961–1979); unpublished data, National Center for Health Statistics (for 1980–1982).

Sources of population data: Grove and Hetzel (1968) (for 1933–1960); *Vital Statistics of the United States* (1961–1979) (for 1961–1979); unpublished data, National Center for Health Statistics (for 1980–1982).

Abbreviations: S = suicide; H = homicide; MVA = motor-vehicle accidents; NMVA = non-motor-vehicle accidents; NS = not significant.

*p < .001; **p < .01; ***p < .05.

adulthood. The youngest (0–14 years) and oldest (65–84 years) age groups will be noted only briefly in this chapter for the following reasons. The younger age groups (0–14 years) demonstrated some significant correlations; however, due to the difficulty in distinguishing the role of the parent's behavior and the victim's behavior in the death, more detailed examination of the correlations between population changes and death rates among the youngest age groups is beyond the scope of this chapter. With respect to the oldest age groups (65–84 years), although statistical trends similar to those reported previously were found (i.e., decreases in suicide rates accompanied increases in the proportion of older people) (Holinger & Offer, 1982), the correlations did not reach statistical significance.

The results will be presented first by the type of violent death, second, by age, and third, in relation to the economy.

Results by Type of Violent Death

Suicide rates showed significant positive correlations with the shifts in population ratios of 15- to 24-year-olds; that is, the suicide rates increased among that age group as their proportion in the total U.S. population increased, and the rates decreased as the proportion of the 15- to 24-year-olds decreased. Suicide rates showed significant inverse correlations with the shifts in population ratios for those aged 35–44 and 55–64; that is, increases in the proportion of 35- to 44-year-olds in the United States were associated with decreases in the suicide rates in those groups. Correlations between suicide rates and population ratios for 25- to 34-year-olds were not significant. A similar pattern was found for homicide rates: significant positive correlations between homicide rates and population shifts for 15- to 24-year-olds, nonsignificant correlations for 25- to 34-year-olds, and significant inverse correlations for those aged 35–44, 45–54, and 55–64. Significant inverse correlations were found between motor-vehicle-accident mortality rates and population shifts for 15- to 24-, 25- to 34-, and 55- to 64-year-olds. Correlations between non-motor-vehicle accidents and population shifts were significantly positive for those aged 15–24, 25–34, 35–44, and 45–54.

Results by Age

The results in Table 12-1 can also be examined by age. The 15- to 24-year-olds had significant positive correlations between all forms of violent death and population shifts, with the exception of motor-vehicle accidents, which were significantly negatively correlated. The 25- to 34-year-olds showed nonsignificant correlations for suicide and homicide rates, significant inverse correlations for motor-vehicle accidents, and significant positive correlations for non-motor-vehicle accident rates. The patterns for the three age groups of 35–64 years are somewhat similar to each other: All three groups show significant inverse correlations between suicide and homicide rates and population shifts, with the exception of suicide rates among 45- to 54-year-olds; correlations for motor-vehicle-accident rates were not significant except for the inverse correlation for 55- to 64-year-olds; and all had positive correlations for non-motor-vehicle-accident rates, except for 55- to 64-year-olds, which showed no significant correlations.

Figures 12-1 and 12-2 focus on suicide and homicide rates, and these figures present examples from two age groups in order to depict the differences between the younger and adult age groups. Figure 12-1 shows the changes over time in mortality rates for suicide and homicide rates for 15- to 24-year-olds, and the proportion of that age group from 1933 to 1982 in the United States. The mortality rates and proportion of 15- to 24-year-olds in the population can be seen to be rather parallel: Increases (and decreases) in the proportion of 15- to 24-year-olds are accompanied by increases (and decreases) in their suicide and homicide rates. Figure 12-2 shows the relationship between suicide and homicide rates and population changes among 35- to 44-year-olds. For the 35–44 age group, rates can be seen to have time trends somewhat opposite to the population changes: Decreases in the proportion of 35- to 44-year-olds are accompanied by increases in their suicide and homicide rates. For 35- to 44-year-olds, suicide and homicide rates were high during the early 1930s, decreased into the mid-1950s, increased again from the mid-1930s to the mid-1970s, and leveled off recently. In contrast, the proportion of 35- to 44-year-olds reached high levels during the 1940s, decreased throughout the 1950s and 1960s into the mid-1970s, and recently increased.

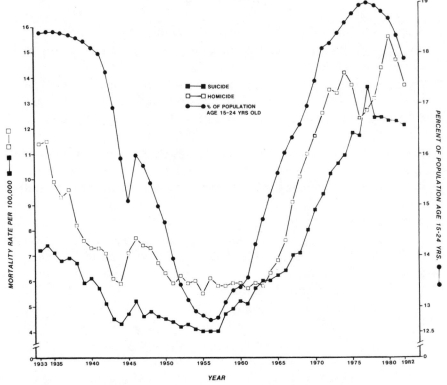

Figure 12-1. Violent death rates and population changes, 15- to 24-year-olds, United States, 1933–1982. *Sources of data*: Same as Table 12-1 (for 1933–1976); unpublished data, National Center for Health Statistics (for 1977–1982).

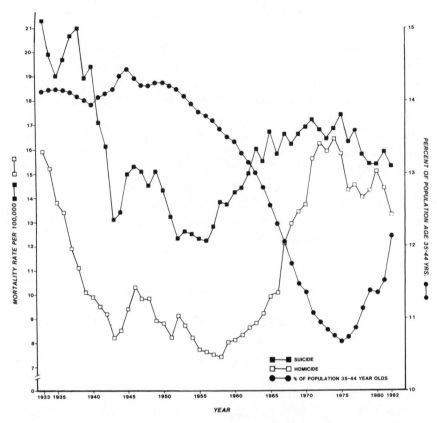

Figure 12-2. Violent death rates and population changes, 35- to 44-year-olds, United States, 1933–1982. *Sources of data*: Same as Figure 12-1.

Violent Deaths and the Economy

Finally, violent deaths were studied in relation to economic factors (economic conditions being defined by unemployment data, as in Brenner, 1971, 1979) and birth rates (indicators of population changes). Figure 12-3 shows that increases in the unemployment rate are accompanied by increases in the suicide, homicide, and motor-vehicle-accident mortality rates, while the birth rates decrease, United States, 1900–1979. Table 12-2 presents the correlation coefficients for these trends: The unemployment rates demonstrated significant positive correlations with suicide, homicide, and motor-vehicle-accident mortality rates, a significant negative correlation with the birth rate, and nonsignificant correlation with non-motor-vehicle-accident rates.

VIOLENT DEATHS AND POPULATION SHIFTS

Suicide and Homicide Mortality and Population Changes

The data suggest that significant positive correlations exist between adolescent and young adult (15- to 24-year-olds) suicide and homicide rates and the proportion of that age group in the United States, whereas significant negative correlations exist between suicide and homicide rates among middle and older adult age groups (35- to 64-year-olds) and their proportions in the population. These results may be understandable if one views the correlations as shifting from positive to negative as age increases. However, these findings and the resulting hypotheses regarding prediction should be viewed with caution due to both the methodologic problems inherent in utilizing national mortality data as well as the number of years required to adequately test such epidemiologic propositions over time.

One seems obligated to attempt preliminary explanations of the findings at this point. At least three levels of interpretation seem necessary and need to be subjected to further hypothesis testing: an epidemiologic–sociological level, a psychodynamic–clinical level, and a nosological level.

On the epidemiologic–sociological level, suicide and homicide rates may increase with increases in the proportion of 15- to

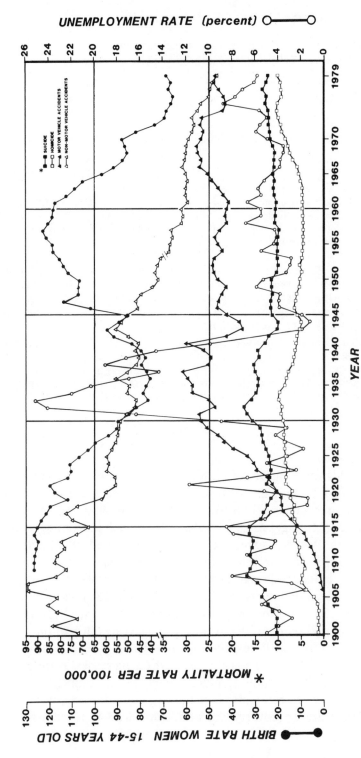

Figure 12-3. Violent death rates, birth rates, and unemployment rates, United States, 1900–1979. *Sources of data:* Same as Table 12-2.

187

Table 12-2. Correlation Coefficients between Violent Death Rates, Birth Rates, and Unemployment Rates, United States, 1900–1979

	S	H	MVA	NMVA	BR
H	+.33**				
MVA	−.34**	+.36*			
NMVA	+.43**	−.42*	−.82*		
BR	NS	−.71*	−.68*	+.49*	
UR	+.59*	+.37*	+.29**	NS	−.41*

Sources of suicide, homicide, and accident data: Vital Statistics—Special Reports (1956) (for 1900–1953); same as in Table 12-1 for 1954–1976; *Vital Statistics of the United States* (1977–1978) (for 1977–1978); unpublished data, National Center for Health Statistics (for 1979). Motor-vehicle-accident mortality data were not officially compiled by the United States until 1906.

Sources of birth rate data: Data not available prior to 1909; U.S. Bureau of the Census (1975) (for 1909–1970); *Vital Statistics of the United States* (1971) (for 1971); U.S. Bureau of the Census (1980) (for 1972); U.S. Bureau of the Census (1982–1983) (for 1973–1979).

Source of unemployment data: U.S. Bureau of the Census (1975) (for 1900–1970); U.S. Bureau of the Census (1982–1983) (for 1971–1979).

Abbreviations: S = suicide, 1900–1979; H = homicide, 1900–1979; MVA = motor-vehicle accidents, 1906–1979; NMVA = non-motor-vehicle accidents, 1900–1979; BR = birth rate = total live births per 1,000 population of women 15–44 years old, 1909–1979; UR = unemployment rate = percentage of civilian labor force unemployed, in thousands of persons age 16 years and over (except 1900–1947 [14 years and over]), 1900–1979; NS = not significant.

$*p < .001$; $**p < .01$.

24-year-olds for a variety of reasons. For example, increased competition for jobs, college positions, and academic and athletic honors come an increased number of adolescents who fail to attain such places (Holinger & Offer, 1982, 1984). Such reasoning is consistent with Barker's extensive data on large and small schools (Barker, 1968; Barker & Gump, 1964). In addition, the younger members of the 15–24 age group may be the least powerful and attractive force in society with respect to political pressure, jobs, and so on. On the other hand, the adults in the 35–64 group are much more powerful politically and, with the exception of the older adults, attractive with respect to employment (e.g., experience, schooling completed). Thus the population increases in the adult age group may lead not so much to increased competition and failure as to more economic benefits (e.g., greater and more successful pressure on government and union leaders to enlarge the job market, obtain more health services). Therefore, suicide and homicide rates would decrease with the increased population ratio in the adult age groups.

Explanations of the findings at the other two levels follow somewhat similar reasoning. For example, on the psychodynamic–clinical level, depressed adolescents with marginal ego capacities and an inadequately internalized sense of self-esteem may be at greater risk of suicide during times of increased numbers of adolescents due to the heightened competition for much-needed external sources of self-esteem (e.g., academic honors, places on athletic teams, etc.). On the nosological level, when the proportion of young people is high, adolescents with thought disorders or major affective disorders may be at greater risk of suicide not only for the above reasons, but also because of a relative decrease in psychiatric services, counselors, and the like, available for diagnosis and treatment.

The absence of significant correlations between suicide and homicide and population changes in the 25- to 34-year-olds might be explained as follows: As age increases, from 15–24, 25–34, 35–44 years old and up, the correlations shift from positive to negative, with the 25- to 34-year-olds being in the middle of the shift and the correlations "washing out" in the transition. This washout may occur because although the 25- to 34-year-olds are more attractive to employers than the 15- to 24-year-olds, they are not old enough to generate the political power to allow an increase in their numbers to create substantially greater economic benefits.

Accident Mortality and Population Changes

Three trends might be noted in examining accident mortality patterns and population changes. First, motor-vehicle-accident and non-motor-vehicle-accident mortality rates tend to respond in opposite directions in relation to population changes within almost all age groups: Motor-vehicle death rates tend to decrease with increases in population, whereas non-motor-vehicle death rates increase with population increases. Second, unlike suicide and homicide rates, there is no shift in the relationship between accidental deaths and population changes as age increases (i.e., as one follows the correlations from adolescence into the adult age groups).

The third trend involves the 15- to 24-year-olds and requires more detailed comment, as this group has been studied more extensively than the others. The finding in question is the significant negative correlation between motor-vehicle-accident rates and population shifts for 15- to 24-year-olds, particularly in the context of the significant positive correlations for suicide and homicide. Turner *et al.* (1981) have reported increases (and decreases) in economic conditions among adolescents and young adults which correspond closely to the respective decreases (and increases) in the population shifts in that age group. The significant inverse correlation between motor-vehicle-accident rates and population shifts in 15- to 24-year-olds may relate to the economic conditions and the youthful age group involved: During times of economic prosperity—and, simultaneously, a low youthful population (e.g., during the 1940s and 1950s)—there may be more opportunity for youngsters to own or use (and die in) motor vehicles, while in economic depression—and, simultaneously, a high youthful population (e.g., during the early 1930s and 1970s) there may be less opportunity for motor-vehicle use by youngsters, leading to the inverse correlation.

POTENTIAL PREDICTION: PSYCHIATRIC AND PUBLIC HEALTH IMPLICATIONS

One of the main features of published reports utilizing a population model has been the potential prediction of suicide, specifically among the young (Holinger & Offer, 1982, 1984; Hendin, 1982). Several researchers (Holinger & Offer, 1982, 1984; Maris, 1985; Hendin, 1982) have explicitly or implicitly predicted that as the absolute numbers and proportion of 15- to 24-year-olds began to level off and decrease during the late 1970s and 1980s, the suicide rates for those ages (which had been increasing over the previous 20 years with the increase in the youthful population) would begin to level off and decrease as well. This hypothesis has some support from recent data on suicide rates for 15- to 24-year-olds per 100,000 population in the United States*: 1977, 13.6; 1978, 12.4;

*Sources of data: *Vital Statistics of the United States* (1977–1979) (for 1977–1979 data); National Center for Health Statistics (1981) (for 1980 and 1981 data); National Center for Health Statistics (1984) (for 1982 data); National Center for Health Statistics (1983) (for 1983 data, based on a 10% sample of deaths).

1979, 12.4; 1980, 12.3; 1981, 12.3; 1982, 12.1; 1983, 11.7. The 1977 suicide rate of 13.6 is the highest rate ever recorded for 15- to 24-year-olds in the United States, and that peak, subsequent leveling off, and slight decrease in rates correspond to the leveling off and beginnings of the decrease in the youthful population.

It is interesting to note that these recent data do not lend support to one of the apparent implications of the cohort studies (Hellon & Solomon, 1980; Solomon & Hellon, 1980; Murphy & Wetzel, 1980). Cohort analyses have provided data to demonstrate the increase in suicide rates among the young (Solomon & Hellon, 1980; Hellon & Solomon, 1980; Murphy & Wetzel, 1980; Klerman, Lavori, Rice, Reich, Endicott, Andreasen, Keller, & Hirschfeld, unpublished data). Solomon and Hellon (1980), studying Alberta, Canada, during the years 1951–1977, identified 5-year age cohorts, and the suicide rates were followed as the cohorts aged. Suicide rates increased directly with age, regardless of gender. Once a cohort entered the 15- to 19-year-old age range with a high rate of suicide, the rate for that cohort remained consistently high as it aged. Murphy and Wetzel (1980) found the same phenomenon, in reduced magnitude, in birth cohorts of much greater size in the United States. Not only does each successive birth cohort start with a higher suicide rate, but at each successive 5-year interval it has a higher rate than the preceding cohort had at that age. Klerman *et al.* (unpublished data) have noted a similar cohort effect in their study of depressed patients.

However, there are similarities and differences between the population-model and the cohort-effect studies. The similarities are found in the emphasis on recent increases in suicide rates among the younger age groups. The differences are found in the predictive aspects. The cohort studies suggest that the suicide rates for the age groups under study would continue to increase as they are followed over time. Implicitly, the cohort studies also seem to suggest that the suicide rates for younger age groups would continue to increase as each new 5-year adolescent age group comes into being.

The predictions by the population model are different. The population model suggests that the suicide rates for younger age groups will begin leveling off and decreasing, inasmuch as the population of younger people has started to decrease, and the data presented above tend to support this idea. In addition, the population model suggests that as the current group of youngsters gets older, suicide rates will increase less than predicted by the cohort studies. It is well known that male suicide rates increase with age in the United States while female rates increase with age until about 65 and then decrease slightly (Kramer et al., 1972; Holinger & Klemen, 1982). Therefore, one would expect an increase in suicide rates with age consistent with this long-established pattern. However, the current group of adolescents and young adults make up an unusually large proportion of the U.S. population. The population model alone suggests that the larger the proportion of adults in the population, the lower will be their suicide rates. Thus, the population model would suggest that the suicide rates for the adult populations would decrease over the next several decades compared with adult rates in the past, consistent with the movement of the "baby boom" population increase through those adult age groups. This is not to say that the suicide rates for the older age groups will be less than for younger groups, but rather that the older groups of the future might be expected to have smaller suicide rates than the older groups of the past.

There are important psychiatric and public health implications in the population model. Based on current population projections, the decrease in the numbers and proportion of 15- to 24-year-olds will be ending in the mid-1990s, with another increase in 15- to 24-year-olds beginning at that time (U.S. Bureau of the Census, 1984). Thus the population model would suggest that the government, schools, employers, health services, and so on should be ready to respond to that increase in terms of increased psychiatric services, counselors, jobs, and high school and college expansion. A preventive response will thus be created, rather than an "after-the-fact" reactive model.

The issue of prediction should also be noted with respect to the older age groups. Epidemiologic trends indicate that suicide rates in the United States tend to demonstrate age effects (Holford, 1983): Male rates increase with age, while female rates show an increase throughout adulthood and a slight decrease in the oldest age groups (MacMahon, Johnson, & Pugh, 1963; Maris, 1985; Kramer et al., 1972). However, cohort effects can interact with these age effects, as described by Holford (1983) and others (Klerman et al., unpublished data). As the population of the older age groups has attained a higher proportion of the total U.S. population, their suicide rates have decreased to the lowest rates ever recorded for those age groups (Holinger & Offer, 1982). For example, as the population of 65- to 69-year-olds has increased to comprise around 4% of the total population, the suicide rates for that group have decreased to their lowest level, about 18 per 100,000 population (National Center for Health Statistics, 1984; Holinger & Offer, 1982; U.S. Bureau of the Census, 1984). These data would lead to the prediction that as the proportion of older people increases, their suicide rates would decrease, but probably not to the lower rates seen among the young (due to the fact that suicide rates increase with age). Again, important psychiatric and public health implications would result from these findings should the predictions hold up. For example, older people will be at particularly increasing risk of suicide when their proportions decrease, and health agencies, government, and business could respond with very specific services in mental and physical health, employment, and housing areas.

IMPLICATIONS FOR FUTURE RESEARCH

Four areas of future research appear particularly important with respect to violent deaths, their potential for prediction, and population changes. First, it is critical that the epidemiologic data be increasingly accurate, in terms of both mortality data (local and national) as well as the population bases from which mortality rates are derived. Epidemiology that utilizes national mortality data is a relatively young field in the United States; only since 1933 have complete population data, not just samples, been available for all states in the United States. Therefore, many more decades of data and study will be needed to test various hypotheses involved in these epidemiologic trends.

Second, prospective studies are needed to specifically test the hypotheses regarding the potential for the prediction of violent deaths using population shifts. To this end, mathematical models need to be developed that could predict violent death rates based on projections of the future population. These predictions of rates could then be measured against the actual findings over the next several years. Such models are currently being developed and will be the subject of future communications.

Third, at least two types of cross-cultural studies of violent mortality would be useful in enhancing an understanding of this leading cause of death: (1) further long-term cross-cultural comparisons of suicide, homicide, and accident rates, with a focus on period, cohort, and age effects; and (2) cross-cultural studies examining violent deaths and population changes specifically, in order to evaluate the predictive and preventive aspects of the population model.

Finally, an attempt has been made in this chapter to examine violent death mortality rates primarily from the perspective of a single variable—population changes. This focus on one variable has been undertaken because of its potential for prediction, with changes in population for the various age groups being known years in advance. Yet it is apparent that understanding something as complex as violent deaths (whether from an intrapsychic or an epidemiologic perspective) requires a concept of a general systems approach. From an epidemiologic perspective, the work of Easterlin (1980) on population changes and Brenner (1971, 1979) and others (Wasserman, 1987; MacMahon et al., 1963) on the economy become important. The relationship between economy and mortality rates is well documented, with poor economic conditions (as indicated by high unemployment rates) being related to higher mortality rates (Brenner, 1971, 1979; Wasserman, 1984; MacMahon et al., 1963). In addition, the birth rate in the United States (which, with immigration and increased life expectancy, will be responsible for most of the relevant population changes) tends to be inversely related to economic changes in the United States: Bad economic conditions correspond to low birth rates, and vice versa (Turner et al., 1981). An interacting system emerges within which violent death mortality may be understood from an epidemiologic perspective, and this system includes such variables as economic conditions, birth rates, and population shifts. However, despite the well-documented relationship between the economy and mortality rates, one cannot predict future violent death rates from this relationship because of the difficulty in predicting future economic conditions. Thus another important area of future research emerges: Further work is needed to determine if the population model discussed in this chapter will enable predictions not only of violent death rates but also of economic conditions for specific age groups (as per Easterlin's [1980] work), inasmuch as the population shifts for certain age groups are known years ahead.

CONCLUSIONS

CHAPTER THIRTEEN

SUMMARY AND DISCUSSION

The descriptive epidemiology and potential prediction of violent deaths have now been presented, along with an examination of the extent to which self-destructive tendencies may explain the epidemiologic patterns of violent deaths. It should be emphasized that these data suggest that time trends of suicide, homicide, and accidental deaths are understandable and are not random patterns.

Furthermore, it would appear that the patterns and predictions of violent deaths can be productively understood from a self-destructive perspective, that is, the concept of self-destructiveness has great explanatory power in the area of violent deaths. In fact, the term "violent deaths" is probably a misnomer because of the implication that the death is caused by external forces. As has been described, clinical data repeatedly demonstrate that homicides (people who are killed, not the killers) and accidental death as well as suicides result to some extent from various conscious and unconscious self-destructive motives in the victim. Perhaps one should use the term "self-destructive deaths" for these causes of mortality.

However, there is a factor that seems to make it difficult to examine scientifically the violent deaths from the self-destructive perspective, and that is the pejorative sense that so often accompanies any thoughts and feelings about self-destructive tendencies and suicide. For most people in Western culture, suicide and self-destructiveness seem to elicit feelings of abhorrence, revulsion, embarrassment, and shame. One almost gets a sense that the topic should be discussed in whispers. Yet it is precisely this emotional reaction to self-destructiveness that betrays its importance and power, as well as the elusiveness and difficulty in studying it. Aggression seems to trigger less emotional reaction. Freud demonstrated the tremendous negative reactions to sex in his culture, the importance of sex in various psychiatric conditions, and the degree to which thoughts and feelings about sex had undergone cultural as well as individual repressions. Similarly, Kohut (1971), in his studies of narcissistic character disorders, noted the pejorative attitudes toward the investment of the self and the needs to be special, admired, and appreciated. He contended that Western culture, with its altruistic concerns, fostered this pejorative attitude, and he suggested that the human being's wish to be special and admired was not only natural but that severe difficulties could arise if these emotional needs were not recognized and fulfilled in childhood. It would seem that the study of self-destructiveness has suffered the same fate as sex and narcissism in culture and the scientific community: That self-destructiveness has not been studied as seriously as it might because of the attitude of abhorrence surrounding self-destructiveness and perhaps death itself.

SUMMARY OF DATA

In order to organize the findings of this study and try to make some theoretical sense out of them, the data must first be summarized and presented according to the three main issues of the book: the epidemiology (distribution and frequency) of violent deaths (Section II); the extent to which all forms of violent death reflect self-destructive tendencies (Section III); and the prediction of violent death patterns for populations (Section IV).

The Epidemiology of Violent Deaths

The focus here is on the larger patterns. Descriptions of the more specific patterns for suicides, homicides, and accidents can be found in the appropriate chapters of Section II. Three major patterns emerge from the epidemiologic data.

The "Typological" Factor

First, the data seem to suggest that a certain proportion of the population is at risk of dying of a violent death, but that the type of violent death is dependent on one's age, race, and sex. For example, whites are at a much greater risk of dying by suicide, whereas nonwhites are much more likely to die of homicide; young people are more at risk of dying by homicide and older people by suicide, motor-vehicle accidents, and non-motor-vehicle accidents. Thus, race and age appear to determine the *type* of violent death from which one is most likely to die; sex seems to determine the *degree* of risk of dying from a particular type of violent death (e.g., females have lower rates than males for virtually every type of violent death at every age).

The "Societal" Factor

Second, neither age, race, nor sex protects against the large upswings and downswings seen in the time trends for suicides, homicides, and accidents. The societal factor will be used to account for these remarkably consistent peaks and valleys in rates. The societal factor is probably a mixture of variables, the most prominent of which are the economy, war, and population shifts.*

The "Generational" Factor

Third, within each specific type of violent death, the age patterns are usually similar regardless of sex and race considerations. One exception to this is suicide: Male rates tend to increase with age, whereas female rates increase to a peak at 35–64 years and then decrease.†

---

*The societal and generational factors should be distinguished from age, period, and cohort effects as used in epidemiology. Age effects involve changes in age-specific rates of mortality or illness over the life span of the individual (Holford, 1983); period effects involve changes in rates of mortality or illness during a particular historical period (Holford, 1983); and cohort effects involve differences in rates of mortality or illness among individuals defined by some shared temporal experience, for example, year or decade of birth (Holford, 1983). Age, period, and cohort effects can interact with each other, and these interactions may need analysis in order to understand an epidemiologic pattern. The societal factor roughly corresponds to period effects, and the generational factor to age effects. However, the terms "societal" and "generational" factors are used to convey an enlargement of the period and age concepts and to accentuate the consistency of these effects throughout the various forms of violent death.

†See previous footnote.

The Extent to Which All Forms of Violent Deaths Reflect
Self-Destructive Tendencies

First, the data are consistent with the hypothesis that self-destructive tendencies and violent deaths are related. The evidence appears to support the idea that suicides, homicides, and motor-vehicle accidents in particular have epidemiologic patterns that are very similar over time. Stated differently, the data seem to disprove a hypothesis that there is no relationship between self-destructiveness and violent deaths.

Second, contrary to popular opinion the violent death rate has tended to decrease over the 20th century and is currently near the lowest rate ever recorded. In addition, the violent death rate, with peaks in infancy and older age groups, tends to remain remarkably constant throughout all of adulthood (age groups 25–69). Finally, nonwhite males have the highest violent death rates.

The Prediction of Violent Death Patterns for Populations

The data suggest that suicide, homicide, motor-vehicle-, and non-motor-vehicle-accident mortality rates can be predicted for specific age groups on the basis of the population shifts of those groups. In particular, in the younger age groups, suicide, homicide, and non-motor-vehicle-accident mortality rates tend to be positively correlated with the corresponding population changes (i.e., those violent death rates increase and decrease as the population increases and decreases, respectively), while in the adult age groups suicide and homicide mortality rates tend to be inversely related to changes in the corresponding population. Inasmuch as the population for a certain age group is known years ahead of time, this model allows for the prediction of violent death rates for certain age groups.

INTERACTIONS BETWEEN THE EPIDEMIOLOGIC AND INTRAPSYCHIC PERSPECTIVES

The main methodological issue in this study involves the difficulty in understanding the relationship between the epidemiologic–sociological model and the intrapsychic model. As one works with both the clinical data (i.e., through the treatment of patients) as well as with the epidemiologic data, it becomes apparent that these two perspectives shed light on each other. Specifically, the clinical data suggest hypotheses with respect to self-destructiveness that are valuable in understanding the epidemiologic data, and the epidemiologic data appear to enhance the understanding of certain clinical data. For example, the clinical data increasingly indicated that, in addition to suicide, those who became involved in accidents (accidental deaths) or got themselves killed (homicide) had conscious or unconscious self-destructive tendencies. That is, these deaths were psychologically determined rather than being just accidents or entirely out of the individual's control.* Freud (1901), Menninger (1938), and Farberow (1979) are among those who have documented the self-destructiveness and psychological determinism behind such clinical episodes. These ideas, derived from clinical intrapsychic data, were then utilized to study the epidemiologic data. In order to study self-destructiveness on an epidemiologic level, it appears one has to go beyond suicide and examine homicide and accidents. How would the epidemiologic data look if one assumed that to some extent self-destructive tendencies were involved in homicide and accidents as well as in suicides? Sections II and III of this book tend to demonstrate that suicide, homicide, and accident rates are rather parallel over time. These results call into question traditional understanding of the relationships between suicide and homicide; specifically, the positive correlations found here contradict Henry and Short's (1954) findings of an inverse relationship. In addition, an appreciation of the clinical data (i.e., self-destructiveness underlying homicide and accidental deaths) makes more understandable the epidemiologic finding of parallel rates for violent deaths.

It should be reiterated that the data presented in this book are epidemiologic data; that is, they involve the distribution and frequency of violent deaths. The epidemiologic data are deaths—self-destructiveness by definition. However, it should be mentioned that attempts to understand the epidemiologic data and patterns may

---

*"Self-destructive tendencies" in this sense is a phenomenological term; that is, the person gets killed. The term does not imply a particular motive, for example, that the victim really wanted to die or really wanted to be helped or cared for. This issue of phenomenology and motives will be taken up in more detail below.

involve turning to intrapsychic hypotheses (Holinger & Offer, 1982, 1984). In focusing on the epidemiologic data and addressing motivational issues below, it might be noted that descriptively there is a wide range of self-destructive behaviors. We have called this a "continuum of self-destructive behavior" (Holinger & Offer, 1981). Such self-destructive behavior can range from subtle and minor self-sabotage (forgetting something, tripping over the curb), to more serious damage (self-mutilation, not addressing one's health needs), to overt self-destruction, that is, suicide. These behaviors may be conscious or unconscious. In addition to the notion of a continuum of self-destructive behaviors, the epidemiologic data might be examined from another perspective: To what extent are there self-destructive tendencies in all violent deaths? To address the question in this way begins to lead to an examination of motivation behind the deaths. One might calculate the number of violent deaths that could be said to result from conscious or unconscious self-destructive tendencies by applying an appropriate percentage (as derived from the literature) to each form of violent death: for example, 100% of suicides, 25% of homicides, 25% of motor-vehicle accidents, and 25% of non-motor-vehicle accidents. This would give a rate for violent deaths that might most closely approximate the rate of those that were due to conscious or unconscious self-destructive tendencies.* A distinction should be made here between deriving a rate of violent deaths that could be said to have self-destruction as a primary motivation and the idea that some degree of self-destructiveness is present in every violent death. Again, in attempting to understand the epidemiologic patterns, one is inexorably drawn to intrapsychic hypotheses and motivational factors, and the different levels of conceptualization must be clarified.

In examining the epidemiologic–sociological perspective on violent deaths, one must also ask what it means for a group of people to be at risk of dying a violent death. Certainly people of different ages, sexes, and races have higher rates of one kind of violent death than another. For example, white males have the highest suicide rates, and nonwhite males have the highest homi-

---

*I am indebted to Leo Levy, Ph.D., for this conceptualization of how one might calculate the violent death rate.

cide rates. Descriptively one can say that a particular group has a higher rate of one kind of violent death, but to say that those in a group are at higher risk of dying a violent death begins to shift to an individual perspective. This introduction of the individual perspective into the epidemiologic model has two aspects. First, to say that a group is at particular risk of dying from, for example, suicide, means that there are certain members in that group who have only marginal strengths, resources, adaptive capacities—intrapsychic ego capacities. Second, as has been shown throughout this book, data indicate that no type of violent death, or any race, sex, or age group escape the impact of increases and decreases in rates based on certain social factors, for example, economic factors or population changes. Thus to adequately understand a group being at risk in an epidemiologic sense appears to involve introducing not only an intrapsychic perspective (i.e., certain members in that group functioning marginally regarding various ego capacities), but also an appreciation that certain social forces, for example, economic conditions, will be involved and have an impact on the members of that group and on the rates for that group.

Similar conceptual problems are encountered when one tries to understand epidemiologic data that suggest that violent death rates remain rather steady throughout adulthood (after high rates in infancy, a decrease during childhood, and an increase throughout adolescence), with an increase in older age groups. How does one understand this epidemiologic finding? Does it suggest that society will tolerate a certain extent of violent death but no more? Or does it reflect a constant degree of affective illness (e.g., depression with its self-destructive results)? Again, the question involves what models and levels of abstraction one uses to attempt to understand epidemiological data.

In understanding epidemiologic data it has been helpful to use the idea that to some extent self-destructive tendencies underlie violent deaths. Conscious and unconscious self-destructive tendencies may have explanatory usefulness in understanding such concerns as war, some popular psychology movements (e.g., PMA [Positive Mental Attitude]), and similar issues. For example, in understanding war perhaps there has been an overemphasis on aggression, and one needs to pay more attention to the self-destructive motivation behind it. The soldiers who volunteer to fight and die, for instance.* War itself, paradoxically, may be an expression of unconscious self-destructive tendencies, rather than reflecting externally directed aggression (intrapsychically). PMA and similar movements are, not infrequently, external evidence of intrapsychic efforts to deny depression and unconscious self-destructive tendencies.

It is hoped that the discussion above indicates the potential use of intrapsychic hypotheses in enhancing an understanding of epidemiologic data if one is aware of the different levels of abstractions and data involved. While the intrapsychic perspective will be the subject of future communications and is not the main focus of this epidemiologic study of violent deaths and self-destructiveness, it is appropriate to convey here a sense of the complexity of this perspective. The problem involves the phenomenologic and motivational distinctions. For example, violent death data reflect those who have died, and many intrapsychic hypotheses have been advanced to explain the motivation for such self-destruction: for example, killing oneself to gain revenge against a disappointing and hated parent, anger redirected inwardly at introjects, masochism (pleasure in unpleasure), narcissistic gratification (dying to save someone else, or dying in a war—this self-destruction, while phenomenologically a death, intrapsychically could be seen as maintaining the self, enhancing one's self-esteem through death, avoiding humiliation), and so on. Thus while a death results and is descriptively "self-destructive," the motivation, conscious or unconscious, may be to kill the self or to preserve it in some way, even through death. Additional complications in sorting out the motivations occur because of the increasing understanding that an individual may have different "selves" in the id, ego, and superego structures (Kohut, 1971). Thus defining "self-destructive" on an epidemiologic level is a very different task from understanding the concept intrapsychically. While the yield from carrying ideas from the intrapsychic field to epidemiology may be great, understanding self-destructiveness on an individual intrapsychic level must be done with great care and sophistication.

---

*This attention to self-destructiveness is not meant to deny the role of aggression, self-esteem, self-cohesion, and so on in individuals and groups in war, but rather to focus on the self-destructive component.

FUTURE CONSIDERATIONS

Two final questions must be noted as issues for the future; evolution and self-destructiveness, and violent deaths specifically among the young. First, one must ask: Do self-destructive tendencies in man have any evolutionary value, or are they an aberration (an evolutionary mistake), or are they irrelevant from an evolutionary perspective? Or to address the issue in other words: Has man evolved (in part) because of self-destructive tendencies, or in spite of these tendencies, or are such tendencies not relevant to man's evolution?

This question requires far more research and elaboration of the various aspects of self-destruction than had been presented here. However, the hypothesis that self-destructive tendencies intrapsychically reflect aggressive impulses turned back upon the self may be useful in beginning to ask how, contrary to common sense, self-destructive tendencies could possibly be an aid to the preservation of the species. It seems conceivable that as man struggles to control his destructive aggression—regardless of the hypotheses of the origin of aggression (e.g., the result of frustration, or innate, etc.)—the psychological mechanism by which aggression is turned back upon the self may be the result of an evolutionary process necessary to allow for a civilized society. Uncontrolled aggressive impulsiveness would lead to chaos and an absence of social interaction as we know it, and the capacity to turn such aggression in on the self may be a necessary concomitant of human society—at least until human beings developmentally become better able to separate thoughts and feelings from action.

Second, while much has been written elsewhere about violent deaths among younger groups specifically, especially regarding epidemiology and prediction (e.g., Holinger & Offer, 1982, 1984; Holinger & Luke, 1984), brief mention is needed here regarding some of the topics considered above. Some have suggested that one motivation for war is that of the older generation killing off the younger generation (or those in power destroying their younger potential rivals), an idea stemming from Freud's elaboration of intrapsychic oedipal issues on a social level. The recent studies correlating violent deaths among the young to changes in their population may be related to this idea: All forms of youthful violent death rates except motor-vehicle accidents tend to increase with increases in the youthful population. The population of 15- to 24-year-olds peaked in the late 1970s. At this time the Vietnam War had ended, and without a war the young became statistically at higher risk of dying from different forms of deaths: suicide, homicide, and accidents. These patterns also appear to be related to the economy: Violent deaths are positively correlated with bad economic conditions. As the population of 15- to 24-year-olds increases, competition for jobs, college positions, and so on increases, and there are more failures and thus more self-destructive deaths. During the economic depression of the early 1930s, the population of 15- to 24-year-olds reached another peak, then decreased throughout the 1940s and 1950s and began to increase in the 1960s. It is difficult to connect war to these changes in population: The peak population of 15- to 24-year-olds occurred several years prior to U.S. involvement in World War II, and the Vietnam War occurred prior to the peak in 15- to 24-year-olds in the 1970s. It would seem, however, that when the population of 15- to 24-year-olds is high and their ratio in the total U.S. population is high, the young are at particular risk of dying by violent death (Holinger & Offer, 1982, 1984; Holinger, 1981). The hypothesis being formulated involves whether or not, in the absence of war, the young will kill themselves through suicides, homicides, and accidents at a proportionately higher rate as their population increases beyond a certain critical mass. Further research to evaluate this hypothesis is currently under way and will be the subject of future communications.

VIOLENT DEATH RATES, UNITED STATES, 1900–1984
By Type of Mortality, Sex, and Race*

SUICIDE RATES

Year	Total	White males	White females	Nonwhite males	Nonwhite females
1984	12.4	21.3	5.9	10.8	2.6
1983	11.3	19.3	5.6	10.7	2.6
1982	11.6	19.4	5.8	10.8	2.6
1981	11.5	18.9	6.0	11.2	3.0
1980	11.9	19.9	5.9	10.6	2.6
1979	12.1	19.6	6.5	12.0	3.1
1978	12.5	20.2	6.9	11.1	3.1
1977	13.3	21.4	7.3	11.4	3.5
1976	12.5	19.8	7.2	11.0	3.2
1975	12.7	20.1	7.4	10.6	3.3
1974	12.1	19.2	7.1	10.2	3.0
1973	12.0	18.8	7.0	10.0	3.0
1972	12.0	18.5	7.3	10.3	3.3
1971	11.7	17.9	7.3	8.6	3.4
1970	11.6	19.0	7.1	8.5	2.9
1969	11.1	17.2	6.8	8.1	2.8
1968	10.7	16.9	6.3	7.3	2.4
1967	10.8	16.8	6.5	7.6	2.7
1966	10.9	17.2	6.3	7.8	2.4
1965	11.1	17.4	6.6	7.7	2.5
1964	10.8	17.2	6.1	7.2	2.2
1963	11.0	17.8	6.3	7.9	2.2
1962	10.9	17.8	5.9	7.2	2.2
1961	10.4	17.1	5.3	7.6	1.9

Sources of data: Same as Figure 4-1; unpublished data, National Center for Health Statistics (for 1981–1984); data by sex and race not available prior to 1910.

Year	Total	White males	White females	Nonwhite males	Nonwhite females
1960	10.6	17.6	5.3	7.2	2.0
1959	10.6	17.7	5.0	7.5	1.9
1958	10.7	18.0	5.1	7.1	1.8
1957	9.8	16.5	4.6	6.8	1.4
1956	10.0	16.9	4.8	6.1	1.6
1955	10.2	17.2	4.9	6.1	1.5
1954	10.1	17.5	4.5	6.8	1.5
1953	10.1	17.2	4.6	6.4	1.3
1952	10.0	16.9	4.7	6.1	1.3
1951	10.4	17.3	5.0	6.6	1.7
1950	11.4	19.0	5.5	7.0	1.7
1949	11.4	19.1	5.5	7.1	1.5
1948	11.2	18.4	5.7	6.9	1.5
1947	11.5	18.9	6.0	6.5	1.6
1946	11.5	18.7	6.2	6.1	1.8
1945	11.2	18.5	6.3	5.7	1.5
1944	10.0	16.0	5.9	4.8	1.4
1943	10.2	16.4	5.9	4.8	1.3
1942	12.0	19.7	6.3	6.0	2.0
1941	12.8	20.8	6.8	6.6	1.7
1940	14.4	23.5	7.3	7.2	2.1
1939	14.1	23.4	7.1	6.5	2.0
1938	15.3	25.3	7.4	7.4	2.5
1937	15.0	24.5	7.6	7.4	2.5
1936	14.3	23.3	7.3	7.0	2.4
1935	14.3	23.3	7.2	7.4	2.7
1934	14.9	24.6	7.3	6.9	2.6
1933	15.9	26.8	7.3	7.7	2.2
1932	17.4	29.4	7.7	8.6	2.5
1931	16.8	28.2	7.6	8.0	2.5
1930	15.6	25.9	7.4	7.6	2.4
1929	13.9	22.5	7.1	7.6	2.3
1928	13.5	22.1	6.6	7.2	2.4
1927	13.2	21.2	6.6	7.0	2.4
1926	12.6	20.0	6.6	6.2	2.6
1925	12.0	19.1	6.2	6.1	2.0
1924	11.9	19.2	5.9	6.3	2.3
1923	11.5	18.1	6.2	5.6	1.8
1922	11.7	18.7	6.1	6.3	2.1
1921	12.4	20.0	6.1	6.9	2.3
1920	10.2	15.4	6.1	5.2	2.0

Year	Total	White males	White females	Nonwhite males	Nonwhite females
1919	11.5	17.5	6.7	6.0	2.0
1918	12.3	19.0	6.5	8.4	2.5
1917	13.0	20.1	6.9	7.2	2.5
1916	13.7	21.5	6.8	7.9	2.0
1915	16.2	24.8	7.7	13.3	5.1
1914	16.1	24.5	7.8	14.6	4.6
1913	15.4	23.6	7.2	12.7	4.7
1912	15.6	23.8	7.4	13.8	5.2
1911	16.0	24.1	7.6	19.3	5.3
1910	15.3	23.2	7.2	16.9	6.0
1909	16.0				
1908	16.8				
1907	14.5				
1906	12.8				
1905	13.5				
1904	12.2				
1903	11.3				
1902	10.3				
1901	10.4				
1900	10.2				

HOMICIDE RATES

Year	Total	White males	White females	Nonwhite males	Nonwhite females
1984	8.4	8.3	2.9	40.9	9.8
1983	8.6	8.4	2.8	40.9	9.8
1982	9.7	9.5	3.1	52.2	10.5
1981	10.4	10.3	3.1	58.5	11.4
1980	10.7	10.9	3.2	57.8	12.1
1979	10.0	9.9	3.0	56.2	12.2
1978	9.4	9.2	2.9	52.6	11.8
1977	9.2	8.7	2.9	53.6	12.0
1976	9.1	8.3	2.7	55.8	12.5
1975	10.0	9.1	2.9	62.6	13.8
1974	10.2	8.9	2.8	67.2	14.5
1973	9.8	8.3	2.8	65.8	14.6
1972	9.4	7.7	2.3	70.1	13.4
1971	9.1	7.3	2.3	67.7	13.9

Year	Total	White males	White females	Nonwhite males	Nonwhite females
1970	8.3	6.8	2.1	60.8	12.3
1969	7.7	6.0	2.0	58.1	11.7
1968	7.3	5.9	1.9	54.6	11.6
1967	6.8	5.3	1.9	49.6	11.9
1966	5.9	4.5	1.8	43.5	10.6
1965	5.5	4.4	1.6	40.1	10.0
1964	5.1	3.9	1.6	37.4	9.2
1963	4.9	3.9	1.5	35.7	9.1
1962	4.8	3.8	1.6	35.5	8.9
1961	4.7	3.6	1.5	33.6	8.9
1960	4.7	3.6	1.4	34.5	9.9
1959	4.6	3.5	1.4	35.0	9.4
1958	4.5	3.4	1.4	34.9	9.3
1957	4.5	3.2	1.3	36.5	9.2
1956	4.6	3.3	1.3	37.1	10.3
1955	4.5	3.4	1.2	36.9	9.5
1954	4.8	3.5	1.4	40.6	9.5
1953	4.8	3.5	1.4	41.3	9.6
1952	5.2	3.7	1.3	45.4	10.8
1951	4.9	3.6	1.4	41.3	10.7
1950	5.3	3.9	1.4	45.5	11.2
1949	5.4	4.1	1.4	45.8	11.4
1948	5.9	4.5	1.5	51.0	11.7
1947	6.1	4.8	1.5	51.5	11.9
1946	6.4	4.9	1.5	54.4	12.4
1945	5.7	4.9	1.3	48.0	10.7
1944	5.0	4.0	1.2	44.1	9.7
1943	5.1	4.2	1.2	42.5	9.9
1942	5.9	4.4	1.3	53.5	12.1
1941	6.0	4.5	1.3	55.0	12.6
1940	6.3	5.0	1.4	55.5	13.0
1939	6.5	5.3	1.4	56.0	13.8
1938	6.9	5.8	1.7	56.4	13.2
1937	7.7	6.5	2.0	62.7	14.3
1936	8.1	6.9	1.9	66.7	15.6
1935	8.5	7.7	2.0	67.2	14.0
1934	9.7	9.2	2.2	74.2	15.0
1933	9.8	9.7	2.4	70.7	14.5
1932	9.1	9.3	2.2	63.9	15.0
1931	9.3	9.3	2.3	66.3	14.9
1930	8.9	8.9	2.4	62.4	14.7

Year	Total	White males	White females	Nonwhite males	Nonwhite females
1929	8.4	7.9	2.2	60.7	14.6
1928	8.7	8.2	2.1	64.4	14.5
1927	8.5	8.0	2.2	65.8	15.4
1926	8.5	8.1	2.1	69.0	15.6
1925	8.4	8.2	2.1	65.5	14.2
1924	8.2	7.9	2.2	61.4	13.6
1923	7.9	7.8	2.0	59.1	13.3
1922	8.1	8.7	2.0	52.2	12.6
1921	8.1	9.4	2.4	49.4	12.7
1920	6.8	7.5	2.0	45.9	10.8
1919	7.2	8.2	2.1	46.5	10.7
1918	6.5	7.7	1.9	44.6	11.0
1917	6.9	8.2	2.2	47.2	10.1
1916	6.3	7.7	2.0	43.9	9.7
1915	5.9	7.3	2.2	45.4	12.9
1914	6.2	7.8	2.3	49.4	10.6
1913	6.1	7.6	2.1	49.8	10.3
1912	5.4	7.0	2.1	43.3	10.9
1911	5.5	7.3	2.0	46.7	11.7
1910	4.6	6.1	1.9	32.1	11.1
1909	4.2				
1908	4.8				
1907	4.9				
1906	3.9				
1905	2.1				
1904	1.3				
1903	1.1				
1902	1.2				
1901	1.2				
1900	1.2				

MOTOR-VEHICLE-ACCIDENT MORTALITY RATES

Year	Total	White males	White females	Nonwhite males	Nonwhite females
1984	19.6	29.1	11.5	25.8	8.1
1983	18.5	27.8	10.3	26.1	8.1
1982	19.3	29.3	10.5	26.7	8.3
1981	21.8	33.4	11.7	30.1	8.7

Year	Total	White males	White females	Nonwhite males	Nonwhite females
1980	23.5	35.9	12.8	31.5	9.3
1979	23.8	36.6	12.8	32.3	9.6
1978	24.0	36.2	13.1	34.1	10.6
1977	22.9	34.1	12.7	33.8	9.8
1976	21.9	32.5	12.1	32.9	10.0
1975	21.5	32.2	11.4	33.8	10.0
1974	22.0	33.0	11.4	34.5	10.6
1973	26.5	38.4	14.5	43.5	14.0
1972	27.0	38.9	15.3	44.7	13.7
1971	26.4	38.0	14.7	43.8	14.3
1970	26.9	39.1	14.8	44.3	13.9
1969	27.6	40.0	15.1	47.0	14.5
1968	27.5	40.0	14.8	46.3	13.9
1967	26.7	39.0	14.7	42.6	13.8
1966	27.1	39.5	14.8	43.0	14.0
1965	25.4	37.1	13.9	39.7	12.8
1964	24.5	35.7	13.8	37.9	11.6
1963	23.1	34.3	12.7	36.6	11.0
1962	22.0	32.5	12.1	34.6	10.8
1961	20.8	30.8	11.0	32.8	10.3
1960	21.3	31.5	11.2	34.4	10.1
1959	21.5	31.9	11.1	35.4	10.2
1958	21.3	31.8	10.9	35.4	9.7
1957	22.7	33.9	11.3	38.4	11.8
1956	23.7	35.3	11.6	42.6	11.9
1955	23.4	35.0	11.5	40.1	12.1
1954	22.1	33.1	10.8	38.3	11.4
1953	24.0	35.8	11.7	43.3	11.9
1952	24.3	36.5	11.7	42.7	11.8
1951	24.1	36.5	11.4	41.7	12.0
1950	23.1	35.1	10.9	38.2	10.8
1949	21.3	32.7	10.0	34.8	8.9
1948	22.1	34.3	10.2	33.8	8.3
1947	22.8	35.9	10.5	32.4	7.7
1946	23.9	37.9	10.7	33.9	9.0
1945	21.2	35.3	9.1	31.2	7.1
1944	18.3	29.8	7.7	29.7	6.6
1943	17.7	28.9	7.2	28.7	5.6
1942	21.1	33.8	8.8	33.6	7.3
1941	30.0	46.2	13.9	48.3	11.0
1940	26.2	40.5	12.3	38.6	9.4

Year	Total	White males	White females	Nonwhite males	Nonwhite females
1939	24.7	38.0	11.6	37.1	9.5
1938	25.1	38.5	11.8	37.5	10.0
1937	30.8	47.3	14.7	44.1	11.1
1936	29.7	45.4	14.2	44.7	11.3
1935	28.6	43.9	13.7	40.5	9.6
1934	28.6	44.3	13.5	39.0	10.0
1933	25.0	38.1	12.4	33.9	8.7
1932	23.6	35.8	12.0	29.8	8.9
1931	27.1	41.0	13.9	34.7	10.4
1930	26.7	40.3	13.7	34.9	9.4
1929	25.5	38.4	13.2	33.6	9.5
1928	23.2	34.8	12.3	27.6	8.5
1927	21.6	32.0	11.6	27.6	8.0
1926	19.9	29.4	10.7	25.2	7.9
1925	16.8	24.7	9.4	20.1	6.8
1924	15.3	22.6	8.4	19.0	5.6
1923	14.6	22.1	7.9	15.1	4.3
1922	12.4	19.2	6.5	10.5	3.2
1921	11.3	17.3	6.1	8.9	2.4
1920	10.3	15.8	5.5	8.4	2.2
1919	9.3	14.4	5.0	7.4	2.0
1918	9.3	14.6	4.4	9.0	2.3
1917	8.6	13.6	4.1	7.2	1.6
1916	7.1	11.3	3.2	5.7	1.1
1915	5.8	9.0	2.6	5.6	2.0
1914	4.2	6.6	1.9	3.5	0.4
1913	3.8	6.0	1.7	3.6	1.1
1912	2.8	4.3	1.3	4.0	0.6
1911	2.1	3.3	0.9	2.4	0.6
1910	1.8	2.7	0.8	1.5	0.3
1909	1.2				
1908	0.8				
1907	0.7				
1906	0.4				
1905					
1904					
1903					
1902					
1901					
1900					

ACCIDENT MORTALITY RATES EXCLUDING MOTOR-VEHICLE ACCIDENTS (NON-MOTOR-VEHICLE-ACCIDENT MORTALITY RATES)

Year	Total	White males	White females	Nonwhite males	Nonwhite females
1984	19.7	26.1	12.8	32.7	12.8
1983	16.8	24.0	8.0	36.5	13.0
1982	17.3	24.9	8.2	37.8	12.2
1981	18.0	25.7	8.4	40.2	12.7
1980	23.2	30.4	14.4	42.9	16.9
1979	23.1	30.6	14.3	42.4	15.5
1978	24.4	32.1	15.4	44.1	16.3
1977	24.8	32.7	15.7	45.4	16.8
1976	25.0	33.0	15.8	45.8	16.3
1975	26.8	35.5	16.7	50.2	17.9
1974	27.5	36.1	17.5	50.7	18.7
1973	28.7	37.4	18.2	55.0	19.6
1972	28.4	36.7	18.1	55.1	20.1
1971	28.6	36.6	18.2	57.4	21.4
1970	29.5	38.2	18.3	60.7	21.6
1969	30.0	38.7	19.0	58.7	22.8
1968	30.0	37.7	19.4	61.9	23.2
1967	30.4	38.6	19.9	59.8	22.9
1966	30.9	38.6	20.2	61.7	26.1
1965	30.4	38.0	20.1	59.0	24.5
1964	29.7	37.2	19.6	57.4	25.0
1963	30.3	37.8	20.3	57.8	27.1
1962	30.3	37.9	20.3	57.6	27.1
1961	29.6	37.2	19.5	55.4	25.8
1960	31.0	38.6	20.4	60.6	28.3
1959	30.7	38.7	19.9	58.7	27.3
1958	31.0	38.7	20.2	59.0	29.5
1957	33.2	41.5	22.2	62.4	29.5
1956	33.0	41.6	21.9	61.0	27.6
1955	33.5	42.3	22.3	60.7	28.7
1954	33.8	42.8	22.4	61.4	28.8
1953	36.1	46.1	23.5	67.3	29.9
1952	37.5	47.2	24.9	70.6	31.7
1951	38.4	49.2	25.3	68.4	30.9
1950	37.5	47.4	25.4	65.7	29.1
1949	39.3	50.2	27.1	65.0	26.7
1948	44.8	56.4	32.3	71.4	28.8
1947	46.4	59.5	32.4	72.5	29.7

Year	Total	White males	White females	Nonwhite males	Nonwhite females
1946	45.9	59.4	31.9	70.7	28.1
1945	50.9	70.2	33.7	74.5	28.7
1944	53.0	74.5	33.3	76.2	29.1
1943	55.7	77.8	34.7	76.7	30.9
1942	50.1	67.7	32.2	76.9	28.7
1941	45.9	60.1	30.8	72.9	26.4
1940	47.0	60.0	32.5	75.0	30.4
1939	45.6	58.4	31.8	71.7	27.0
1938	46.7	59.9	32.5	72.0	28.8
1937	50.4	66.3	32.9	81.0	31.2
1936	55.7	72.3	37.3	88.4	35.8
1935	49.3	64.5	32.5	78.1	31.6
1934	50.8	67.2	32.5	83.1	32.0
1933	46.9	61.6	30.5	76.8	29.0
1932	47.2	62.4	30.2	78.8	28.6
1931	50.7	69.3	30.5	79.9	31.2
1930	53.1	72.8	30.8	91.4	33.1
1929	54.2	74.9	30.6	96.1	34.9
1928	54.9	75.8	30.8	98.9	36.5
1927	55.5	76.8	30.4	109.4	34.6
1926	57.3	78.8	31.9	109.1	39.5
1925	59.7	82.7	33.3	109.5	40.8
1924	58.5	81.2	32.4	102.3	44.7
1923	59.7	84.0	32.9	101.6	38.5
1922	55.9	78.4	31.5	88.6	37.2
1921	55.5	77.6	31.1	91.0	35.1
1920	59.7	83.1	33.2	99.0	42.7
1919	68.1	88.5	32.6	101.0	40.7
1918	72.2	106.8	35.9	118.1	45.8
1917	77.4	112.6	38.5	129.6	53.4
1916	74.5	110.7	35.6	118.6	43.9
1915	67.7	99.5	33.1	116.8	44.4
1914	72.5	107.0	34.8	125.6	48.9
1913	79.9	119.9	36.4	138.6	49.2
1912	78.0	116.2	36.6	137.8	45.0
1911	81.5	120.7	39.0	140.7	52.9
1910	82.4	126.1	35.8	136.2	41.0
1909	77.5				
1908	82.1				
1907	94.1				
1906	94.0				

Year	Total	White males	White females	Nonwhite males	Nonwhite females
1905	81.3				
1904	85.4				
1903	81.4				
1902	72.5				
1901	83.8				
1900	72.3				

ACCIDENT (TOTAL) MORTALITY RATES

Year	Total	White males	White females	Nonwhite males	Nonwhite females
1984	39.3	55.2	24.3	58.6	21.0
1983	35.3	51.8	18.3	62.5	21.0
1982	36.6	54.1	18.7	64.5	20.5
1981	39.8	59.1	20.2	70.4	21.4
1980	46.7	66.3	27.2	74.4	26.3
1979	46.9	67.2	27.1	74.7	25.1
1978	48.4	68.3	28.5	78.2	26.8
1977	47.7	66.7	28.4	79.1	26.6
1976	46.9	65.6	27.9	78.7	26.3
1975	48.4	67.7	28.0	84.1	28.0
1974	49.5	69.1	28.9	85.3	29.3
1973	55.2	75.9	32.7	98.5	33.6
1972	55.4	75.6	33.4	99.8	33.8
1971	55.0	74.6	33.0	101.2	35.7
1970	56.4	77.2	33.1	105.0	35.5
1969	57.6	78.7	34.1	105.7	37.3
1968	57.5	77.7	34.3	108.2	37.2
1967	57.2	77.6	34.6	102.4	36.7
1966	58.0	78.1	35.0	104.6	40.0
1965	55.7	75.1	34.0	98.6	37.3
1964	54.3	72.9	33.4	95.3	36.6
1963	53.4	72.1	33.0	94.4	38.0
1962	52.3	70.4	32.4	92.2	37.9
1961	50.4	68.0	30.5	88.2	36.0
1960	52.3	70.0	31.5	95.0	38.7
1959	52.0	70.6	31.0	94.5	33.0
1958	52.3	70.6	31.1	94.7	31.3
1957	56.0	75.5	33.5	101.0	38.4

Year	Total	White males	White females	Nonwhite males	Nonwhite females
1956	56.7	76.9	33.5	103.6	34.4
1955	56.9	77.3	33.8	100.9	34.8
1954	55.9	75.9	33.2	99.7	34.4
1953	60.0	81.9	35.1	110.9	40.8
1952	61.7	83.7	36.6	113.4	35.4
1951	62.5	85.6	36.8	110.1	35.0
1950	60.6	82.5	36.6	103.9	39.9
1949	60.6	82.9	37.1	99.8	35.7
1948	66.9	90.7	42.5	105.2	37.2
1947	69.2	95.5	42.9	104.9	37.5
1946	69.7	97.2	42.6	104.6	37.1
1945	70.1	105.5	42.8	105.7	35.9
1944	71.3	104.4	41.0	105.9	35.7
1943	73.4	106.6	41.9	105.4	36.5
1942	71.3	101.4	41.0	110.4	36.0
1941	75.9	106.2	44.7	121.2	37.4
1940	73.2	100.5	44.8	113.6	39.8
1939	70.4	96.5	43.4	108.8	36.5
1938	71.8	98.4	44.3	109.4	38.8
1937	81.1	113.6	47.6	125.2	42.3
1936	85.4	117.7	51.5	133.1	47.1
1935	77.8	108.4	46.3	118.6	41.1
1934	79.3	111.4	45.9	122.0	42.1
1933	71.9	99.7	42.9	110.7	37.7
1932	70.8	98.2	42.2	108.5	37.5
1931	77.8	110.3	44.4	114.7	41.6
1930	79.8	113.1	44.5	126.3	42.4
1929	79.8	113.3	43.8	129.7	44.3
1928	78.1	110.5	43.1	126.5	45.0
1927	77.1	108.8	41.9	137.0	42.6
1926	77.3	108.2	42.7	134.3	47.3
1925	76.6	107.4	42.6	129.6	47.6
1924	73.9	103.7	40.8	121.3	50.3
1923	74.4	106.1	40.8	116.8	42.8
1922	68.2	97.6	38.0	99.1	40.4
1921	66.7	94.9	37.2	100.0	37.5
1920	70.0	98.9	38.8	107.4	44.9
1919	71.2	102.9	37.6	108.4	42.7
1918	81.4	121.4	40.3	127.1	48.1
1917	86.0	126.2	42.6	136.8	54.9
1916	81.6	122.0	38.8	124.4	45.0

Year	Total	White males	White females	Nonwhite males	Nonwhite females
1915	73.5	108.5	35.7	122.4	46.4
1914	76.7	113.6	36.6	129.1	49.3
1913	83.8	125.9	38.1	142.2	50.3
1912	80.8	120.5	37.9	141.8	45.6
1911	83.6	124.0	39.9	143.1	53.5
1910	84.2	128.8	36.6	137.7	41.3
1909	78.7				
1908	82.9				
1907	94.8				
1906	94.4				
1905	81.3				
1904	85.4				
1903	81.4				
1902	72.7				
1901	83.8				
1900	72.3				

VIOLENT DEATH RATES, UNITED STATES, 1914–1984
By Type of Mortality, Age, Sex, and Race*

SUICIDE RATES

White Males

Year	Age (years)							
	5–14	15–24	25–34	35–44	45–54	55–64	65–74	75–84
1984	1.1	22.0	25.8	23.7	25.3	28.8	35.6	52.0
1983	0.9	20.6	26.2	23.2	25.5	27.4	33.2	52.5
1982	0.9	21.2	26.1	23.6	25.8	27.9	33.1	48.5
1981	0.8	21.1	26.2	24.3	23.9	26.3	30.3	43.8
1980	0.7	21.4	25.6	23.5	24.2	25.8	32.5	45.5
1979	0.6	20.5	25.4	22.4	24.0	26.3	33.4	48.0
1978	0.7	20.8	25.8	22.5	24.7	29.3	35.5	50.9
1977	1.0	22.9	26.7	24.7	27.3	30.9	37.5	48.4
1976	0.7	19.2	23.7	23.6	27.7	31.6	36.2	45.6
1975	0.8	19.6	24.4	24.5	29.7	32.1	36.1	44.8
1974	0.8	17.8	23.3	23.8	28.3	32.1	34.9	46.0
1973	0.7	17.4	21.8	22.8	28.4	32.4	37.0	46.3
1972	0.5	15.5	20.9	23.0	29.7	33.5	38.4	48.0
1971	0.5	14.4	19.4	23.2	28.6	34.6	37.8	47.0
1970	0.5	13.9	19.9	23.3	29.5	35.0	38.7	45.5
1969	0.5	12.6	18.3	22.4	28.6	34.9	37.0	46.7
1968	0.5	11.3	17.2	23.2	28.8	36.1	36.2	44.2
1967	0.5	10.8	17.2	23.8	29.2	36.5	34.6	43.8
1966	0.5	9.9	17.2	22.7	30.1	38.4	38.8	51.1

*Sources of data: Same as Figure 4-1; unpublished data, National Center for Health Statistics (for 1981–1984); data for 1917 by age, sex, and race not available; data by age, sex, and race not available prior to 1914.

	Age (years)							
Year	5–14	15–24	25–34	35–44	45–54	55–64	65–74	75–84
1965	0.5	9.6	17.7	23.4	30.8	39.7	39.3	49.5
1964	0.5	9.3	17.0	22.2	31.8	38.5	39.0	50.6
1963	0.5	9.2	16.9	23.6	33.0	40.2	40.3	52.6
1962	0.5	8.7	16.5	22.9	33.4	40.5	41.3	57.1
1961	0.4	7.9	14.7	22.4	32.8	39.7	39.9	53.2
1960	0.5	8.6	14.9	21.9	33.7	40.2	42.0	55.7
1959	0.5	7.8	14.5	21.7	32.6	42.0	47.9	57.8
1958	0.4	7.5	14.4	22.2	33.9	42.1	48.4	59.3
1957	0.4	6.4	12.7	20.2	30.2	38.3	45.5	56.3
1956	0.3	6.3	13.0	19.1	30.1	41.8	48.0	59.0
1955	0.2	6.1	12.7	19.8	31.7	43.1	46.9	55.5
1954	0.2	6.8	13.6	19.9	33.0	41.8	47.1	53.3
1953	0.4	6.8	13.0	20.5	31.0	38.7	48.1	56.6
1952	0.2	6.8	12.6	19.6	29.7	38.6	47.5	57.2
1951	0.3	6.7	12.8	20.4	30.3	39.8	50.4	54.1
1950	0.3	6.6	13.8	22.4	34.1	45.9	53.2	61.9
1949	0.4	6.9	13.3	24.0	33.6	46.6	51.2	59.6
1948	0.4	6.8	13.3	21.8	33.3	44.7	48.8	58.1
1947	0.5	6.8	13.8	23.3	32.6	45.5	48.3	67.6
1946	0.5	7.7	14.7	25.4	32.4	42.8	45.7	56.4
1945	0.4	7.7	16.7	23.3	29.0	38.6	44.7	58.4
1944	0.4	6.2	14.0	20.1	25.8	33.8	40.0	57.4
1943	0.4	6.5	13.5	19.9	26.2	37.1	44.0	60.2
1942	0.4	7.2	17.4	25.3	33.0	46.8	49.9	61.1
1941	0.3	7.8	18.3	26.4	35.8	49.2	55.2	65.7
1940	0.4	8.8	19.9	30.1	44.1	58.8	58.2	65.9
1939	0.5	8.5	19.8	29.3	44.8	58.2	60.2	70.4
1938	0.3	9.4	22.2	33.1	50.1	63.6	61.9	68.5
1937	0.5	9.5	21.5	32.2	48.5	59.2	61.6	73.8
1936	0.4	9.1	21.0	30.7	44.0	57.3	61.6	73.0
1935	0.3	9.5	20.7	29.0	47.0	58.5	63.6	75.8
1934	0.3	9.6	21.3	31.0	48.1	63.6	78.4	78.1
1933	0.2	9.1	20.4	33.2	56.3	74.7	84.1	80.2
1932	0.3	9.4	23.0	36.5	62.1	85.9	92.2	88.5
1931	0.3	9.2	21.8	36.4	61.2	81.4	88.6	80.1
1930	0.3	9.6	21.6	36.2	55.7	70.6	75.3	76.1
1929	0.3	8.9	19.2	31.8	46.7	68.1	72.6	76.8
1928	0.2	8.1	19.3	30.1	48.2	58.6	72.1	77.0
1927	0.3	8.3	18.4	30.0	45.2	56.8	66.3	68.5

			Age (years)				
Year	5–14	15–24	25–34	35–44	45–54	55–64	65–74	75–84
1926	0.3	7.7	16.8	29.6	42.0	53.0	64.7	67.7
1925	0.3	7.4	17.0	27.3	40.3	51.1	63.0	61.5
1924	0.2	7.7	17.1	28.8	40.5	52.3	59.0	58.9
1923	0.3	6.3	16.9	27.3	38.4	48.0	55.3	65.2
1922	0.3	7.4	17.8	27.4	40.0	49.3	59.7	60.1
1921	0.4	8.5	19.4	29.9	42.5	52.2	56.6	60.7
1920	0.2	7.5	15.7	22.7	30.2	38.3	46.6	52.2
1919	0.3	7.7	19.9	27.1	31.7	43.3	49.4	59.7
1918	0.2	9.5	24.1	29.0	33.3	45.2	49.8	53.9
1916	0.3	10.8	22.1	31.1	41.8	59.6	63.2	65.4
1915	0.3	11.7	26.2	35.8	50.6	68.2	66.8	63.1
1914	0.3	12.6	27.0	35.3	52.1	64.1	60.6	59.4

White Females

			Age (years)				
Year	5–14	15–24	25–34	35–44	45–54	55–64	65–74	75–84
1984	0.3	4.7	6.6	8.4	10.0	9.1	7.8	6.8
1983	0.3	4.6	7.2	8.2	9.9	9.1	7.9	6.6
1982	0.3	4.5	7.5	9.2	10.4	9.5	7.4	6.1
1981	0.3	4.9	7.7	9.5	11.1	9.4	7.3	5.5
1980	0.2	4.6	7.5	9.1	10.2	9.1	7.0	5.7
1979	0.3	4.9	7.8	10.1	11.6	9.9	7.8	6.7
1978	0.2	5.0	8.5	10.9	12.1	10.3	8.4	7.7
1977	0.2	5.5	9.3	11.2	13.6	11.2	9.4	7.5
1976	0.2	4.9	8.6	11.0	13.8	12.1	8.9	7.8
1975	0.2	4.9	8.9	12.6	13.8	11.7	9.5	7.8
1974	0.2	4.8	8.7	12.1	14.1	11.0	8.5	7.3
1973	0.2	4.3	8.5	12.2	13.7	12.0	9.1	7.7
1972	0.2	4.6	9.2	12.6	13.4	13.3	9.2	7.8
1971	0.2	4.6	8.9	13.0	14.5	12.6	10.3	7.3
1970	0.1	4.2	9.0	13.0	13.5	12.3	9.6	7.2
1969	0.2	3.8	8.1	12.7	13.3	11.8	9.8	7.5
1968	0.1	3.4	7.5	11.5	13.4	11.6	8.1	6.5
1967	0.1	3.4	7.9	11.5	13.0	12.3	9.9	6.9

	Age (years)							
Year	5–14	15–24	25–34	35–44	45–54	55–64	65–74	75–84
1966	0.1	3.2	7.8	11.3	12.9	11.5	9.7	7.4
1965	0.1	3.0	7.6	12.0	13.6	22.3	10.0	7.9
1964	0.1	2.9	7.3	10.9	12.5	10.9	10.4	6.7
1963	0.1	3.1	7.5	10.9	12.9	11.6	9.5	7.7
1962	0.1	2.9	7.2	9.5	12.4	11.1	8.8	7.6
1961	0.1	2.3	6.1	8.3	10.8	10.4	9.1	7.6
1960	0.1	2.3	5.8	8.1	10.9	10.9	8.8	9.2
1959	0.0	2.1	5.7	7.5	9.3	10.5	10.4	7.5
1958	0.1	2.4	5.9	7.1	10.3	9.9	10.1	6.6
1957	0.1	1.8	5.0	7.1	8.7	10.0	8.7	6.3
1956	0.1	2.0	4.7	6.6	9.6	10.5	9.7	6.9
1955	0.1	2.0	4.9	6.6	10.9	10.4	9.7	8.5
1954	0.1	1.8	4.4	6.8	8.2	9.5	8.9	6.4
1953	0.0	2.3	4.8	6.5	9.0	9.3	8.4	7.7
1952	0.1	2.1	4.9	6.8	9.4	9.2	9.1	7.2
1951	0.1	2.3	5.0	7.7	9.7	9.3	9.1	8.4
1950	0.1	2.7	5.2	8.2	10.5	10.7	10.6	8.4
1949	0.1	2.0	5.1	8.2	10.4	11.5	10.0	7.6
1948	0.1	3.1	5.5	9.0	10.7	10.6	9.4	9.7
1947	0.1	2.7	6.0	8.9	11.8	10.9	11.5	8.8
1946	0.1	3.4	6.3	9.4	11.7	11.9	10.3	8.7
1945	0.1	3.0	6.8	9.5	12.0	11.4	10.9	8.9
1944	0.1	3.3	6.1	9.0	10.5	11.5	9.6	10.4
1943	0.2	3.2	6.1	8.4	10.8	12.4	11.2	9.1
1942	0.1	3.2	7.1	9.3	11.8	12.0	9.7	12.2
1941	0.2	4.1	8.1	10.3	12.8	12.5	10.7	8.3
1940	0.2	3.9	8.6	11.5	14.0	12.1	12.9	9.0
1939	0.2	3.9	7.6	11.0	14.3	13.7	12.4	7.5
1938	0.0	4.6	8.5	11.7	14.3	14.0	11.4	9.0
1937	0.1	5.1	9.0	11.6	14.6	14.4	11.5	9.8
1936	0.2	5.0	9.8	10.9	13.3	13.4	11.6	9.0
1935	0.2	5.4	9.4	10.9	13.0	13.8	11.9	7.9
1934	0.1	5.7	9.2	11.1	13.8	13.3	10.9	9.9
1933	0.1	5.9	9.0	11.3	12.9	14.0	12.1	9.1
1932	0.1	5.9	9.9	11.2	13.9	15.0	14.7	9.0
1931	0.1	5.9	9.9	11.8	14.2	15.2	12.3	10.5
1930	0.1	6.4	9.8	11.4	13.2	14.5	12.7	10.0
1929	0.1	6.0	9.3	10.8	12.9	14.1	12.3	10.7
1928	0.1	6.1	8.8	10.3	12.5	11.9	11.8	8.2

	Age (years)							
Year	5–14	15–24	25–34	35–44	45–54	55–64	65–74	75–84
1927	0.2	5.3	8.8	10.6	12.4	12.4	10.9	9.4
1926	0.2	6.1	8.6	10.2	12.6	12.3	10.7	10.3
1925	0.2	5.0	8.4	9.9	12.3	11.3	10.7	6.9
1924	0.2	5.4	7.6	9.5	11.1	11.9	10.1	8.0
1923	0.2	5.7	8.1	9.4	11.3	12.9	9.5	10.9
1922	0.1	6.0	7.6	9.6	11.4	11.9	10.7	10.7
1921	0.2	5.7	8.0	9.2	11.5	11.0	10.2	9.3
1920	0.2	5.5	0.2	10.0	11.7	11.1	9.9	8.6
1919	0.2	6.1	8.5	10.5	12.9	13.4	11.9	10.6
1918	0.3	5.8	9.1	10.1	11.5	13.4	11.2	10.9
1916	0.2	7.2	9.3	9.7	12.4	12.9	11.5	8.5
1915	0.3	8.1	10.4	11.6	13.3	14.0	14.0	10.8
1914	0.2	9.3	10.3	11.5	12.6	15.5	11.7	9.5

Nonwhite Males

	Age (years)							
Year	5–14	15–24	25–34	35–44	45–54	55–64	65–74	75–84
1984	0.6	12.8	19.6	15.3	11.7	13.3	14.1	15.7
1983	0.5	13.2	18.7	13.4	12.0	11.4	13.3	17.5
1982	0.8	12.3	20.0	14.5	11.7	11.0	12.7	14.0
1981	0.2	12.6	20.8	15.4	12.0	13.1	10.6	17.7
1980	0.3	13.8	21.1	14.9	12.1	12.1	11.0	11.3
1979	0.3	16.0	24.2	16.9	13.6	12.1	13.5	12.7
1978	0.4	14.8	23.7	17.0	13.2	10.5	11.7	14.0
1977	0.4	15.5	25.7	16.0	11.7	13.3	11.8	13.2
1976	0.3	14.7	22.8	16.8	13.5	12.3	13.4	13.2
1975	0.1	14.4	24.6	16.0	12.8	11.5	11.3	13.4
1974	0.4	12.9	22.9	15.6	11.9	12.5	14.5	17.1
1973	0.3	14.0	22.6	14.3	13.4	12.2	11.6	13.1
1972	0.0	16.7	20.9	15.8	13.2	11.9	11.6	12.4
1971	0.5	11.5	17.6	14.9	10.3	11.9	15.0	7.9
1970	0.2	11.3	19.8	12.6	14.1	10.5	10.2	11.9
1969	0.2	9.9	17.8	15.8	12.1	10.6	14.5	16.2
1968	0.2	8.2	16.0	12.6	12.3	12.4	14.9	11.9
1967	0.2	8.2	17.7	14.7	11.6	13.3	12.3	12.6

	Age (years)							
Year	5–14	15–24	25–34	35–44	45–54	55–64	65–74	75–84
1966	0.1	8.6	17.9	11.4	14.1	14.4	14.1	15.4
1965	0.2	8.5	14.2	15.0	13.5	14.2	15.3	15.9
1964	0.1	8.0	16.2	12.7	11.8	12.3	13.4	12.6
1963	0.3	7.5	15.9	14.9	13.6	12.7	18.1	19.0
1962	0.1	7.5	12.8	12.8	12.4	14.6	16.7	13.7
1961	0.1	7.6	16.3	11.5	14.0	14.9	13.2	16.6
1960	0.1	5.3	12.9	13.5	12.8	16.9	12.6	11.3
1959	0.2	6.2	14.3	11.5	13.7	15.3	18.7	23.4
1958	0.2	5.1	12.6	13.0	12.6	15.7	17.7	11.7
1957	0.0	5.4	12.9	11.2	11.6	12.1	21.2	15.7
1956	0.0	5.5	10.7	11.2	9.7	12.4	12.0	11.7
1955	0.1	6.2	9.5	10.1	10.4	12.7	12.7	12.9
1954	0.1	5.3	12.7	11.1	11.3	12.1	15.6	13.7
1953	0.1	4.1	10.0	10.7	12.5	11.8	13.8	22.7
1952	0.3	4.3	10.7	9.1	9.8	13.9	12.3	11.2
1951	0.3	5.1	10.7	10.9	11.4	11.5	11.2	15.4
1950	0.1	5.3	10.1	11.3	11.7	16.8	15.0	7.9
1949	0.1	4.6	9.9	11.3	12.0	16.4	15.8	15.3
1948	0.0	5.0	9.1	12.2	14.1	10.9	14.5	12.6
1947	0.3	5.0	8.9	11.1	9.1	13.8	14.3	16.5
1946	0.2	5.0	9.4	8.8	9.9	12.8	10.7	12.6
1945	0.0	5.1	9.1	8.8	9.1	9.1	12.2	14.6
1944	0.1	3.9	7.6	7.2	8.0	11.1	6.7	7.7
1943	0.4	4.9	7.8	6.2	6.9	10.3	6.5	8.2
1942	0.2	5.0	9.3	9.7	8.0	14.5	9.2	10.1
1941	0.1	5.1	10.3	10.5	12.5	11.7	11.3	12.1
1940	0.4	5.1	11.5	10.6	14.8	12.6	13.5	8.5
1939	0.0	3.9	10.1	11.8	13.1	12.0	9.3	16.9
1938	0.3	5.5	9.8	12.7	14.0	17.2	9.0	24.4
1937	0.4	4.4	10.7	13.7	13.2	15.9	13.0	12.5
1936	0.4	5.5	9.2	13.2	10.8	17.8	11.2	7.3
1935	0.2	5.1	10.7	13.0	14.8	17.8	10.8	9.4
1934	0.1	6.3	11.9	11.3	13.8	16.7	10.6	25.0
1933	0.1	5.9	11.2	16.3	17.5	13.8	17.4	13.7
1932	0.2	5.9	11.9	16.1	16.8	24.9	16.3	25.8
1931	0.1	4.6	12.7	14.2	14.6	20.0	14.9	11.0
1930	0.1	4.4	11.9	13.4	14.3	16.5	23.0	15.6
1929	0.2	5.7	11.6	11.9	16.6	13.8	17.5	22.3
1928	0.0	5.2	10.8	14.0	14.2	15.8	9.9	15.6

| | Age (years) | | | | | | | |
Year	5–14	15–24	25–34	35–44	45–54	55–64	65–74	75–84
1927	0.2	4.3	12.8	12.8	12.4	12.6	16.5	7.6
1926	0.2	3.8	9.7	10.3	12.1	14.0	14.5	10.8
1925	0.2	4.8	9.7	12.0	8.2	9.1	16.6	19.3
1924	0.2	4.1	9.6	13.6	10.2	13.8	11.8	11.1
1923	0.0	3.5	7.5	11.9	13.2	10.4	12.0	5.7
1922	0.1	4.6	9.2	14.1	10.7	9.9	13.2	20.5
1921	0.1	6.3	10.8	12.8	10.3	10.3	19.0	10.4
1920	0.2	3.7	8.5	8.3	10.7	10.0	12.5	10.7
1919	0.0	5.2	11.8	10.9	8.8	9.8	8.0	3.6
1918	0.2	6.7	14.8	15.7	8.6	16.1	23.8	17.6
1916	0.0	4.8	15.5	15.4	12.6	11.2	14.9	12.2
1915	0.0	7.2	24.0	20.2	18.7	19.5	23.1	18.6
1914	0.4	8.4	26.9	23.6	13.9	29.7	26.3	19.1

Nonwhite Females

| | Age (years) | | | | | | | |
Year	5–14	15–24	25–34	35–44	45–54	55–64	65–74	75–84
1984	0.3	2.9	3.7	3.6	4.3	3.7	3.2	1.3
1983	0.6	3.0	3.3	4.1	3.6	3.1	1.9	3.5
1982	0.1	2.9	4.1	4.0	3.4	3.1	2.3	2.4
1981	0.2	3.0	5.3	5.1	3.5	3.3	3.1	1.6
1980	0.1	2.7	4.9	4.6	3.8	2.7	2.1	2.7
1979	0.1	3.8	5.5	4.3	3.7	4.5	3.4	5.1
1978	0.2	3.2	5.6	4.7	4.6	3.8	2.7	3.7
1977	0.2	4.0	6.8	5.1	5.2	4.4	1.9	3.4
1976	0.4	4.0	6.5	4.7	4,3	2.8	4.0	2.2
1975	0.2	3.9	6.5	4.9	4.5	4.1	3.3	2.6
1974	0.2	3.9	6.3	4.5	4.0	3.4	2.4	2.3
1973	0.1	4.1	5.3	5.4	3.2	4.4	2.4	3.8
1972	0.2	5.6	5.7	5.2	3.8	3.7	1.5	5.0
1971	0.2	5.2	6.7	6.0	4.1	3.0	2.3	4.4
1970	0.2	4.1	5.8	4.3	4.5	2.2	3.5	3.2
1969	0.2	4.1	6.1	4.8	3.7	2.3	2.8	2.6
1968	0.1	3.1	4.6	4.5	3.6	2.8	3.0	3.8
1967	0.1	4.0	5.9	4.2	3.5	3.3	3.3	2.4

	Age (years)							
Year	5–14	15–24	25–34	35–44	45–54	55–64	65–74	75–84
1966	0.1	2.9	6.2	3.1	3.5	3.6	3.7	2.5
1965	0.1	3.1	6.0	4.2	4.1	2.8	2.5	3.5
1964	0.0	2.0	4.6	4.1	3.4	4.0	3.1	2.8
1963	0.2	2.6	5.0	4.0	2.7	2.3	5.0	1.5
1962	0.0	3.0	4.6	3.9	3.3	3.9	2.0	3.2
1961	0.2	2.0	3.5	3.9	2.7	3.2	1.9	1.6
1960	0.0	1.5	3.5	3.7	3.2	2.4	2.8	4.2
1959	0.1	2.2	3.8	2.8	2.8	4.4	2.8	1.8
1958	0.0	1.7	3.6	2.8	3.0	3.0	3.0	3.2
1957	0.0	1.3	2.5	2.3	1.2	4.0	2.4	2.0
1956	0.0	1.2	2.6	3.0	2.9	3.3	3.4	1.4
1955	0.0	1.8	2.8	1.7	2.7	2.6	3.1	1.5
1954	0.0	1.5	2.7	2.0	2.8	2.8	3.2	0.8
1953	0.2	2.0	2.1	1.6	1.8	1.8	2.6	0.9
1952	0.1	1.3	2.7	2.5	1.6	2.1	0.3	0.9
1951	0.0	2.4	2.6	2.7	2.2	2.7	2.7	1.9
1950	0.1	1.7	2.8	2.2	4.0	1.2	2.5	2.9
1949	0.2	1.7	2.5	2.6	2.1	2.2	1.8	2.0
1948	0.1	1.8	3.1	2.4	2.2	0.8	1.5	0.0
1947	0.1	2.6	3.1	2.5	1.7	1.5	0.8	0.0
1946	0.0	2.3	2.8	2.8	3.4	2.2	1.6	0.0
1945	0.0	2.2	2.0	2.3	1.5	1.1	0.4	2.4
1944	0.1	2.0	2.1	2.0	1.8	1.2	2.5	2.5
1943	0.1	1.0	1.7	2.7	1.4	1.9	0.9	3.9
1942	0.1	2.8	4.0	2.9	2.1	1.3	0.9	0.0
1941	0.1	2.5	2.6	1.8	2.9	2.3	1.9	2.9
1940	0.0	0.0	3.3	3.5	3.0	3.2	1.4	1.5
1939	0.1	2.7	3.2	2.4	3.7	1.8	2.3	4.8
1938	0.1	2.9	5.3	3.1	2.9	4.1	3.0	0.0
1937	0.1	3.4	4.7	3.0	3.8	2.9	1.6	1.7
1936	0.3	3.0	4.9	2.7	2.8	2.3	2.2	10.4
1935	0.1	3.6	6.3	4.0	1.2	2.0	1.2	5.3
1934	0.1	4.3	5.1	4.2	3.2	2.8	2.5	3.6
1933	0.1	4.0	3.9	3.5	3.4	2.9	1.3	1.9
1932	0.2	3.7	4.5	4.7	2.6	4.0	1.5	0.0
1931	0.0	3.5	5.2	3.0	2.1	4.6	2.4	4.2
1930	0.1	3.6	3.8	3.7	2.9	2.9	3.4	2.1
1929	0.0	3.3	4.2	3.6	2.6	3.4	1.7	2.2
1928	0.2	2.9	5.3	3.2	2.3	3.4	5.4	2.2

				Age (years)				
Year	5–14	15–24	25–34	35–44	45–54	55–64	65–74	75–84
1927	0.1	2.8	4.8	4.3	3.2	2.4	0.0	0.0
1926	0.2	2.8	5.1	3.9	4.3	3.1	1.1	5.3
1925	0.0	2.3	3.9	3.2	3.4	1.6	2.2	0.0
1924	0.1	3.2	4.9	3.0	2.9	2.2	1.1	0.0
1923	0.0	2.5	3.6	3.6	1.5	1.1	0.0	2.9
1922	0.2	3.1	3.3	3.4	3.6	2.4	0.0	0.0
1921	0.0	3.7	4.9	2.9	1.8	2.1	1.3	0.0
1920	0.1	3.7	2.9	2.3	3.3	1.5	1.4	3.6
1919	0.0	2.5	4.6	3.2	1.8	0.8	2.7	0.0
1918	0.0	3.8	4.1	3.4	2.7	2.7	8.1	4.3
1916	0.0	3.8	3.6	2.2	3.1	1.2	2.2	0.0
1915	0.0	5.4	10.4	8.2	5.5	5.3	0.0	8.8
1914	0.0	7.8	8.9	5.6	2.8	1.8	6.7	0.0

HOMICIDE RATES

White Males

					Age (years)					
Year	0–1	1–4	5–14	15–24	25–34	35–44	45–54	55–64	65–74	75–84
1984	4.9	1.9	0.9	11.1	14.1	11.8	9.4	6.3	4.2	4.2
1983	3.3	1.7	0.9	11.5	14.9	12.4	9.1	6.4	4.6	4.6
1982	5.8	1.9	0.8	13.1	16.2	13.9	10.9	7.1	5.0	5.2
1981	4.7	1.6	0.9	14.4	17.6	15.1	12.1	7.9	5.2	5.1
1980	4.3	2.0	0.9	15.5	18.9	15.5	11.9	7.8	6.9	6.3
1979	4.0	1.7	1.0	14.4	16.8	13.9	11.2	7.4	6.0	5.4
1978	3.5	1.7	1.0	12.4	15.3	13.9	10.4	7.6	5.5	4.7
1977	4.2	1.9	0.9	11.5	14.4	13.8	9.7	7.8	5.7	5.4
1976	3.9	1.7	0.9	10.6	14.2	13.6	9.6	7.3	5.8	5.5
1975	5.0	1.9	0.8	11.2	15.6	14.4	11.3	8.9	7.1	6.6
1974	3.7	1.7	1.0	11.4	15.8	14.1	10.9	8.1	6.2	6.7
1973	4.0	1.8	0.8	10.5	15.3	12.7	9.8	8.5	6.3	5.7
1972	4.1	1.5	0.6	9.5	13.9	13.0	9.6	8.2	5.2	4.5
1971	3.8	1.5	0.6	8.6	14.0	12.5	9.1	7.6	6.2	5.3
1970	2.9	1.4	0.5	7.9	13.0	11.0	9.0	7.7	5.6	5.1
1969	3.5	1.4	0.5	7.6	11.6	10.1	7.1	6.9	5.2	4.1
1968	3.9	1.0	0.5	7.5	11.0	9.8	8.0	6.4	5.6	4.3

Year	\multicolumn{10}{c}{Age (years)}
	0–1	1–4	5–14	15–24	25–34	35–44	45–54	55–64	65–74	75–84
1967	5.6	0.9	0.5	6.3	10.4	8.8	6.9	5.7	5.0	3.8
1966	5.2	0.8	0.5	5.0	8.2	7.6	6.3	5.4	3.7	2.8
1965	5.3	1.0	0.5	4.9	7.8	7.3	6.0	5.2	3.5	3.5
1964	4.6	1.1	0.6	4.4	7.0	6.1	5.7	4.7	2.9	3.0
1963	4.2	1.1	0.5	4.2	7.3	6.4	5.1	4.4	3.4	3.1
1962	4.3	0.7	0.5	3.9	6.9	6.0	5.7	4.6	3.4	3.1
1961	3.9	0.8	0.5	3.9	6.4	5.8	5.4	4.1	3.4	3.9
1960	3.8	0.6	0.4	4.4	6.2	5.5	5.0	4.3	3.4	2.7
1959	3.2	0.8	0.5	4.1	5.5	5.5	5.0	4.3	3.7	3.1
1958	2.5	0.5	0.5	3.9	5.5	4.8	5.1	4.1	3.7	2.6
1957	3.1	0.3	0.4	3.8	5.6	4.9	4.3	4.0	3.6	2.5
1956	2.5	0.6	0.5	4.0	5.4	4.8	4.2	4.3	3.4	2.7
1955	3.3	0.4	0.4	3.5	5.3	5.7	4.6	4.2	3.1	3.4
1954	3.0	0.5	0.4	3.9	5.4	5.7	5.1	3.6	3.1	3.3
1953	2.7	0.6	0.4	3.7	5.4	5.7	5.2	3.7	3.1	3.4
1952	3.8	0.7	0.5	3.8	5.6	5.8	5.3	4.0	3.9	3.6
1951	3.7	0.4	0.4	3.6	5.6	5.5	5.5	4.3	3.5	3.0
1950	4.3	0.4	0.4	3.7	5.4	6.4	5.5	4.4	4.1	3.5
1949	3.9	0.7	0.5	4.0	6.1	6.6	5.5	4.8	4.1	4.5
1948	4.0	0.6	0.5	4.2	6.8	7.4	6.1	5.2	4.6	3.9
1947	5.1	0.7	0.4	4.4	7.4	7.8	6.0	5.5	4.6	4.1
1946	5.3	0.6	0.4	5.2	7.6	7.3	6.9	5.6	4.4	2.9
1945	5.6	0.7	0.6	5.3	8.1	7.8	6.8	5.2	4.3	3.1
1944	4.1	0.4	0.5	3.8	6.5	6.3	5.6	4.7	3.5	3.0
1943	5.1	0.4	0.5	3.7	6.1	6.3	5.9	5.4	4.0	3.2
1942	4.6	0.5	0.4	4.1	6.6	6.8	6.1	5.5	4.1	3.6
1941	5.4	0.6	0.5	3.7	7.1	7.3	6.4	5.1	4.3	2.4
1940	5.1	0.7	0.5	4.0	8.0	7.8	7.0	6.2	4.9	4.4
1939	5.3	0.5	0.5	4.4	8.4	8.3	7.3	5.9	6.5	3.2
1938	5.0	0.5	0.5	5.2	9.4	9.6	8.0	6.8	5.8	4.2
1937	6.2	0.8	0.6	5.9	10.7	10.3	9.1	7.5	6.0	4.1
1936	6.0	0.6	0.5	6.4	11.2	11.9	9.3	8.0	6.1	4.7
1935	7.0	0.6	0.5	6.9	12.5	12.8	11.0	10.0	5.4	5.1
1934	6.2	0.5	0.6	8.5	14.9	15.0	12.8	10.6	7.4	5.2
1933	8.4	0.6	0.6	8.5	16.3	16.0	13.6	10.5	7.6	8.6
1932	7.3	0.8	0.7	8.8	16.3	14.7	12.1	0.8	8.2	6.6
1931	5.5	0.8	0.7	9.6	16.4	15.8	12.4	10.7	6.8	5.3
1930	6.0	1.0	0.8	8.9	15.6	14.9	12.2	9.9	7.3	4.5
1929	5.6	0.7	0.7	7.6	14.1	13.8	10.9	8.7	5.9	3.7

| | Age (years) | | | | | | | | | |
Year	0–1	1–4	5–14	15–24	25–34	35–44	45–54	55–64	65–74	75–84
1928	6.4	0.7	0.6	7.9	14.9	14,2	11.2	9.1	5.6	4.5
1927	8.6	0.8	0.8	7.4	14.4	13.5	10.9	8.1	6.4	4.6
1926	8.7	0.7	0.5	8.5	14.7	14.3	10.3	7.8	5.6	2.7
1925	7.8	0.7	0.7	8.5	15.1	14.4	10.3	7.5	5.8	3.6
1924	6.8	0.6	0.6	7.8	14.4	13.7	10.7	8.3	6.5	3.9
1923	8.1	0.4	0.7	7.4	14.6	13.9	10.7	6.3	5.3	4.8
1922	6.6	0.5	0.7	8.0	16.4	15.4	12.9	8.0	5.6	2.5
1921	7.3	0.8	0.7	8.4	17.9	16.6	12.6	9.2	6.8	6.1
1920	8.6	0.6	0.6	7.5	14.2	12.6	9.4	7.2	4.6	2.5
1919	7.7	1.2	0.9	8.0	15.2	14.2	10.8	7.0	4.9	4.5
1918	7.7	0.9	1.0	7.3	14.5	13.9	9.5	6.6	5.5	2.0
1916	8.7	0.6	0.8	7.1	14.6	13.3	10.1	5.9	4.2	4.2
1915	9.4	0.7	0.8	7.2	12.3	12.9	8.5	6.6	5.7	4.4
1914	9.6	0.3	0.7	8.6	14.4	12.6	9.1	7.1	4.1	3.1

White Females

| | Age (years) | | | | | | | | | |
Year	0–1	1–4	5–14	15–24	25–34	35–44	45–54	55–64	65–74	75–84
1984	4.0	1.7	0.9	4.3	3.9	3.4	2.7	2.2	1.9	2.9
1983	3.7	1.2	0.7	3.7	4.1	3.5	2.9	2.2	2.0	3.1
1982	4.2	1.7	1.0	4.4	4.3	4.0	2.9	2.2	2.4	2.9
1981	4.9	1.8	1.0	4.3	4.3	3.6	3.2	2.2	2.1	3.6
1980	4.3	1.5	1.0	4.7	4.3	4.1	3.0	2.1	2.5	3.3
1979	2.8	1.7	0.7	4.3	4.0	3.6	2.9	2.1	2.6	2.9
1978	3.6	1.4	0.9	4.1	4.0	3.6	3.0	2.0	2.1	3.4
1977	4.1	1.6	0.9	3.9	3.9	4.0	2.8	2.5	2.3	3.1
1976	4.0	1.6	0.7	3.6	3.6	3.2	2.8	2.2	2.2	3.8
1975	3.5	1.2	0.8	4.0	4.1	4.0	3.0	2.4	2.3	3.8
1974	3.7	1.4	0.6	3.8	4.3	3.9	2.8	2.4	2.6	3.1
1973	3.7	1.6	0.7	3.8	3.9	4.1	2.8	2.1	2.3	3.4
1972	3.3	1.2	0.6	3.2	3.3	3.2	2.6	2.0	1.7	2.7
1971	4.3	1.3	0.6	2.5	3.6	3.2	2.5	2.3	1.9	2.5
1970	2.9	1.2	0.5	2.7	3.4	3.2	2.2	2.0	1.7	2.5
1969	3.6	1.3	0.5	2.4	3.2	2.6	2.3	1.8	1.8	1.6

Year	Age (years)									
	0–1	1–4	5–14	15–24	25–34	35–44	45–54	55–64	65–74	75–84
1968	4.2	1.1	0.5	2.2	2.8	2.9	2.2	1.8	1.5	1.9
1967	4.7	0.9	0.5	2.2	2.8	3.2	2.3	1.5	1.5	2.3
1966	4.7	0.9	0.4	2.0	3.0	2.4	2.3	1.9	1.6	1.8
1965	3.6	0.8	0.4	1.8	2.5	2.3	2.0	1.6	1.3	1.3
1964	4.0	0.9	0.4	1.6	2.7	2.4	1.9	1.5	1.5	1.4
1963	4.1	0.9	0.4	1.4	2.3	2.2	1.9	1.4	1.3	1.7
1962	4.2	0.9	0.5	1.7	2.2	2.5	1.8	1.4	1.5	1.6
1961	3.3	0.8	0.4	1.5	2.4	2.5	2.1	1.2	1.1	2.1
1960	3.5	0.5	0.3	1.5	2.0	2.2	1.9	1.5	1.1	1.2
1959	2.9	0.7	0.4	1.4	2.4	2.2	1.8	1.1	1.2	1.3
1958	2.8	0.7	0.3	1.6	1.7	2.2	1.9	1.2	1.3	2.1
1957	2.2	0.5	0.3	1.4	1.9	2.2	1.7	1.5	0.9	1.1
1956	2.6	0.6	0.2	1.4	1.9	2.8	1.8	1.2	1.0	1.3
1955	2.5	0.4	0.3	1.2	1.7	1.9	1.9	1.1	0.8	1.4
1954	3.0	0.6	0.4	1.4	1.9	2.1	2.0	1.0	1.0	1.1
1953	3.1	0.6	0.3	1.2	2.0	2.1	1.7	1.1	1.2	0.9
1952	3.0	0.5	0.3	1.4	1.8	2.3	1.7	1.1	0.9	0.8
1951	4.3	0.5	0.4	1.3	1.9	2.0	1.7	1.1	1.0	1.3
1950	3.9	0.6	0.4	1.3	1.9	2.2	1.6	1.3	1.1	1.2
1949	3.6	0.3	0.3	1.4	1.8	2.1	1.9	1.2	0.7	1.7
1948	4.9	0.4	0.4	1.6	1.9	2.3	1.6	1.2	1.2	1.2
1947	4.9	0.5	0.3	1.3	2.0	2.0	1.9	1.1	1.2	0.9
1946	4.7	0.7	0.3	1.6	2.2	2.2	1.7	1.4	0.8	1.6
1945	6.0	0.7	0.5	1.4	1.7	1.8	1.2	0.9	0.8	0.7
1944	4.0	0.6	0.3	1.1	1.6	1.8	1.2	1.1	0.7	1.2
1943	4.8	0.7	0.5	1.3	1.7	1.5	1.2	1.2	0.7	1.5
1942	3.9	0.3	0.4	1.2	1.7	1.9	1.4	1.0	1.0	1.2
1941	4.0	0.3	0.4	1.5	1.8	1.6	1.5	1.0	0.8	1.1
1940	4.6	0.5	0.4	1.3	1.8	1.9	1.5	1.2	1.2	1.5
1939	3.5	0.4	0.4	1.2	2.0	2.0	1.6	1.4	1.0	1.7
1938	3.9	0.6	0.4	2.3	2.7	2.2	1.8	1.1	0.9	1.0
1937	6.1	0.8	0.5	2.6	3.1	2.5	1.7	1.2	1.4	1.4
1936	4.5	0.6	0.3	2.4	2.8	2.5	2.2	1.2	1.3	2.3
1935	5.4	0.4	0.5	2.8	3.1	2.6	1.7	1.6	1.3	1.8
1934	6.8	0.6	0.5	2.8	3.5	3.1	2.0	1.6	1.3	1.5
1933	7.3	0.7	0.6	3.0	3.7	3.1	2.3	1.7	1.5	2.2
1932	6.5	0.7	0.5	2.6	3.4	3.1	2.1	2.3	1.7	1.8
1931	7.0	0.6	0.6	3.5	3.5	3.3	2.1	1.6	1.0	1.0
1930	6.1	0.7	0.6	3.6	3.5	3.3	2.2	1.5	1.5	1.3

	Age (years)									
Year	0–1	1–4	5–14	15–24	25–34	35–44	45–54	55–64	65–74	75–84
1929	7.0	0.8	0.6	3.2	3.4	3.1	2.0	1.3	1.2	2.3
1928	6.5	0.6	0.4	2.9	3.6	3.0	2.0	1.2	1.1	0.8
1927	8.0	0.6	0.7	2.9	3.8	3.2	1.8	1.4	1.4	0.7
1926	6.1	0.6	0.5	2.7	3.6	2.8	2.2	1.1	1.3	1.5
1925	6.9	0.4	0.3	3.3	3.5	3.0	2.0	1.1	1.5	1.4
1924	7.2	0.8	0.3	3.1	3.8	3.4	1.9	1.2	1.1	1.8
1923	6.1	0.8	0.4	2.8	3.4	2.4	2.0	1.3	1.1	0.8
1922	6.3	0.6	0.4	2.8	3.4	2.8	2.1	1.3	0.9	1.2
1921	7.3	0.6	0.7	3.5	3.9	3.3	1.9	1.1	1.3	1.7
1920	6.9	0.8	0.5	3.0	3.4	2.3	1.7	0.6	0.9	1.1
1919	7.0	0.6	0.3	2.7	3.9	2.8	1.6	1.2	1.0	1.0
1918	7.8	0.9	0.6	2.4	3.1	2.4	1.6	0.9	1.1	0.6
1916	6.3	0.6	0.4	3.0	3.0	2.6	1.9	1.1	1.2	0.5
1915	10.9	0.7	0.6	2.7	3.6	2.6	1.5	1.7	1.5	2.0
1914	6.1	0.5	0.7	2.7	4.0	3.0	2.1	1.1	1.0	2.1

Nonwhite Males

	Age (years)									
Year	0–1	1–4	5–14	15–24	25–34	35–44	45–54	55–64	65–74	75–84
1984	17.2	4.3	2.9	52.7	78.4	62.8	47.4	35.0	26.6	24.9
1983	12.1	6.4	2.7	57.4	84.2	66.2	49.7	40.8	24.9	28.3
1982	14.3	7.7	3.0	63.0	101.2	74.0	63.0	42.4	32.2	22.9
1981	10.2	7.6	3.8	68.5	112.9	86.6	71.9	46.5	32.9	29.4
1980	15.6	6.4	2.7	74.5	120.9	90.6	72.2	48.9	31.3	25.5
1979	15.2	5.5	2.9	68.1	120.1	94.4	74.4	52.3	29.5	22.8
1978	12.0	7.7	3.2	66.0	116.2	91.9	65.5	45.8	29.5	22.5
1977	14.5	8.2	2.9	65.5	117.2	97.4	68.5	52.5	33.0	24.8
1976	14.7	5.8	3.0	70.2	112.3	100.5	74.2	57.5	37.3	22.2
1975	13.7	7.3	2.6	82.0	140.4	111.6	87.7	57.7	37.9	25.0
1974	12.3	6.0	2.9	88.3	149.8	125.5	96.8	65.3	40.4	24.5
1973	10.9	7.3	3.9	85.1	153.4	124.0	92.3	61.8	40.4	25.4
1972	12.6	4.5	3.7	97.9	160.9	139.9	99.0	64.1	31.0	17.2
1971	12.1	6.6	3.5	99.4	159.6	130.2	91.8	57.2	32.8	25.7
1970	13.4	4.6	3.9	92.0	137.3	110.8	90.3	55.1	37.0	17.1
1969	11.5	3.7	2.7	88.0	138.4	122.9	83.5	50.1	39.9	9.3

Year	Age (years)									
	0–1	1–4	5–14	15–24	25–34	35–44	45–54	55–64	65–74	75–84
1968	7.8	3.5	2.9	77.1	137.3	114.6	81.8	52.7	34.3	15.9
1967	12.4	2.0	2.4	69.6	126.5	107.5	71.7	45.2	32.1	13.6
1966	11.7	2.7	1.8	61.1	104.2	95.4	67.8	40.7	27.5	15.4
1965	11.2	2.4	2.2	51.8	104.1	86.5	58.7	36.7	30.7	16.4
1964	9.8	1.9	1.3	49.6	89.6	86.9	58.1	34.6	21.5	14.7
1963	9.3	1.8	1.5	45.2	87.7	54.7	37.5	37.5	17.9	12.6
1962	10.5	1.7	1.2	48.2	85.2	76.3	56.1	36.0	21.0	11.8
1961	9.3	2.1	1.5	44.2	81.3	71.0	5.13	29.9	21.8	15.3
1960	10.1	1.6	1.4	43.7	84.7	72.3	51.5	29.1	18.6	16.7
1959	9.7	1.5	1.3	42.8	84.2	77.1	50.7	31.9	23.1	15.6
1958	8.3	1.5	0.9	41.9	82.8	72.9	53.8	32.7	22.5	10.9
1957	4.9	1.7	1.5	43.6	85.7	73.8	55.5	32.1	28.9	14.9
1956	6.6	0.9	1.6	46.3	86.9	78.3	48.4	30.9	22.0	10.9
1955	6.1	1.1	1.4	43.1	88.2	71.8	52.4	35.2	18.9	8.9
1954	10.1	1.4	1.6	47.3	94.1	80.1	57.1	32.9	22.7	15.4
1953	5.8	1.1	1.4	51.4	89.8	88.9	53.7	26.5	21.6	12.7
1952	5.6	1.3	1.2	54.2	106.1	92.4	52.8	31.8	21.3	18.7
1951	5.9	1.5	0.8	50.0	91.8	80.8	51.5	32.5	16.6	11.5
1950	5.9	0.9	1.8	56.6	105.6	60.4	52.8	32.3	20.9	11.9
1949	6.9	1.3	2.1	58.0	98.0	82.3	57.6	31.6	18.2	15.3
1948	7.9	1.1	1.7	67.3	110.9	89.5	62.3	25.7	20.6	16.8
1947	7.7	0.8	2.5	70.4	111.1	88.2	57.6	29.1	19.4	9.9
1946	10.0	1.5	2.7	65.4	113.3	100.1	63.9	33.9	21.3	14.9
1945	7.5	0.8	1.7	64.3	112.1	87.3	59.4	24.5	20.9	14.6
1944	6.8	0.6	1.9	55.4	100.6	85.0	48.1	26.2	15.3	15.4
1943	3.4	1.0	3.5	58.2	87.8	77.7	47.9	19.6	13.4	6.8
1942	7.2	1.2	2.4	66.6	122.4	91.9	56.3	27.6	16.0	13.0
1941	5.4	1.3	1.5	70.9	123.9	91.0	57.9	28.7	23.0	13.6
1940	4.2	0.4	1.8	70.2	128.5	92.3	56.5	28.2	18.5	24.2
1939	7.5	0.4	1.9	72.3	123.2	92.2	60.3	32.6	25.9	13.5
1938	8.4	1.2	2.4	70.7	123.4	98.2	54.3	34.4	25.7	19.1
1937	6.0	0.6	2.3	83.9	134.5	105.5	62.7	38.5	23.0	28.6
1936	13.0	2.0	2.7	73.8	149.9	120.3	73.7	37.4	29.0	14.6
1935	10.1	0.0	2.3	82.1	151.2	119.0	65.5	35.8	33.4	18.8
1934	5.1	1.0	2.2	95.8	175.5	126.2	78.4	46.9	35.9	13.4
1933	15.2	1.6	2.8	91.8	152.8	130.5	78.1	48.8	29.5	29.4
1932	11.7	1.1	2.3	82.0	141.5	113.6	63.9	46.8	27.2	34.4
1931	8.0	1.0	2.3	83.5	146.8	118.6	63.8	37.4	37.7	8.8
1930	9.7	1.2	3.0	75.8	138.2	109.7	66.3	38.1	26.7	26.8

| | Age (years) | | | | | | | | | |
Year	0–1	1–4	5–14	15–24	25–34	35–44	45–54	55–64	65–74	75–84
1929	13.7	0.4	2.8	74.8	139.6	108.8	56.9	35.7	28.2	6.7
1928	10.2	0.8	3.1	79.1	144.7	119.3	65.4	34.2	27.5	8.9
1927	9.0	1.6	2.5	77.6	148.2	120.3	62.2	39.8	21.7	30.6
1926	14.7	1.4	3.1	85.1	157.3	117.7	70.6	32.8	22.7	26.9
1925	11.8	1.0	2.6	76.6	153.6	116.1	66.5	30.1	19.4	24.8
1924	12.8	1.5	4.0	81.6	134.9	107.5	55.7	33.1	32.8	5.6
1923	8.7	1.2	3.4	73.4	132.5	105.1	65.8	28.2	14.8	11.4
1922	7.5	0.5	1.8	63.4	116.7	94.8	53.5	28.5	34.9	20.5
1921	11.2	1.3	2.6	60.3	102.6	81.6	52.3	42.2	27.0	34.6
1920	10.9	1.6	3.0	65.6	98.0	74.2	40.5	25.1	16.1	17.8
1919	7.8	1.6	3.4	62.6	93.3	80.2	46.8	28.8	29.8	32.0
1918	15.7	0.8	3.8	60.5	89.9	76.6	41.6	29.5	21.0	8.8
1916	18.1	1.6	3.2	64.7	88.1	73.7	36.4	20.6	16.7	18.3
1915	30.4	2.0	0.8	63.8	79.4	68.2	35.4	26.5	14.4	27.9
1914	46.0	3.1	2.1	59.7	98.0	67.4	38.2	23.4	23.4	19.1

Nonwhite Females

| | Age (years) | | | | | | | | | |
Year	0–1	1–4	5–14	15–24	25–34	35–44	45–54	55–64	65–74	75–84
1984	13.3	5.7	2.7	13.1	16.4	12.4	7.2	6.0	6.1	8.5
1983	13.9	5.5	1.6	14.0	17.2	12.5	8.5	5.6	6.4	10.0
1982	12.2	5.8	1.9	13.6	17.9	13.7	10.2	7.2	7.3	8.4
1981	12.4	5.0	2.0	15.5	19.6	14.4	10.7	10.2	5.9	8.1
1980	11.1	5.7	2.0	16.6	22.1	15.7	11.4	8.2	7.7	6.4
1979	9.4	6.9	1.8	16.8	20.8	16.2	12.4	9.5	9.3	9.6
1978	12.0	6.6	2.7	16.1	20.9	16.8	9.4	8.6	8.5	7.4
1977	10.9	6.3	2.4	16.9	21.8	16.8	11.4	9.7	6.6	7.7
1976	13.3	7.0	1.5	17.0	22.8	18.3	13.5	11.0	6.9	10.5
1975	12.5	6.3	1.9	18.8	25.0	21.6	16.3	10.0	8.6	8.3
1974	17.5	5.4	2.0	20.5	27.9	23.1	15.2	9.6	8.2	8.0
1973	13.5	6.1	1.7	19.9	28.3	25.5	16.9	10.4	8.4	6.8
1972	13.6	3.8	2.0	18.5	27.7	21.3	15.1	11.0	7.3	6.4
1971	11.6	5.7	2.2	17.9	27.1	26.6	17.2	11.2	5.9	2.6
1970	10.2	5.8	1.9	16.3	23.3	22.6	16.1	7.8	7.1	5.1
1969	4.5	2.7	1.0	15.8	27.4	23.8	13.9	9.8	6.0	3.3

Year	Age (years)									
	0–1	1–4	5–14	15–24	25–34	35–44	45–54	55–64	65–74	75–84
1968	8.0	2.9	1.3	16.1	26.2	23.6	13.3	8.5	5.9	4.2
1967	12.3	2.5	1.5	16.0	27.1	23.0	15.2	9.2	6.8	1.2
1966	7.6	2.9	1.3	12.6	24.7	22.1	13.3	7.7	3.9	7.5
1965	10.4	2.4	1.0	11.6	24.0	21.3	12.5	7.0	3.3	3.5
1964	12.4	2.4	1.4	11.1	20.5	19.4	10.5	6.8	4.2	0.9
1963	8.5	1.9	1.3	10.9	20.4	19.6	10.5	5.5	6.1	3.5
1962	8.4	1.3	0.8	11.0	21.1	20.0	8.5	5.9	3.3	4.2
1961	10.0	2.3	0.8	10.6	20.4	19.1	9.5	5.6	2.6	4.3
1960	13.0	1.7	1.0	11.3	22.9	19.6	12.3	6.6	3.1	3.0
1959	4.6	1.2	0.7	12.2	23.2	19.6	8.8	6.2	5.0	2.5
1958	6.6	1.1	0.8	12.3	20.6	18.1	11.9	5.4	4.8	3.2
1957	6.3	1.5	0.5	11.9	21.2	17.7	10.6	5.0	5.2	2.0
1956	8.4	1.6	0.5	12.9	23.0	19.3	10.7	7.6	6.2	1.4
1955	6.8	1.2	0.6	12.3	21.3	17.4	10.0	6.0	3.1	3.8
1954	5.6	0.9	0.7	12.6	20.6	16.5	12.2	2.5	5.7	8.2
1953	4.0	1.0	0.8	12.2	21.5	17.2	9.5	5.5	4.2	2.7
1952	7.3	0.6	0.7	13.2	25.1	19.4	10.3	4.7	3.9	4.6
1951	7.2	1.2	0.7	15.2	24.3	16.6	10.3	4.2	3.0	4.8
1950	6.4	1.5	1.2	15.8	25.8	17.7	8.7	3.2	3.9	3.9
1949	5.5	1.2	0.8	17.3	22.7	18.1	10.7	6.3	3.2	6.0
1948	6.4	1.0	1.3	16.4	24.4	19.8	9.2	4.3	5.5	7.2
1947	2.7	0.3	0.8	17.2	26.6	18.1	10.2	6.8	2.6	2.2
1946	9.2	1.7	1.1	18.5	26.1	18.9	9.4	3.3	5.1	8.0
1945	8.8	0.6	0.8	16.6	22.2	16.7	7.4	3.4	2.4	2.4
1944	7.7	0.3	1.4	14.9	21.6	14.1	5.1	3.0	1.3	1.2
1943	1.4	1.2	1.1	14.9	21.3	15.1	6.4	3.1	1.7	0.0
1942	2.9	1.0	0.6	21.9	26.8	13.8	7.3	3.5	2.7	5.6
1941	10.1	1.1	1.1	22.0	25.6	17.4	5.8	2.3	3.3	8.7
1940	4.9	0.9	1.1	21.4	27.1	17.2	9.3	4.3	2.9	0.0
1939	8.1	0.6	1.0	22.8	31.2	16.8	7.9	5.4	2.8	1.6
1938	1.6	1.1	1.1	21.1	28.9	17.1	8.6	4.4	3.9	3.3
1937	10.1	0.4	1.3	23.7	30.2	16.9	9.5	4.8	5.8	1.7
1936	6.8	1.7	1.3	25.4	34.8	18.5	8.8	5.6	5.0	1.7
1935	3.3	0.8	0.9	20.8	32.5	19.1	7.9	5.8	3.6	7.1
1934	8.3	0.2	1.7	23.7	33.3	17.6	10.6	8.1	7.0	7.3
1933	10.0	0.8	1.2	23.4	32.7	19.2	8.1	5.8	2.0	5.6
1932	7.1	0.8	1.3	23.2	36.2	17.1	8.2	8,3	2.8	4.1
1931	7.0	0.6	1.6	25.4	32.5	17.5	5.9	6.9	3.2	8.3
1930	7.8	1.0	1.5	23.6	31.4	17.9	10.2	7.1	2.5	10.6

	Age (years)									
Year	0–1	1–4	5–14	15–24	25–34	35–44	45–54	55–64	65–74	75–84
1929	8.5	0.2	1.1	22.1	34.2	19.6	8.6	5.5	5.2	2.2
1928	4.5	0.8	1.6	25.2	31.3	18.9	5.2	3.4	3.6	2.2
1927	8.7	0.9	1.5	26.2	32.3	18.8	9.6	5.9	4.1	5.0
1926	4.1	1.2	1.1	28.9	33.0	17.3	8.1	5.7	3.3	0.0
1925	3.2	1.0	1.1	23.5	30.7	20.8	6.2	2.7	5.5	0.0
1924	10.5	1.0	0.9	24.4	27.7	17.7	6.6	3.3	5.6	2.8
1923	10.7	1.0	1.2	23.7	27.1	14.8	9.1	7.4	4.5	0.0
1922	6.3	0.8	1.2	22.7	26.1	13.6	7.8	3.6	4.6	5.9
1921	8.6	0.8	1.2	21.0	25.7	17.8	7.4	4.9	4.0	3.5
1920	7.9	2.5	1.0	19.0	22.1	14.1	4.0	1.5	2.7	10.8
1919	10.3	1.0	1.5	18.4	22.3	13.0	4.7	4.5	1.4	3.5
1918	7.7	0.8	1.2	20.3	20.6	13.2	6.7	2.7	3.2	0.0
1916	23.8	0.5	1.3	14.7	18.1	14.3	8.0	2.4	0.0	5.9
1915	33.8	0.0	2.4	22.4	22.0	9.3	12.7	3.6	3.3	17.6
1914	19.0	1.0	0.4	17.1	17.3	17.5	4.6	3.6	0.0	0.0

MOTOR-VEHICLE-ACCIDENT MORTALITY RATES

White Males

	Age (years)									
Year	0–1	1–4	5–14	15–24	25–34	35–44	45–54	55–64	65–74	75–84
1984	3.9	7.5	8.4	59.1	37.3	24.3	21.7	20.9	24.0	41.8
1983	5.7	8.3	8.4	57.0	37.0	24.3	21.2	19.9	22.5	39.8
1982	5.9	8.2	8.5	60.8	38.5	26.3	22.4	20.8	23.1	39.6
1981	6.2	8.1	9.9	67.6	46.3	29.9	25.5	24.0	26.3	43.8
1980	7.0	9.5	9.8	73.8	46.6	30.7	26.3	23.9	25.8	43.6
1979	7.4	9.7	10.6	75.4	46.0	30.7	26.5	25.5	29.0	46.4
1978	7.5	11.0	11.3	75.4	44.5	29.7	25.3	25.4	29.4	48.5
1977	8.6	10.3	10.4	71.0	40.2	27.3	24.9	25.6	28.8	49.6
1976	6.8	11.4	10.5	66.4	37.9	26.3	24.3	24.8	29.5	50.8
1975	8.0	10.9	10.8	64.6	38.2	27.7	24.0	24.4	30.3	52.3
1974	6.8	10.2	10.6	66.7	39.6	27.8	26.2	27.0	31.4	49.6
1973	11.4	12.6	13.2	74.8	45.8	33.0	31.1	33.3	39.7	65.1
1972	9.2	11.8	13.0	75.2	45.7	33.1	32.9	35.0	43.1	74.8
1971	10.2	11.1	12.8	72.6	45.9	33.7	32.5	35.2	44.0	66.6

	Age (years)								
Year	0–1	1–4	5–14	15–24	25–34	35–44	45–54	55–64	65–74	75–84
1970	9.1	12.2	12.6	75.2	47.0	35.2	34.6	39.0	46.2	69.2
1969	10.7	12.4	11.8	82.0	49.5	35.5	34.5	37.9	48.3	67.0
1968	10.1	11.2	12.5	80.7	49.5	35.1	35.8	39.6	49.2	73.6
1967	9.0	12.1	11.5	78.4	48.5	34.7	36.1	39.6	50.1	70.3
1966	9.8	12.1	12.2	78.7	49.9	35.7	36.8	40.9	49.7	72.8
1965	9.9	11.1	11.5	71.6	45.8	35.2	35.4	39.5	49.6	72.9
1964	9.4	11.1	11.1	67.9	45.8	33.4	34.1	38.0	50.5	70.6
1963	8.0	11.2	10.4	65.4	42.7	32.4	34.0	37.9	47.3	72.0
1962	8.6	10.2	10.6	63.3	39.9	30.3	30.9	36.0	46.4	66.9
1961	7.2	10.9	9.8	60.6	38.3	28.6	29.8	33.4	44.9	64.4
1960	8.8	11.3	10.3	62.7	38.6	28.4	29.7	34.4	45.5	66.8
1959	8.2	10.5	10.1	63.6	39.0	28.8	30.5	34.7	50.0	68.4
1958	8.8	10.7	10.5	61.6	38.8	30.0	29.5	34.3	50.6	69.2
1957	9.4	10.3	10.3	67.1	42.3	31.3	31.8	38.2	53.2	75.1
1956	9.4	9.9	11.0	72.0	42.9	31.9	33.4	38.9	55.3	76.8
1955	9.5	11.3	10.5	68.5	42.7	32.8	32.0	39.6	53.7	75.7
1954	8.8	12.4	10.4	62.0	40.5	29.6	30.6	37.0	51.3	80.1
1953	10.9	13.7	10.8	65.4	42.9	32.2	33.1	41.0	57.0	84.2
1952	9.7	13.6	11.2	64.8	43.3	33.3	33.5	42.6	60.6	81.9
1951	9.8	13.8	12.0	60.6	42.4	33.9	34.6	42.0	59.6	84.7
1950	9.1	13.2	12.0	58.3	39.1	30.9	31.6	41.9	59.1	86.4
1949	6.9	13.7	12.3	52.1	35.1	27.3	29.4	40.0	57.5	83.6
1948	5.6	14.7	14.1	54.5	34.6	28.2	30.4	41.8	63.1	92.0
1947	5.9	1.45	14.2	54.8	36.0	29.5	32.3	45.9	68.0	100.6
1946	7.4	16.1	15.8	58.4	38.2	29.5	33.5	47.4	70.1	105.5
1945	4.8	14.0	16.1	51.7	39.8	30.0	31.5	45.9	66.1	92.3
1944	4.4	13.0	13.7	39.3	30.4	26.1	27.9	42.5	57.6	77.7
1943	4.7	13.5	12.9	34.7	29.3	24.5	29.6	41.1	55.5	79.7
1942	4.9	12.9	13.3	41.7	32.9	29.1	35.4	51.5	67.2	86.6
1941	8.8	16.7	18.0	56.3	46.2	40.0	48.2	65.1	95.5	133.0
1940	5.7	15.4	16.0	45.7	40.0	34.3	43.8	62.8	86.5	121.1
1939	6.8	14.4	14.4	43.4	37.4	33.6	41.2	59.4	81.3	119.3
1938	7.0	15.1	15.4	40.6	36.1	33.0	45.5	63.3	86.5	124.4
1937	8.8	16.7	18.1	52.9	44.5	43.0	56.1	77.9	101.3	142.3
1936	5.5	18.4	18.2	48.2	45.2	41.7	55.0	75.0	95.7	133.0
1935	5.2	17.3	17.7	45.6	44.9	41.7	54.3	70.8	93.4	127.0
1934	6.7	16.7	18.1	45.1	43.2	42.1	55.4	72.3	96.2	129.7
1933	5.4	17.7	18.0	38.4	37.8	35.4	45.1	60.7	82.8	114.5
1932	5.0	17.0	16.3	35.8	34.6	34.3	41.2	58.6	81.7	119.1

				Age (years)						
Year	0–1	1–4	5–14	15–24	25–34	35–44	45–54	55–64	65–74	75–84
1931	6.4	19.3	20.4	44.9	38.7	38.8	46.7	66.2	89.7	113.8
1930	8.6	18.5	20.9	44.1	38.8	36.7	46.9	63.4	93.4	124.4
1929	6.2	19.3	22.6	40.9	34.4	34.7	45.6	59.9	85.9	134.0
1928	5.3	18.5	22.2	35.9	31.0	32.6	39.8	55.4	78.6	114.4
1927	6.7	19.1	22.9	32.2	28.0	30.0	35.4	50.0	70.6	98.8
1926	6.2	15.3	23.0	27.9	24.4	27.2	35.0	40.9	65.1	95.5
1925	4.0	15.5	22.1	21.9	19.6	21.6	27.6	37.1	59.2	82.9
1924	5.2	15.3	22.2	19.3	18.2	20.1	25.5	31.6	50.8	71.4
1923	3.1	13.7	21.6	18.3	17.9	21.0	25.5	32.3	48.4	68.3
1922	2.2	13.3	21.4	14.8	16.1	16.5	20.3	26.4	41.5	60.7
1921	1.8	13.4	20.6	12.6	14.1	15.8	17.8	22.6	37.2	44.6
1920	1.5	12.2	20.8	12.5	13.2	12.3	14.9	19.9	31.4	43.8
1919	1.6	10.7	19.6	11.0	10.9	11.9	13.0	19.5	28.8	37.7
1918	2.3	9.3	17.2	11.5	11.8	13.3	16.0	21.6	27.1	30.1
1916	1.0	6.4	12.6	9.1	10.0	10.7	12.8	17.7	20.7	23.4
1915	0.9	4.5	10.3	7.4	7.4	8.6	10.5	12.9	17.5	21.5
1914	1.3	3.2	8.2	4.8	5.3	6.5	8.3	9.6	12.9	11.0

White Females

				Age (years)						
Year	0–1	1–4	5–14	15–24	25–34	35–44	45–54	55–64	65–74	75–84
1984	4.4	5.4	5.1	20.1	11.0	9.4	8.9	10.3	13.0	20.6
1983	4.8	6.0	4.7	18.8	10.7	8.8	8.5	9.3	12.6	17.9
1982	5.6	7.0	5.0	18.9	10.6	8.8	8.5	9.3	12.6	17.3
1981	6.5	6.8	5.1	21.8	12.4	9.9	9.5	10.7	13.3	18.0
1980	7.1	7.7	5.7	23.0	12.2	10.6	10.2	10.5	13.4	19.0
1979	6.2	8.9	6.1	22.8	12.1	10.6	9.8	10.3	13.7	18.9
1978	8.5	8.6	6.4	23.8	12.2	9.6	9.6	11.2	14.9	20.4
1977	7.8	8.9	6.6	22.7	11.1	9.6	9.5	11.1	14.7	21.0
1976	8.4	8.4	6.4	20.5	10.4	8.9	9.2	10.8	15.0	21.6
1975	8.4	8.2	6.1	18.4	10.5	8.6	8.9	10.5	14.4	20.9
1974	8.3	8.5	6.2	18.5	10.0	8.6	9.2	11.0	14.6	20.9
1973	9.5	9.6	7.6	22.3	12.7	11.7	12.2	15.2	20.3	26.8
1972	7.7	9.9	8.0	23.2	12.7	12.5	14.0	16.2	23.3	26.8

	Age (years)									
Year	0–1	1–4	5–14	15–24	25–34	35–44	45–54	55–64	65–74	75–84
1971	8.9	9.7	7.6	22.0	13.0	12.0	12.9	15.6	22.3	27.7
1970	10.2	9.6	6.9	22.7	12.7	12.3	14.3	16.1	22.1	28.1
1969	11.3	10.1	6.9	23.1	13.0	13.2	13.8	17.1	23.7	27.6
1968	9.0	9.6	6.8	22.7	12.9	12.3	13.6	17.0	24.2	28.0
1967	9.1	9.2	6.5	22.1	12.8	12.1	14.0	17.5	24.8	29.1
1966	9.3	8.7	6.6	22.0	13.2	12.2	14.3	18.7	24.8	27.4
1965	7.8	8.8	6.0	19.6	11.8	12.3	14.1	17.9	23.3	28.0
1964	10.0	9.0	5.8	19.3	11.9	12.1	13.7	18.0	23.1	27.8
1963	8.9	8.7	5.4	18.1	10.6	10.9	13.0	16.4	21.9	26.3
1962	7.9	8.6	5.3	16.7	10.1	10.7	12.1	16.2	21.3	25.5
1961	7.9	8.1	4.9	14.7	9.3	9.2	11.4	14.8	18.9	23.8
1960	7.5	8.3	5.3	15.6	9.0	8.9	11.4	15.3	19.3	23.8
1959	9.5	8.3	5.0	14.8	9.6	8.8	11.1	14.5	21.2	25.0
1958	7.3	8.0	5.5	14.3	8.6	8.9	11.0	14.4	22.0	25.2
1957	8.5	8.0	5.3	15.0	9.2	9.6	11.6	15.5	21.3	25.1
1956	7.8	8.6	5.4	16.3	9.6	9.5	11.4	14.8	22.4	24.9
1955	8.5	9.2	5.2	15.6	9.8	9.1	11.5	15.8	20.5	27.2
1954	6.9	9.1	5.5	13.2	8.4	8.7	11.2	14.5	20.2	25.7
1953	7.8	9.9	5.7	15.5	9.1	9.1	11.9	15.3	22.0	27.1
1952	9.0	9.8	6.0	15.3	9.0	9.7	12.1	16.0	19.8	26.3
1951	7.9	8.9	6.2	13.5	9.5	9.1	11.0	15.9	21.3	26.8
1950	7.8	10.1	5.6	12.6	9.0	8.1	10.8	15.0	20.9	25.4
1949	6.9	9.9	5.8	11.1	7.4	7.3	9.2	14.4	19.9	27.2
1948	6.5	10.3	6.5	12.6	6.9	7.0	9.4	14.3	18.5	26.3
1947	4.2	10.5	6.7	12.6	6.9	8.0	9.9	14.2	19.6	29.3
1946	5.6	10.3	7.3	13.1	8.2	7.1	9.7	14.0	20.0	28.7
1945	4.1	9.1	6.7	11.1	6.9	7.1	7.8	11.1	15.5	23.9
1944	2.9	9.5	5.9	8.8	5.8	5.2	6.6	9.4	14.4	20.7
1943	3.8	9.0	5.5	7.6	4.8	5.3	6.9	9.5	13.6	17.9
1942	3.8	9.5	5.1	10.1	6.5	6.3	9.1	11.8	18.1	22.0
1941	7.0	12.1	7.8	15.2	10.6	10.0	14.2	19.8	32.0	41.1
1940	6.3	10.3	7.4	12.7	9.0	9.0	12.3	18.9	29.4	38.6
1939	7.6	11.4	6.3	10.9	8.5	8.6	11.9	18.1	30.6	37.6
1938	5.8	9.8	6.6	10.9	8.6	8.7	12.7	18.9	31.5	41.6
1937	8.5	12.4	8.0	14.9	11.0	11.6	15.4	22.4	36.2	48.9
1936	7.0	12.2	8.2	14.3	10.8	11.0	15.2	22.9	34.4	44.0
1935	6.0	10.8	7.8	14.1	10.5	10.6	15.3	22.7	32.1	45.5
1934	4.9	9.9	8.3	12.7	10.4	10.0	14.0	22.9	36.1	44.9
1933	5.5	10.1	8.1	11.7	8.6	9.2	13.4	21.1	32.0	44.2

				Age (years)						
Year	0–1	1–4	5–14	15–24	25–34	35–44	45–54	55–64	65–74	75–84
1932	4.0	9.6	8.0	11.1	8.2	8.6	13.0	20.9	32.9	42.3
1931	6.9	12.3	9.4	13.1	9.1	10.3	15.8	23.9	38.0	45.9
1930	5.7	11.8	9.4	12.3	9.0	9.3	15.9	24.1	40.2	52.0
1929	5.7	12.5	9.8	12.0	8.4	9.0	14.6	23.8	36.4	41.1
1928	6.7	11.4	10.1	9.9	7.2	9.3	14.7	22.0	33.4	45.8
1927	5.5	10.9	10.1	9.3	7.0	8.7	12.3	20.3	32.8	42.1
1926	5.7	10.1	9.8	8.8	6.6	7.9	12.1	18.0	27.4	36.0
1925	4.0	9.5	9.0	7.2	4.8	6.6	9.9	18.2	26.2	35.5
1924	2.8	9.0	8.7	6.2	4.7	6.2	8.5	15.5	23.3	27.1
1923	2.4	8.4	8.6	5.5	4.5	6.0	8.2	13.4	21.3	23.7
1922	3.2	7.5	7.8	4.6	3.5	4.0	6.4	11.9	17.4	19.8
1921	2.4	7.4	7.5	3.4	3.3	3.9	6.6	11.0	17.2	16.9
1920	2.3	6.9	6.5	3.8	2.9	3.3	6.0	9.8	14.1	16.4
1919	1.2	6.1	6.2	3.2	2.8	3.5	5.4	8.6	10.6	13.9
1918	1.9	5.3	5.3	3.0	2.6	2.8	4.9	7.8	9.1	13.1
1916	1.2	3.8	3.3	2.2	1.9	2.6	3.8	5.3	6.4	7.8
1915	0.5	3.0	2.9	1.8	1.6	2.0	3.3	4.9	5.0	6.3
1914	0.3	2.3	2.1	1.5	1.1	1.7	1.7	3.1	4.1	4.9

Nonwhite Males

				Age (years)						
Year	0–1	1–4	5–14	15–24	25–34	35–44	45–54	55–64	65–74	75–84
1984	5.5	9.9	8.1	33.7	35.1	21.5	27.8	29.8	32.7	43.6
1983	3.8	10.5	8.6	30.6	34.9	31.0	30.8	29.4	31.0	42.8
1982	6.5	10.5	8.2	30.9	35.0	31.4	32.1	32.1	34.1	41.6
1981	6.9	9.8	9.0	33.4	40.5	38.1	36.9	33.8	41.8	42.9
1980	8.8	13.5	10.4	38.7	44.1	38.8	37.5	38.8	41.2	50.7
1979	4.3	14.1	11.1	38.7	46.6	41.7	39.2	41.0	40.6	40.3
1978	7.4	14.6	10.9	42.4	51.0	42.9	38.4	42.2	42.9	64.4
1977	6.9	14.5	12.8	42.7	50.6	39.2	38.7	45.4	40.1	52.1
1976	8.9	14.7	11.8	40.2	49.2	42.0	40.3	41.9	41.4	52.6
1975	9.5	16.2	13.3	38.8	51.8	42.7	40.9	44.8	49.2	49.1
1974	6.0	13.7	13.2	43.5	49.4	43.9	42.6	45.4	52.6	49.1
1973	8.2	22.2	14.7	54.5	63.6	59.0	56.4	57.9	60.5	56.3

Year	Age (years)									
	0–1	1–4	5–14	15–24	25–34	35–44	45–54	55–64	65–74	75–84
1972	10.4	19.9	13.9	57.3	68.7	59.0	60.5	62.0	54.2	66.0
1971	14.6	17.2	16.2	58.3	66.4	53.0	54.0	62.4	63.0	64.4
1970	10.8	17.0	15.7	60.3	67.4	57.7	60.6	59.9	57.5	56.5
1969	9.6	16.5	15.8	67.2	72.2	65.2	62.9	69.4	68.3	65.2
1968	6.2	17.0	15.1	66.1	76.2	59.6	62.8	65.1	75.5	65.2
1967	7.8	17.0	14.7	61.6	68.7	53.9	54.4	59.3	74.6	57.3
1966	12.3	15.3	13.9	61.3	69.5	57.6	58.3	57.5	70.3	65.1
1965	5.9	16.4	12.6	55.2	65.7	54.0	52.5	58.2	62.8	50.3
1964	7.4	14.7	13.4	49.1	59.5	53.8	53.3	52.6	67.5	51.6
1963	5.6	14.6	12.2	52.9	57.9	49.6	48.1	51.3	58.5	50.0
1962	8.6	12.4	11.5	49.6	53.7	46.6	45.7	51.0	60.2	45.0
1961	6.0	12.3	11.2	46.5	50.9	42.8	42.3	48.1	53.2	52.1
1960	7.5	13.1	10.7	50.7	51.7	43.1	49.1	47.6	49.1	56.0
1959	6.3	11.7	11.9	46.9	53.2	49.5	52.3	51.3	55.7	43.3
1958	6.1	11.6	10.7	47.5	55.2	50.2	46.5	50.2	67.2	43.8
1957	9.2	13.1	10.8	47.8	61.3	51.4	51.1	58.1	62.4	73.9
1956	14.5	10.8	10.9	56.8	66.5	60.9	54.6	59.1	68.3	62.5
1955	10.6	13.5	10.0	54.6	62.5	54.3	52.5	55.9	64.2	53.2
1954	14.2	13.0	10.2	47.9	58.7	48.2	54.8	54.4	57.1	61.5
1953	11.1	17.5	12.6	53.2	66.1	56.6	57.3	55.1	67.5	82.7
1952	8.8	15.6	11.3	53.8	63.6	54.4	58.6	59.7	60.1	71.0
1951	6.4	13.4	13.1	40.7	62.3	54.3	52.8	55.2	67.5	75.0
1950	8.9	11.7	10.8	44.3	55.4	46.9	52.0	57.0	58.8	66.4
1949	6.4	12.6	13.0	40.3	46.9	42.3	45.8	43.6	59.6	72.4
1948	8.4	12.6	11.5	27.6	39.9	41.5	48.7	51.7	57.4	76.8
1947	4.4	11.3	11.2	37.5	35.9	40.0	44.8	48.7	65.9	65.9
1946	3.6	14.1	14.0	37.4	40.1	40.1	46.8	50.5	54.0	62.1
1945	3.4	11.1	11.4	33.5	39.1	40.5	42.2	48.8	51.7	69.5
1944	4.1	12.3	13.1	32.0	38.6	35.2	40.5	36.7	56.1	59.0
1943	2.0	12.9	11.3	29.7	33.0	34.2	42.3	43.5	55.3	56.2
1942	3.6	11.2	11.6	36.3	43.9	40.1	50.0	48.9	52.9	49.3
1941	10.0	12.0	17.2	52.7	59.4	60.6	66.8	73.4	93.5	90.9
1940	5.0	9.9	13.7	41.8	48.0	45.0	58.4	57.8	72.1	85.5
1939	3.3	11.0	14.4	35.6	43.8	47.7	56.1	62.5	69.2	67.7
1938	5.9	11.4	12.8	38.4	45.5	51.6	49.6	65.7	69.1	76.5
1937	7.7	11.9	14.4	43.6	50.3	58.4	66.3	80.2	90.2	109.0
1936	8.6	10.6	13.0	42.0	51.2	68.0	65.4	83.9	81.9	98.9
1935	3.4	12.5	11.8	38.0	50.2	57.2	57.8	71.9	82.5	101.3
1934	5.1	12.1	16.7	40.6	54.5	53.1	63.1	77.1	91.8	96.0

Year	\multicolumn{10}{c}{Age (years)}

Year	0–1	1–4	5–14	15–24	25–34	35–44	45–54	55–64	65–74	75–84
1933	4.2	11.8	15.8	34.9	45.4	48.2	52.6	64.3	80.6	108.0
1932	7.2	11.1	14.2	28.3	38.9	45.5	48.4	54.6	67.2	58.1
1931	2.7	8.6	16.1	31.6	44.6	45.2	51.3	58.4	76.8	65.8
1930	3.5	9.4	14.6	37.3	41.2	44.7	52.0	58.2	67.5	87.2
1929	3.9	10.9	14.4	31.6	41.3	41.9	52.6	59.9	60.1	100.6
1928	4.6	9.1	14.1	25.0	29.9	37.2	44.1	43.5	63.5	60.3
1927	6.0	12.7	16.3	22.6	30.3	35.5	42.4	37.2	61.5	101.9
1926	2.1	9.4	15.1	24.8	29.7	32.7	33.5	33.6	51.8	45.8
1925	4.3	9.2	14.0	18.4	20.5	27.6	28.6	25.1	43.4	46.8
1924	2.1	10.0	12.4	18.0	19.3	23.1	28.8	24.7	35.5	63.9
1923	3.3	6.2	10.5	14.3	17.0	20.2	19.5	23.0	17.5	31.3
1922	1.1	5.4	8.3	7.0	12.9	13.1	14.6	14.9	22.7	20.5
1921	2.5	4.1	9.2	6.3	8.1	10.3	12.5	13.0	15.7	27.7
1920	2.7	3.8	9.6	8.1	9.0	7.5	6.2	15.6	12.6	14.3
1919	0.0	2.6	7.2	5.3	7.5	9.3	6.9	15.6	20.6	10.7
1918	0.0	6.8	10.2	7.3	7.0	9.4	8.9	11.9	22.4	30.7
1916	0.0	3.1	5.7	3.9	5.3	7.5	5.1	9.4	18.6	6.1
1915	0.0	1.0	4.2	5.6	4.3	5.8	9.4	11.2	8.7	18.6
1914	0.0	1.0	4.2	3.2	4.7	2.8	0.7	5.7	8.8	19.1

Nonwhite Females

Year	\multicolumn{10}{c}{Age (years)}

Year	0–1	1–4	5–14	15–24	25–34	35–44	45–54	55–64	65–74	75–84
1984	5.3	7.3	4.2	9.4	9.1	8.4	7.9	9.3	10.1	13.7
1983	5.9	7.3	4.4	9.7	8.2	7.9	9.6	8.1	10.3	15.0
1982	5.3	8.0	5.2	9.6	9.4	8.8	8.0	8.6	10.6	8.8
1981	3.7	8.4	5.4	9.6	9.9	8.9	9.1	9.5	10.7	13.2
1980	4.8	9.9	5.7	9.5	11.9	9.7	9.7	10.4	8.9	12.8
1979	5.7	10.0	5.3	11.3	9.9	10.0	10.1	11.3	11.2	14.2
1978	11.3	13.1	5.8	12.4	11.3	10.7	10.8	13.4	10.1	13.6
1977	6.8	10.1	5.7	12.3	10.4	9.5	10.0	12.5	9.0	15.8
1976	10.8	11.4	5.8	10.8	11.2	10.4	10.7	11.6	13.1	12.7
1975	7.8	11.3	6.2	10.5	10.2	10.2	12.2	12.7	12.1	15.7
1974	8.1	11.6	6.9	10.7	12.4	10.9	10.7	13.9	13.0	14.7

	Age (years)									
Year	0–1	1–4	5–14	15–24	25–34	35–44	45–54	55–64	65–74	75–84
1973	14.3	13.5	7.9	16.2	16.3	15.1	17.2	14.2	17.5	14.0
1972	14.4	11.5	9.5	14.8	13.2	16.2	17.9	14.3	17.4	17.0
1971	10.1	13.7	7.9	16.2	16.8	16.3	17.4	15.8	19.8	14.8
1970	11.3	12.3	9.1	14.9	14.7	16.6	16.6	16.7	17.2	14.6
1969	7.8	12.3	8.4	19.2	15.9	15.7	16.6	17.6	21.7	15.8
1968	10.0	11.0	7.8	15.2	17.1	17.8	15.6	17.1	22.5	18.5
1967	10.6	10.4	8.7	16.1	15.7	14.1	17.7	17.9	19.5	20.7
1966	8.3	11.0	7.3	17.8	17.1	15.5	18.6	15.4	20.7	16.3
1965	6.6	9.8	7.1	15.5	14.8	15.2	16.1	15.7	21.5	11.9
1964	6.7	8.0	6.5	12.4	14.1	13.9	13.9	17.0	19.2	16.7
1963	5.3	8.6	6.0	11.6	14.0	11.3	15.3	16.1	16.7	16.1
1962	7.5	9.1	6.5	12.0	10.1	13.6	13.9	14.2	17.0	14.3
1961	4.8	8.1	5.9	12.4	11.9	11.6	11.4	14.6	14.4	20.1
1060	7.8	9.4	5.9	11.2	10.3	11.0	12.8	14.4	14.4	11.3
1959	5.6	8.4	5.5	11.3	12.3	11.6	12.9	12.7	20.8	12.3
1958	5.1	9.5	4.0	10.6	11.2	11.9	12.3	12.0	19.2	15.4
1957	7.0	9.0	5.7	13.1	14.4	12.7	14.6	17.9	20.4	18.1
1956	10.1	9.2	6.4	12.4	12.9	14.1	14.3	20.7	17.3	14.2
1955	8.9	10.9	5.4	13.5	13.5	13.4	14.1	17-3	22.6	18.8
1954	9.4	11.1	5.3	11.9	11.9	13.3	13.7	16.6	16.8	20.5
1953	11.6	9.7	6.2	13.3	13.5	14.5	14.1	12.9	14.7	21.2
1952	7.8	9.9	4.6	14.4	14.2	10.8	16.6	14.6	17.0	22.2
1951	9.5	9.1	5.6	13.6	12.0	13.5	15.5	16.6	20.2	19.0
1950	6.9	9.4	6.4	12.1	11.4	11.5	11.1	13.9	15.4	22.5
1949	3.5	9.0	5.2	8.8	9.4	7.9	12.7	11.9	16.7	17.0
1948	1.6	8.7	5.3	9.0	8.0	8.8	9.6	10.6	13.2	16.5
1947	3.8	7.3	4.9	8.6	7.7	6.4	10.5	11.9	10.5	15.1
1946	5.7	9.4	6.7	9.8	7.2	8.6	10.6	12.2	13.2	19.3
1945	5.4	6.6	4.6	7.0	6.7	7.0	9.2	8.3	16.9	11.9
1944	4.9	6.5	4.6	6.1	7.4	6.4	7.8	8.2	10.9	12.3
1943	2.1	5.2	3.8	5.2	7.0	5.4	5.4	8.9	8.7	7.8
1942	1.5	5.2	4.7	7.2	8.3	7.9	8.8	9.3	12.3	19.4
1941	9.3	7.2	6.4	11.2	11.4	11.1	13.9	16.9	20.9	30.4
1940	5.7	7.3	6.0	7.7	10.7	9.4	13.3	15.7	17.7	13.7
1939	3.3	7.7	4.3	9.6	9.6	9.7	11.9	20.5	21.2	16.0
1938	4.1	6.7	5.1	8.1	10.3	12.1	15.8	20.9	16.2	21.4
1937	6.7	5.2	5.0	10.6	10.8	14.0	15.3	24.1	22.0	32.2
1936	5.9	7.2	4.7	10.1	13.2	13.4	13.5	22.2	29.0	24.3
1935	6.6	8.6	4.7	7.0	9.9	11.0	14.8	19.0	20.8	21.3

| Year | Age (years) | | | | | | | | | |
	0–1	1–4	5–14	15–24	25–34	35–44	45–54	55–64	65–74	75–84
1934	2.5	8.5	7.4	7.7	11.4	11.5	15.8	24.9	23.4	18.2
1933	2.5	8.1	5.6	7.1	8.3	11.1	14.0	20.2	22.0	20.5
1932	0.9	8.2	6.2	5.4	10.2	11.0	14.9	19.5	25.1	28.5
1931	5.3	6.6	5.4	8.5	11.7	12.2	14.0	26.2	30.4	20.8
1930	0.9	8.9	5.7	7.1	10.3	8.8	13.9	22.7	29.4	17.0
1929	4.7	7.4	6.1	8.2	10.5	10.2	14.5	16.1	20.1	15.2
1928	3.6	7.4	6.4	5.5	7.9	9.5	14.3	17.9	16.1	30.7
1927	4.8	6.0	5.4	4.5	8.0	11.0	14.5	13.6	22.7	12.6
1926	1.0	6.3	5.2	6.5	8.1	9.6	9.7	14.5	20.7	19.6
1925	2.1	5.2	3.9	6.4	7.8	7.5	7.5	12.3	15.5	24.6
1924	3.2	3.9	3.8	3.9	5.9	6.5	8.6	11.0	14.5	13.9
1923	3.2	2.0	3.6	4.5	3.7	4.4	4.1	9.1	11.3	20.1
1922	0.0	4.1	2.4	2.2	2.5	4.7	3.0	5.3	12.7	3.0
1921	1.2	2.8	1.9	1.5	1.6	2.3	3.5	4.2	13.5	7.0
1920	0.0	3.8	2.0	1.3	2.1	1.9	2.5	5.1	4.1	3.6
1919	1.3	2.3	2.7	0.7	1.5	1.7	1.8	4.5	2.7	17.7
1918	1.5	1.6	2.8	1.3	1.2	2.6	3.6	6.3	0.0	4.3
1916	0.0	1.5	1.5	0.7	1.7	0.4	1.2	2.2	2.2	0.0
1915	0.0	5.9	2.4	0.4	2.5	1.6	0.9	0.0	6.6	0.0
1914	0.0	0.0	0.8	0.0	0.0	0.6	0.9	1.8	0.0	0.0

ACCIDENT MORTALITY RATES EXCLUDING MOTOR-VEHICLE ACCIDENTS (NON-MOTOR-VEHICLE-ACCIDENT MORTALITY RATES)

White Males

| Year | Age (years) | | | | | | | | | |
	0–1	1–4	5–14	15–24	25–34	35–44	45–54	55–64	65–74	75–84
1984	16.4	14.2	7.3	20.9	23.8	21.0	24.1	28.7	43.7	103.7
1983	19.0	16.0	7.9	22.4	24.8	22.5	24.8	30.9	43.4	101.5
1982	22.0	16.4	8.3	24.4	26.1	22.2	26.1	31.0	44.8	101.3
1981	19.7	17.6	8.5	24.9	26.2	22.6	27.9	32.7	47.4	103.8
1980	23.9	18.6	8.9	27.9	27.2	24.3	28.4	34.8	51.4	113.7
1979	23.1	18.2	9.8	28.3	26.2	25.3	29.2	35.7	52.4	113.1
1978	28.5	20.1	10.8	29.6	27.2	26.2	30.1	38.1	53.1	124.7
1977	27.7	19.2	11.4	30.0	28.1	26.9	30.8	39.8	55.7	129.3
1976	33.1	19.7	11.4	30.9	28.9	26.8	30.7	41.0	55.7	127.9

	Age (years)								
Year	0–1	1–4	5–14	15–24	25–34	35–44	45–54	55–64	65–74	75–84
1975	30.2	19.2	12.5	34.3	30.6	29.4	35.0	43.6	61.5	137.2
1974	39.0	22.6	13.1	34.2	30.7	30.0	34.8	44.3	62.6	138.8
1973	40.7	21.5	13.2	35.6	31.6	31.4	36.4	48.9	64.6	142.6
1972	45.5	23.7	13.3	32.1	29.7	29.0	37.0	49.5	65.8	146.9
1971	50.7	21.9	12.3	31.7	28.7	32.6	36.7	50.3	68.3	143.5
1970	48.1	21.6	13.2	33.7	30.9	33.6	39.3	51.1	72.9	152.8
1969	56.6	20.6	12.9	33.4	32.0	34.5	40.1	53.6	70.8	151.7
1968	56.0	20.5	13.2	31.0	30.0	32.1	39.4	52.6	74.6	153.5
1967	62.4	21.9	13.3	29.8	30.8	34.1	41.2	54.3	71.6	157.9
1966	66.5	22.5	12.7	29.6	29.8	33.0	42.3	55.0	71.4	166.1
1965	71.6	22.4	12.6	28.3	29.8	31.2	41.8	52.1	72.5	165.5
1964	68.6	20.9	13.0	27.8	28.7	31.7	40.6	51.1	70.4	164.4
1963	72.0	21.0	13.1	27.5	28.0	31.1	41.5	52.2	72.6	166.3
1962	73.1	21.1	12.7	26.8	28.9	31.9	42.2	50.1	72.9	172.4
1961	72.7	21.0	14.0	28.6	28.2	30.5	40.0	49.1	68.3	165.8
1960	76.8	20.6	14.5	29.5	29.1	32.4	42.6	49.7	72.3	171.9
1959	82.8	20.6	14.2	30.0	29.6	32.6	40.8	49.8	75.8	176.2
1958	86.6	20.9	14.4	31.4	29.2	33.7	39.5	48.3	73.2	178.5
1957	77.9	20.5	32.6	30.5	34.4	43.0	43.0	53.4	84.4	203.3
1956	77.8	22.2	15.2	33.9	30.3	33.0	42.1	53.1	86.6	202.5
1955	77.6	21.6	16.1	32.2	30.2	33.6	44.9	54.2	87.7	214.7
1954	86.8	22.4	16.6	33.8	31.1	34.3	43.1	54.6	86.5	211.8
1953	90.2	23.8	18.2	37.4	33.9	35.9	47.6	59.3	88.6	230.6
1952	92.6	24.6	18.3	36.6	34.6	38.0	48.3	62.4	90.8	236.0
1951	99.2	24.6	19.4	36.1	37.6	42.4	48.5	63.0	98.5	236.2
1950	102.3	26.3	18.1	33.4	34.9	39.2	47.4	61.9	95.7	240.3
1949	111.8	28.0	19.1	35.1	35.5	41.9	50.1	66.4	100.2	259.1
1948	99.4	31.2	20.5	38.4	39.2	45.9	55.6	76.5	117.7	314.8
1947	94.3	33.4	23.3	42.4	43.1	50.0	58.5	81.3	122.1	312.2
1946	115.5	35.2	25.0	44.8	41.8	47.5	57.4	80.1	122.0	309.9
1945	104.1	38.1	29.1	74.0	56.9	52.5	59.2	87.7	131.0	342.6
1944	111.0	41.5	29.8	102.4	61.5	52.3	60.3	86.0	127.0	328.7
1943	110.8	45.8	29.3	93.1	64.5	54.3	60.3	86.0	127.0	365.1
1942	115.6	39.9	27.8	57.3	55.5	55.5	69.7	89.1	129.0	332.7
1941	117.6	38.6	24.1	40.3	45.5	52.8	65.5	83.1	127.7	326.6
1940	112.8	39.3	23.4	38.6	43.7	52.8	66.5	87.8	135.7	342.9
1939	103.0	42.4	24.1	38.6	42.9	49.8	65.7	84.3	130.4	344.8
1938	105.9	42.7	23.1	41.3	43.5	52.5	70.5	87.9	132.8	339.2
1937	103.8	44.0	26.9	43.6	50.3	59.0	78.2	103.3	145.9	383.8

	Age (years)									
Year	0–1	1–4	5–14	15–24	25–34	35–44	45–54	55–64	65–74	75–84
1936	114.5	46.3	26.5	43.6	51.3	65.6	91.2	120.0	175.8	425.1
1935	97.1	44.8	26.5	42.5	48.1	60.2	79.9	100.6	146.4	357.4
1934	96.0	44.4	28.0	44.7	48.4	59.7	85.0	109.0	154.8	372.5
1933	84.0	43.9	27.7	44.2	46.8	55.9	75.2	95.6	137.1	315.8
1932	82.1	46.3	27.8	47.0	47.8	57.9	75.9	97.4	136.1	312.7
1931	85.3	49.7	27.5	51.6	55.4	69.0	91.3	110.5	152.7	331.8
1930	92.1	48.0	29.0	56.7	63.7	76.3	94.2	112.6	153.7	318.1
1929	91.6	49.9	32.1	61.1	67.5	80.0	95.3	113.3	151.3	313.3
1928	90.0	53.7	34.1	60.5	66.8	80.9	99.0	110.0	152.7	331.7
1927	83.7	56.2	33.7	63.7	65.5	82.8	99.2	115.1	156.6	326.3
1926	99.3	56.4	33.9	66.4	68.2	87.3	103.0	119.8	157.5	326.0
1925	92.1	58.2	36.4	72.2	72.9	89.5	106.9	120.2	169.0	326.4
1924	91.0	64.7	36.4	71.6	71.3	88.3	101.4	117.0	158.5	317.5
1923	88.5	63.6	37.7	73.5	77.6	90.5	104.3	124.1	168.7	320.5
1922	84.6	64.7	37.7	69.3	71.9	83.0	93.2	111.7	152.8	313.7
1921	86.8	68.9	39.8	71.9	72.0	79.3	86.1	104.2	149.5	303.3
1920	98.2	71.0	42.6	78.9	78.3	84.1	93.2	109.0	160.5	311.8
1919	98.8	75.8	45.6	81.6	84.3	95.1	100.8	120.7	159.1	294.3
1918	103.5	80.9	50.4	98.5	107.8	112.7	126.5	151.5	205.1	330.7
1916	119.3	81.6	45.0	94.2	111.2	130.6	143.6	160.1	200.0	358.6
1915	103.5	84.2	45.5	84.6	100.0	112.9	120.4	135.9	178.6	329.4
1914	115.5	87.1	46.3	93.2	109.8	121.2	129.7	150.4	193.0	329.8

White Females

	Age (years)									
Year	0–1	1–4	5–14	15–24	25–34	35–44	45–54	55–64	65–74	75–84
1984	14.8	8.4	2.7	4.1	4.5	4.6	7.2	9.9	20.1	62.2
1983	15.1	10.0	3.1	4.3	4.6	5.0	6.9	10.3	21.3	63.7
1982	14.9	9.8	3.2	4.2	4.8	5.3	7.9	10.8	21.1	63.6
1981	15.5	10.3	3.2	4.2	4.6	5.7	8.5	10.8	22.1	65.8
1980	18.2	11.4	3.5	5.1	5.0	5.4	8.4	12.1	23.4	73.5
1979	15.8	10.7	3.7	5.2	4.9	6.1	8.9	12.8	23.7	73.3
1978	21.9	12.3	4.4	5.7	5.6	6.9	9.4	14.0	24.8	81.6
1977	19.7	11.9	4.4	5.6	5.2	7.2	10.6	14.9	26.0	86.4

Year	Age (years)									
	0–1	1–4	5–14	15–24	25–34	35–44	45–54	55–64	65–74	75–84
1976	22.8	12.2	4.1	5.8	5.3	6.9	10.6	15.5	25.7	86.6
1975	25.7	13.0	4.4	5.8	6.0	8.1	11.2	15.3	28.6	91.4
1974	28.2	12.5	4.7	6.0	6.0	7.8	11.4	16.3	30.0	100.9
1973	27.5	13.3	5.0	5.9	5.7	7.8	11.7	18.0	31.9	106.6
1972	30.5	12.4	5.0	5.8	5.8	7.9	11.9	17.5	31.0	110.9
1971	34.2	13.4	4.7	5.3	6.2	8.4	12.0	17.6	31.9	112.1
1970	40.6	13.4	4.7	5.3	5.8	7.9	12.3	16.9	33.0	117.6
1969	39.8	13.4	4.7	5.3	5.6	8.5	12.1	17.6	34.8	122.2
1968	48.1	13.7	5.8	4.8	5.2	8.2	11.7	17.0	36.4	130.4
1967	46.7	13.7	4.5	4.9	5.3	8.0	11.9	16.9	36.6	138.3
1966	50.1	14.5	5.0	4.5	5.8	8.2	11.4	16.3	37.6	147.0
1965	51.0	13.4	4.5	4.4	5.5	7.5	12.1	15.9	37.2	151.7
1964	53.1	13.9	4.7	4.0	5.3	7.1	10.9	16.0	37.6	147.5
1963	54.2	14.1	4.7	4.4	4.6	7.6	10.9	16.0	38.6	159.8
1962	56.7	14.2	4.5	4.3	4.7	7.3	11.2	15.3	39.6	162.6
1961	55.1	14.0	4.7	4.1	4.7	6.6	9.8	14.2	38.5	159.1
1960	59.3	14.7	5.0	4.1	5.0	6.8	10.0	14.4	39.9	177.2
1959	63.6	13.8	4.7	4.1	4.6	6.2	10.1	14.1	41.3	171.1
1958	61.1	13.8	5.5	4.2	4.2	6.1	8.8	14.3	43.2	184.3
1957	59.2	15.2	5.4	4.4	4.6	6.6	9.6	16.3	46.9	213.5
1956	56.9	14.7	5.4	4.6	4.4	6.5	9.3	16.4	47.2	218.7
1955	54.8	14.5	5.7	4.4	4.1	7.1	9.3	15.7	47.9	230.2
1954	61.5	15.7	5.8	4.5	4.2	6.5	9.7	16.1	49.6	238.0
1953	66.6	16.5	6.8	4.8	4.5	6.5	9.4	16.2	52.2	259.1
1952	72.1	17.9	6.9	5.6	5.1	7.2	9.9	17.0	55.3	277.1
1951	74.2	18.1	6.7	5.3	5.1	7.2	9.5	18.0	57.8	291.9
1950	75.4	17.0	6.9	5.0	5.0	7.6	10.6	18.5	59.0	295.9
1949	80.2	19.4	7.4	5.5	5.4	7.3	9.9	18.0	65.5	322.7
1948	78.4	20.9	7.5	6.5	6.0	8.1	10.6	22.1	86.1	414.0
1947	74.5	20.9	8.1	7.2	6.8	8.6	10.6	23.0	88.1	421.2
1946	87.9	24.4	9.1	7.4	6.3	9.0	11.8	23.2	86.7	419.4
1945	81.1	27.7	9.9	7.8	7.0	9.0	12.2	26.3	96.1	452.4
1944	80.4	29.0	10.4	8.0	6.9	9.2	12.3	26.2	96.6	461.5
1943	80.7	31.6	11.5	6.9	7.1	9.1	13.2	28.1	105.1	493.2
1942	87.8	30.7	9.6	7.1	7.7	8.3	11.7	26.2	99.6	463.0
1941	84.4	26.9	8.8	5.9	6.1	7.0	11.6	27.4	98.8	467.5
1940	95.3	29.3	8.7	6.5	7.2	8.0	12.4	29.2	111.3	501.0
1939	79.1	29.3	8.7	6.5	6.2	7.8	12.9	30.9	107.5	517.7
1938	81.5	32.0	9.1	6.3	7.0	9.0	14.0	31.7	113.7	525.9

	Age (years)									
Year	0–1	1–4	5–14	15–24	25–34	35–44	45–54	55–64	65–74	75–84
1937	76.0	34.3	10.5	7.6	7.4	8.9	14.5	32.4	118.1	528.3
1936	93.8	37.6	11.1	7.6	8.9	10.9	17.7	40.3	137.2	595.8
1935	77.5	37.4	10.7	8.1	8.2	9.7	15.9	35.7	115.9	499.4
1934	76.2	35.3	10.8	7.8	8.4	9.9	16.2	36.3	121.2	511.5
1933	69.2	37.7	10.3	8.1	8.0	9.9	15.4	34.1	107.2	481.6
1932	66.6	37.7	10.9	8.2	7.5	9.5	15.2	33.9	112.0	456.4
1931	68.6	40.5	10.7	8.2	7.6	9.9	16.2	36.5	111.7	473.4
1930	75.8	39.3	11.3	8.8	8.8	10.3	16.3	34.9	109.8	481.0
1929	71.0	42.7	12.1	9.0	9.5	11.3	16.4	33.4	110.5	457.5
1928	73.1	43.0	12.7	9.3	9.1	10.5	17.7	33.7	108.4	475.7
1927	69.8	46.0	12.8	9.4	9.1	12.5	17.0	33.7	102.6	442.3
1926	83.3	47.8	13.2	9.7	9.7	12.0	20.2	35.3	106.0	468.3
1925	74.3	51.2	14.7	12.4	11.4	14.5	21.1	36.5	105.7	457.3
1924	75.5	52.6	15.6	11.5	10.2	13.4	19.2	35.2	108.8	426.5
1923	71.1	52.5	15.6	11.6	11.3	14.3	20.0	35.5	112.5	453.4
1922	66.9	55.1	15.1	11.3	11.0	12.0	18.7	33.5	103.5	422.2
1921	70.9	55.4	15.4	11.2	10.9	12.3	17.8	35.1	98.5	405.8
1920	76.1	63.8	17.3	11.9	11.0	14.0	18.9	37.0	106.1	422.7
1919	71.9	65.4	18.3	13.1	11.6	13.5	18.8	36.2	94.4	379.8
1918	84.9	65.7	19.7	14.5	13.0	16.4	18.8	36.2	111.6	408.7
1916	105.4	67.4	16.7	12.0	13.3	15.8	23.3	43.9	114.1	403.3
1915	88.2	63.1	15.9	12.1	11.0	13.7	20.8	39.3	108.8	400.6
1914	101.0	66.3	16.4	13.0	12.4	15.3	21.6	40.6	109.6	407.9

Nonwhite Males

	Age (years)									
Year	0–1	1–4	5–14	15–24	25–34	35–44	45–54	55–64	65–74	75–84
1984	34.9	23.4	12.5	20.9	31.0	39.4	41.8	52.0	73.5	123.6
1983	46.0	22.8	11.2	21.2	33.5	40.4	46.8	60.6	80.9	142.8
1982	43.5	23.5	12.7	23.3	36.4	40.0	50.9	62.1	77.6	130.7
1981	37.4	29.6	14.3	25.6	37.1	41.7	56.1	66.4	79.9	129.4
1980	53.5	27.8	15.1	30.3	41.4	46.4	64.0	74.1	90.8	167.0
1979	52.5	31.6	17.4	28.4	42.8	51.4	61.8	65.5	83.9	145.5
1978	64.0	30.3	17.3	32.5	41.7	59.0	61.5	75.2	83.7	141.1

Year	0–1	1–4	5–14	15–24	25–34	35–44	45–54	55–64	65–74	75–84
1977	60.0	28.4	18.1	34.0	49.9	58.0	64.4	75.7	85.2	129.5
1976	66.3	28.5	17.2	35.9	52.0	56.6	64.9	75.3	86.1	132.5
1975	73.4	28.8	20.4	44.3	55.4	64.3	69.3	79.3	87.1	135.3
1974	87.3	30.7	19.4	44.3	55.5	62.5	73.0	82.4	95.4	116.2
1973	103.5	32.9	23.3	49.5	58.8	65.4	74.6	89.2	94.4	143.2
1972	92.6	34.1	20.1	52.1	56.1	70.7	73.8	87.5	109.5	143.2
1971	118.9	37.5	21.6	55.8	61.1	70.1	78.1	79.6	105.5	143.6
1970	131.6	36.1	20.9	60.6	66.1	76.9	86.3	92.1	103.3	147.6
1969	106.7	34.9	23.5	57.9	64.0	72.4	78.5	94.6	124.2	131.4
1968	132.4	39.5	24.7	54.5	66.9	78.7	85.8	97.9	142.7	129.9
1967	149.3	42.6	22.1	47.9	67.5	78.1	83.6	95.9	111.6	141.7
1966	172.2	42.8	24.7	48.0	59.9	74.4	87.0	99.9	128.5	149.2
1965	163.0	42.1	22.7	44.2	58.2	75.9	84.4	88.3	111.9	143.4
1964	159.2	40.6	23.5	45.6	60.2	71.1	80.2	84.4	104.2	118.5
1963	158.0	42.9	23.9	46.0	56.3	66.1	77.3	87.5	110.7	146.6
1962	163.4	40.5	23.9	46.5	55.6	65.0	77.9	85.2	106.9	137.9
1961	164.2	41.0	23.5	43.7	50.8	65.8	76.3	81.2	85.9	125.2
1960	196.8	46.9	27.8	48.1	54.4	67.3	78.8	81.5	93.8	150.8
1959	214.8	46.6	24.8	45.3	53.4	68.3	70.5	88.3	116.5	137.6
1958	232.1	45.2	23.7	48.2	54.0	63.2	68.3	85.8	109.3	159.9
1957	216.2	42.5	27.3	48.9	60.8	67.4	77.4	83.1	122.8	147.0
1956	223.8	42.4	25.6	49.9	53.8	71.0	73.0	86.4	111.7	146.1
1955	198.0	46.9	25.9	45.7	53.3	67.4	82.7	84.0	118.6	145.2
1954	221.9	46.3	26.7	52.1	58.1	60.6	74.5	74.0	117.2	165.8
1953	226.2	50.4	27.3	58.0	62.8	70.4	84.5	91.8	108.2	195.5
1952	225.1	53.0	27.0	59.2	64.0	76.4	89.4	94.1	114.0	197.2
1951	223.7	52.8	31.8	52.6	56.3	72.9	87.1	94.5	119.7	180.8
1950	236.6	53.3	31.0	53.1	54.7	72.3	77.8	86.4	106.8	156.6
1949	228.1	51.0	27.3	53.8	56.8	65.3	80.0	85.4	117.2	187.8
1948	231.6	48.9	28.2	62.2	63.5	76.9	93.0	93.3	122.0	198.9
1947	207.1	53.2	34.4	66.0	64.7	77.0	88.3	101.0	115.1	181.3
1946	204.3	62.3	35.7	58.9	65.5	74.0	85.9	97.4	117.3	163.2
1945	210.2	58.6	34.2	68.3	74.3	80.9	87.9	93.4	116.7	181.7
1944	196.6	62.7	38.5	74.2	67.0	77.1	94.1	91.3	112.2	171.8
1943	214.2	63.9	36.5	81.8	70.6	77.2	85.9	92.3	126.8	190.4
1942	208.6	56.0	36.6	74.7	75.0	88.2	90.9	90.0	120.6	192.8
1941	229.2	50.1	30.8	67.1	76.0	84.3	88.5	93.0	104.8	210.6
1940	271.9	54.2	33.7	67.3	75.0	79.9	88.4	96.5	133.8	221.0
1939	216.2	55.0	36.5	67.8	69.8	75.1	92.1	88.6	112.4	194.6

					Age (years)					
Year	0–1	1–4	5–14	15–24	25–34	35–44	45–54	55–64	65–74	75–84
1938	195.8	50.5	35.6	69.4	75.8	78.6	85.7	92.7	109.2	167.0
1937	213.5	67.1	34.1	75.5	82.6	94.9	100.4	107.4	133.8	232.2
1936	244.5	53.8	38.1	75.8	94.9	102.5	115.2	121.6	167.4	269.1
1935	201.6	52.9	37.8	74.2	81.9	92.4	89.8	101.4	135.8	217.6
1934	211.8	72.5	40.9	82.8	91.2	99.7	116.5	117.8	142.6	245.8
1933	201.5	57.9	42.6	79.4	86.2	89.4	99.7	108.9	131.8	233.6
1932	178.4	66.3	39.1	85.4	89.7	92.7	87.1	106.9	127.6	238.7
1931	177.1	60.5	39.5	77.0	84.6	94.1	102.2	104.7	131.5	182.1
1930	213.6	73.3	38.3	86.8	101.2	114.9	106.1	104.8	166.2	295.1
1929	201.9	70.6	43.9	97.0	109.1	119.9	110.6	107.2	150.0	301.7
1928	214.5	72.9	41.5	104.7	111.5	120.4	117.6	95.1	148.4	267.8
1927	223.3	84.3	47.5	117.7	120.3	133.6	122.9	118.6	142.1	290.4
1926	204.3	94.3	49.0	113,1	119.4	126.0	130.2	132.9	149.1	285.5
1925	184.3	93.1	50.8	120.2	116.6	127.6	128.0	119.9	149.6	297.1
1924	257.5	98.5	45.7	113.4	101.9	111.7	110.4	123.5	142.9	261.2
1923	213.8	96.4	50.1	112.8	107.0	105.4	112.7	102.6	172.5	256.1
1922	228.5	89.0	42.4	100.3	87.6	83.5	102.8	108.8	132.1	204.7
1921	205.8	83.6	48.4	116.0	90.4	89.8	90.7	85.4	131.1	200.5
1920	240.1	107.4	49.1	122.5	98.4	88.6	96.4	110.3	168.9	228.1
1919	208.2	106.8	57.5	114.8	98.1	102.0	102.5	98.7	176.5	245.4
1918	226.7	115.7	54.0	127.2	114.8	138.5	122.8	138.2	200.2	320.6
1916	276.2	131.0	48.4	120.7	123.6	140.5	122.2	142.4	171.2	287.1
1915	269.5	128.9	64.2	109.6	105.7	122.6	122.3	145.0	196.4	251.3
1914	357.3	119.7	55.2	119.9	135.8	136.3	130.5	130.3	163.9	314.6

Nonwhite Females

					Age (years)					
Year	0–1	1–4	5–14	15–24	25–34	35–44	45–54	55–64	65–74	75–84
1984	27.5	15.4	4.5	5.0	7.5	8.4	12.4	16.2	30.4	73.8
1983	28.6	17.1	6.2	5.3	9.2	8.8	13.0	20.0	36.1	80.0
1982	31.3	17.0	6.1	4.9	8.0	9.2	13.2	17.6	32.5	65.3
1981	33.3	18.1	5.9	4.6	9.5	10.1	13.9	18.2	30.5	69.0
1980	42.8	19.7	6.7	6.2	8.0	11.2	14.5	24.1	46.5	110.1
1979	49.3	22.2	6.9	6.4	9.5	10.6	14.7	19.2	34.9	71.9

Year	Age (years)									
	0–1	1–4	5–14	15–24	25–34	35–44	45–54	55–64	65–74	75–84
1978	54.2	23.3	6.8	7.0	8.9	12.7	16.6	24.4	38.4	79.0
1977	49.6	20.6	6.7	8.3	9.9	11.6	17.9	26.7	36.9	88.5
1976	53.4	19.3	6.5	8.4	11.5	12.4	17.7	22.8	33.8	80.9
1975	67.2	23.2	6.9	10.0	11.5	15.6	17.8	23.9	38.2	86.2
1974	66.7	23.5	7.3	9.6	12.6	16.1	21.1	25.5	42.1	76.6
1973	86.5	28.1	7.8	10.6	11.4	15.5	19.1	22.7	46.0	91.4
1972	68.9	26.5	8.5	10.5	13.2	15.2	18.6	25.8	48.9	93.6
1971	98.9	25.9	9.3	11.5	12.4	16.9	19.3	27.4	52.6	98.9
1970	103.5	28.8	8.9	10.6	13.9	16.2	20.0	24.5	52.8	111.9
1969	106.5	29.4	9.2	11.0	12.9	16.5	21.0	27.8	63.3	101.1
1968	108.7	32.6	10.0	8.9	12.5	17.6	19.1	33.3	63.0	101.5
1967	122.3	34.0	8.5	8.4	12.7	18.4	18.4	27.8	57.8	102.8
1966	139.3	38.3	10.2	7.3	14.2	18.1	23.8	31.4	70.5	122.2
1965	153.2	35.7	11.0	7.3	11.7	18.3	20.2	29.2	57.6	94.3
1964	130.0	38.2	11.4	7.9	13.9	15.9	17.3	29.9	54.7	127.4
1963	149.7	37.9	12.9	9.0	14.3	16.4	19.7	31.2	64.6	125.1
1962	153.1	40.7	12.1	7.5	13.2	16.4	18.2	31.6	69.0	124.9
1961	128.7	42.1	11.9	8.5	13.8	17.6	18.7	31.1	54.3	111.4
1960	165.7	42.2	14.0	8.4	12.8	18.3	22.0	36.7	61.4	134.9
1959	194.7	40.2	12.8	7.4	12.8	17.8	19.7	28.9	70.5	114.7
1958	207.6	46.4	14.3	8.8	11.3	15.9	18.8	33.7	84.1	132.1
1957	187.9	44.7	13.1	9.0	12.7	17.6	22.3	31.5	80.9	145.0
1956	183.3	38.4	13.3	9.1	11.3	17.3	19.1	32.1	84.3	141.1
1955	170.9	47.4	13.4	8.2	14.1	15.8	20.6	34.5	76.4	157.1
1954	208.5	44.1	12.0	9.2	13.0	16.4	21.8	31.8	80.4	166.4
1953	193.8	47.3	11.6	11.4	14.7	17.6	24.2	43.1	76.6	170.8
1952	214.2	50.8	15.3	10.4	14.4	17.6	24.0	37.9	83.6	181.5
1951	214.0	46.6	13.4	11.8	13.7	18.4	22.7	36.5	70.7	180.0
1950	200.8	48.9	14.0	10.0	14.4	17.5	19.8	33.9	79.2	143.5
1949	194.0	40.1	13.1	9.9	11.1	14.5	22.2	30.2	70.5	165.0
1948	188.8	48.5	16.3	10.0	13.4	15.9	21.0	38.3	78.0	161.9
1947	198.9	46.8	14.3	13.3	16.4	16.9	24.4	39.4	77.1	143.0
1946	192.9	48.6	17.6	14.3	13.0	17.0	22.6	32.2	71.6	161.4
1945	177.6	48.5	17.5	12.4	13.0	17.6	23.1	37.2	80.6	189.3
1944	180.4	59.6	16.7	12.0	14.4	17.2	21.4	40.1	72.3	185.2
1943	180.0	59.5	17.7	13.0	13.6	15.8	27.8	41.7	98.3	215.6
1942	200.0	51.9	16.0	13.7	13.0	17.1	21.1	41.0	85.9	180.6
1941	205.4	50.4	14.6	10.1	12.7	15.4	21.7	35.3	83.9	147.8
1940	205.7	45.5	14.6	17.6	16.2	16.1	24.6	45.9	97.8	226.2

					Age (years)					
Year	0–1	1–4	5–14	15–24	25–34	35–44	45–54	55–64	65–74	75–84
1939	163.5	49.3	14.6	13.6	13.9	14.4	22.7	47.4	79.7	173.3
1938	174.2	56.8	17.1	13.6	12.2	18.7	27.5	50.8	82.6	171.5
1937	199.6	58.5	20.8	11.8	15.6	18.9	30.9	52.0	96.0	179.4
1936	200.0	66.5	20.3	14.1	19.0	21.7	36.2	68.5	123.4	227.3
1935	173.0	60.6	19.6	13.8	16.4	19.8	34.1	51.4	93.9	192.0
1934	208.7	63.5	19.9	17.2	18.4	23.3	33.5	61.4	91.0	211.3
1933	179.1	61.6	19.9	14.9	16.5	22.2	29.3	60.3	90.5	132.4
1932	164.4	62.0	19.4	14.1	16.2	18.2	27.8	50.1	93.4	205.6
1931	164.7	67.4	19.8	13.5	16.5	19.4	30.7	55.6	93.6	222.6
1930	184.3	66.6	22.3	14.5	16.3	21.5	32.2	67.3	83.1	193.4
1929	189.7	73.2	23.3	16.3	19.1	22.0	32.5	67.9	86.5	177.5
1928	188.1	77.8	24.6	19.2	17.1	23.0	35.7	50.3	96.7	212.6
1927	177.8	75.9	25.0	16.2	15.5	22.1	29.2	55.5	93.7	196.5
1926	177.0	92.8	28.6	19.4	20.5	27.2	34.4	48.3	104.6	194.4
1925	225.1	93.0	26.2	24.0	19.8	23.3	33.8	58.2	82.1	229.4
1924	209.2	113.4	30.4	23.9	20.0	23.7	40.5	53.1	122.8	253.8
1923	177.1	101.7	26.6	18.5	20.8	16.7	28.9	52.4	98.6	235.4
1922	194.5	100.1	26.9	18.8	14.8	20.7	27.9	49.8	90.0	169.2
1921	186.8	85.8	25.8	14.6	14.2	22.1	24.4	52.9	113.0	196.6
1920	208.6	112.4	38.2	19.2	17.8	19.8	32.0	44.4	110.6	238.6
1919	187.2	102.0	30.9	18.0	23.7	20.7	33.1	50.7	95.1	258.5
1918	197.9	111.6	33.4	18.0	21.4	31.7	38.7	64.2	136.4	219.1
1916	208.4	124.3	36.2	19.9	17.8	25.3	25.7	53.9	78.4	231.6
1915	213.9	108.0	36.7	22.8	17.4	25.2	30.9	71.0	98.5	247.0
1914	322.7	118.8	40.4	19.1	19.0	26.5	50.1	55.5	109.8	295.1

ACCIDENT (TOTAL) MORTALITY RATES

White Males

					Age (years)					
Year	0–1	1–4	5–14	15–24	25–34	35–44	45–54	55–64	65–74	75–84
1984	20.4	21.7	15.6	80.0	61.2	45.4	45.8	49.7	67.7	145.5
1983	24.7	24.2	16.3	79.4	61.8	46.8	46.0	50.8	65.9	141.3
1982	27.9	24.6	16.8	85.2	64.6	48.5	48.5	51.9	67.9	140.9
1981	25.9	25.6	18.4	92.6	72.5	52.6	53.5	56.7	73.7	147.7

					Age (years)					
Year	0–1	1–4	5–14	15–24	25–34	35–44	45–54	55–64	65–74	75–84
1980	30.9	28.1	18.7	101.8	73.9	55.0	54.7	58.7	77.3	157.4
1979	30.5	27.9	20.4	103.7	72.3	56.0	55.7	61.3	81.3	159.5
1978	36.0	31.1	22.2	105.0	71.8	56.3	55.4	63.5	82.5	173.1
1977	36.3	29.4	21.7	101.1	68.4	54.1	55.7	65.4	84.5	178.9
1976	39.9	31.0	21.7	97.1	66.8	53.1	55.0	65.8	85.2	178.7
1975	38.2	30.2	23.3	98.9	68.8	57.1	59.0	68.0	91.8	189.5
1974	45.7	32.8	23.7	100.9	70.3	57.8	61.0	71.2	94.0	188.4
1973	52.1	34.1	26.4	110.4	77.4	64.3	67.5	82.3	104.3	207.6
1972	54.7	35.5	26.3	107.3	75.4	62.1	69.8	84.5	108.8	221.8
1971	61.0	33.0	25.1	104.4	74.6	66.3	69.2	85.5	112.3	210.1
1970	57.2	33.8	25.8	108.9	77.9	68.8	74.0	90.0	119.1	222.0
1969	67.4	33.0	24.7	115.4	81.4	70.0	74.7	91.5	119.1	218.6
1968	66.1	31.8	25.7	111.7	79.5	67.3	75.2	92.2	123.8	227.1
1967	71.4	34.0	24.8	108.2	79.3	68.8	77.3	93.9	121.6	228.2
1966	76.3	34.6	25.0	108.2	79.7	68.7	79.1	95.8	121.1	238.9
1965	81.5	33.5	24.1	99.9	75.6	66.4	77.2	91.6	122.1	238.4
1964	78.0	32.0	24.2	95.8	74.4	65.1	74.7	89.1	120.9	235.0
1963	80.0	32.2	23.4	92.9	70.7	63.5	75.5	90.1	120.0	238.3
1962	81.7	31.3	23.4	90.1	68.8	62.2	73.3	86.1	119.2	239.3
1961	79.9	31.9	23.8	89.3	66.4	59.1	69.8	82.5	113.3	230.2
1960	85.6	31.8	24.8	92.2	67.7	60.8	72.3	84.2	117.7	238.7
1959	91.0	31.1	24.3	93.6	68.6	61.4	71.3	84.5	125.8	244.6
1958	95.4	31.6	24.9	93.0	68.0	63.7	69.0	82.6	123.8	247.7
1957	87.4	30.8	25.5	99.6	72.9	65.7	74.8	91.6	137.6	278.4
1956	87.1	32.1	26.2	105.9	73.2	64.8	75.6	92.0	141.9	279.3
1955	87.0	32.9	26.6	100.8	72.9	66.4	76.9	93.8	141.4	290.5
1954	95.7	34.8	27.0	95.8	71.6	63.9	73.7	91.6	137.8	291.9
1953	101.1	37.4	29.0	102.7	76.8	68.2	80.6	100.4	145.6	314.8
1952	102.3	38.3	29.5	101.4	77.9	71.3	81.8	105.0	151.4	317.9
1951	109.0	38.4	31.4	96.7	80.0	76.3	83.1	105.0	158.1	320.9
1950	111.5	39.5	30.1	91.7	74.0	70.1	79.0	103.8	154.8	326.7
1949	118.7	41.7	31.4	87.2	70.6	69.2	79.5	106.4	157.7	342.7
1948	105.0	46.0	34.6	92.9	73.8	74.1	86.0	118.3	180.0	406.8
1947	100.3	47.9	37.5	97.2	79.1	79.5	90.8	127.2	190.1	412.8
1946	122.9	51.3	40.8	103.2	80.0	77.0	90.0	127.5	192.1	415.4
1945	108.9	52.1	45.2	125.7	96.7	82.5	90.7	133.6	197.1	434.9
1944	115.4	54.5	43.5	141.7	91.9	78.4	88.2	128.5	184.6	406.4
1943	115.5	59.3	42.2	127.8	93.8	78.8	96.4	137.6	193.9	444.8
1942	120.5	52.8	41.1	99.0	88.4	84.6	105.1	140.6	196.2	419.3

	Age (years)									
Year	0–1	1–4	5–14	15–24	25–34	35–44	45–54	55–64	65–74	75–84
1941	126.4	55.4	42.1	96.6	91.7	92.8	113.7	148.2	223.2	459.6
1940	118.5	54.8	39.4	84.3	83.7	87.1	110.3	150.6	222.2	464.0
1939	109.8	56.8	38.5	81.9	80.3	83.4	106.8	143.7	211.6	464.0
1938	112.9	57.8	38.6	81.9	79.6	85.4	115.6	151.2	219.3	463.6
1937	112.6	60.7	45.1	96.5	94.8	102.0	134.3	181.2	247.2	526.1
1936	120.0	64.7	44.7	91.8	96.6	107.3	146.3	195.0	271.5	558.1
1935	102.3	62.1	44.2	88.1	93.1	101.9	134.2	171.4	239.8	484.4
1934	102.6	61.1	46.1	89.8	91.7	101.8	140.4	181.3	251.0	502.3
1933	89.4	61.6	45.6	82.5	84.6	91.2	120.3	156.3	219.9	430.3
1932	87.1	63.3	44.1	82.8	82.3	92.3	117.0	156.0	217.8	436.8
1931	91.7	68.9	47.9	96.5	94.2	107.8	138.0	176.7	242.4	465.6
1930	100.7	66.5	49.9	100.8	102.4	113.0	141.1	175.9	247.1	442.4
1929	97.8	69.3	54.7	102.0	101.8	114.8	140.9	173.2	240.2	447.3
1928	95.3	72.3	56.2	96.4	97.8	113.6	138.8	165.4	231.3	446.1
1927	90.4	75.3	56.5	95.9	93.5	112.7	134.7	165.1	227.2	425.1
1926	105.6	71.7	56.9	94.3	92.5	114.5	137.9	160.8	222.6	421.5
1925	96.1	73.7	58.6	94.1	92.5	111.1	134.5	157.3	228.2	409.3
1924	96.2	80.0	58.6	90.9	89.5	108.3	127.0	138.6	209.3	388.9
1923	91.6	77.2	59.3	91.8	95.5	111.4	129.7	156.4	217.1	388.8
1922	86.7	78.1	59.1	84.1	88.1	99.6	113.5	138.1	194.3	374.4
1921	88.6	82.3	60.4	84.5	86.1	95.1	103.9	126.9	186.7	347.9
1920	99.7	83.2	63.4	91.4	91.6	96.4	108.1	128.8	191.9	355.6
1919	100.4	86.5	65.2	92.7	95.2	107.0	113.7	140.2	187.8	332.0
1918	105.8	90.2	67.6	110.0	119.6	126.0	142.5	173.1	232.2	360.9
1916	120.3	88.0	57.5	103.3	121.2	141.3	156.4	177.9	220.7	382.0
1915	104.4	88.6	55.8	92.0	107.5	121.5	131.0	148.8	196.2	350.9
1914	116.8	90.3	54.5	98.0	115.1	127.7	138.0	160.0	205.9	340.8

White Females

	Age (years)									
Year	0–1	1–4	5–14	15–24	25–34	35–44	45–54	55–64	65–74	75–84
1984	19.3	13.8	7.8	24.2	15.5	14.0	16.1	20.2	33.1	82.8
1983	19.9	15.9	7.7	23.1	15.2	13.8	15.4	19.6	33.8	81.5
1982	20.5	16.8	8.2	23.1	15.4	14.1	16.4	20.1	33.7	81.0
1981	22.0	17.2	8.4	26.0	16.9	15.6	18.0	21.6	35.3	83.7

				Age (years)						
Year	0–1	1–4	5–14	15–24	25–34	35–44	45–54	55–64	65–74	75–84
1980	25.3	19.1	9.2	28.0	17.2	16.0	18.7	22.6	36.9	92.6
1979	21.9	19.6	9.7	28.1	17.0	16.7	18.8	23.1	37.4	92.2
1978	30.4	21.0	10.7	29.6	17.8	16.5	19.0	25.2	39.8	102.0
1977	27.5	20.8	10.9	28.3	16.3	16.8	20.1	25.9	40.7	107.4
1976	31.2	20.6	10.5	26.4	15.7	15.8	19.8	26.3	40.7	108.2
1975	34.1	21.1	10.5	24.2	16.5	16.7	20.1	25.8	43.0	112.3
1974	36.5	21.1	10.9	24.5	16.0	16.4	20.6	27.3	44.6	121.7
1973	37.0	22.9	12.6	28.2	18.4	19.5	24.0	33.2	52.1	133.4
1972	38.3	22.2	13.0	29.0	18.5	20.3	25.9	33.7	54.3	137.6
1971	43.1	23.2	12.3	27.3	19.3	20.4	24.9	33.2	54.2	139.8
1970	50.8	23.0	11.5	28.0	18.6	20.2	26.6	33.1	55.1	145.7
1969	51.1	23.4	11.5	28.3	18.6	21.7	25.9	34.7	58.4	149.7
1968	57.1	23.4	11.7	27.5	18.2	20.4	25.3	33.9	60.6	158.7
1967	55.8	22.9	10.9	27.0	18.1	20.2	25.9	34.5	61.4	167.4
1966	59.5	24.2	11.6	26.5	18.1	20.4	25.8	35.0	62.4	174.4
1965	58.8	22.2	10.5	24.0	17.3	19.8	26.2	33.8	60.5	179.7
1964	63.1	22.9	10.5	23.3	17.3	19.2	24.6	33.9	60.7	175.3
1963	63.1	22.8	10.1	22.5	15.2	18.2	23.9	32.3	60.5	186.0
1962	64.6	22.7	9.9	21.0	14.8	18.0	23.4	31.6	60.9	188.1
1961	62.9	22.2	9.6	18.9	14.0	15.9	21.2	29.0	57.4	182.9
1960	66.7	23.0	10.4	19.7	14.0	15.7	21.4	29.6	59.3	201.0
1959	73.1	22.1	9.7	18.9	14.2	15.0	21.2	28.6	62.5	196.1
1958	68.4	21.8	11.0	18.5	12.8	15.0	19.8	28.7	65.2	209.5
1957	67.7	23.1	10.7	19.4	13.8	16.2	21.2	31.7	68.2	238.6
1956	64.7	23.3	10.8	20.9	14.0	16.0	20.7	31.2	69.6	243.6
1955	63.2	23.7	10.9	20.1	13.9	16.2	20.8	31.5	68.4	257.3
1954	68.4	24.8	11.3	17.7	12.6	15.1	20.8	30.6	69.9	263.7
1953	74.3	26.4	12.5	20.3	13.6	15.5	21.3	31.6	74.2	286.2
1952	81.1	27.7	12.9	20.9	14.1	16.9	22.0	33.0	75.1	303.4
1951	82.1	26.9	12.9	18.8	14.6	16.3	21.1	33.9	79.1	318.7
1950	83.1	27.0	12.5	17.6	14.0	15.7	21.4	33.5	79.9	321.3
1949	87.1	29.3	13.2	16.6	12.8	14.6	19.1	32.4	85.4	349.9
1948	84.9	31.2	14.0	19.1	12.9	15.9	20.0	36.4	104.6	440.3
1947	78.7	31.4	14.8	19.8	13.7	16.6	20.5	37.2	107.7	450.5
1946	93.5	34.7	16.4	20.5	14.5	16.1	21.5	37.2	106.7	448.1
1945	85.2	36.8	16.6	18.9	13.9	16.1	20.0	37.4	111.6	476.3
1944	83.3	38.6	16.3	16.8	12.7	14.4	18.9	35.6	111.0	482.2
1943	84.5	40.5	17.0	14.5	11.9	14.4	20.1	37.6	118.7	511.1
1942	91.6	40.2	14.7	17.2	14.2	14.6	20.8	38.0	117.7	485.0

					Age (years)					
Year	0–1	1–4	5–14	15–24	25–34	35–44	45–54	55–64	65–74	75–84
1941	91.4	39.0	16.6	21.1	16.7	17.0	25.8	47.2	130.8	508.6
1940	101.6	39.6	16.1	19.2	16.2	17.0	24.7	48.1	140.7	539.6
1939	86.7	41.3	14.8	16.6	14.9	16.3	24.8	49.1	138.1	555.4
1938	87.3	41.8	15.7	17.2	15.6	17.7	26.7	50.6	145.3	567.5
1937	84.5	46.7	18.5	22.5	18.4	20.4	30.0	54.8	154.4	577.1
1936	100.8	49.7	19.3	21.9	19.7	21.9	32.9	63.3	171.1	639.8
1935	83.5	48.3	18.5	22.2	18.8	20.3	31.2	58.4	148.0	544.9
1934	81.1	45.1	19.2	20.5	18.8	19.9	30.2	59.1	157.4	556.4
1933	74.7	47.8	18.3	19.8	16.6	19.1	28.9	55.2	139.1	525.8
1932	70.7	47.3	18.8	19.3	15.7	18.1	28.2	54.8	144.8	498.7
1931	75.5	52.8	20.1	21.3	16.8	20.2	32.0	60.4	149.8	519.3
1930	81.5	51.1	20.7	21.1	17.8	19.6	32.2	59.0	150.1	533.0
1929	76.7	55.2	21.9	21.0	17.9	20.9	31.0	57.2	146.9	498.6
1928	79.8	54.3	22.8	19.1	16.3	19.8	32.4	55.8	141.8	521.5
1927	75.3	56.9	22.9	18.6	16.1	21.2	29.3	54.0	135.4	484.3
1926	89.0	57.9	23.1	18.5	16.3	19.9	32.3	53.2	133.4	504.2
1925	78.3	60.7	23.7	19.6	16.2	21.1	31.0	54.7	131.9	490.8
1924	78.3	61.6	24.3	17.7	14.8	19.5	27.7	50.7	132.1	453.6
1923	73.6	61.0	24.2	17.1	15.9	20.4	28.2	48.9	126.9	477.1
1922	70.2	62.6	22.9	15.9	14.5	15.9	25.0	45.5	120.9	441.9
1921	73.3	62.8	22.7	14.6	14.3	16.3	24.4	46.1	115.6	422.8
1920	78.4	70.7	23.8	15.6	13.9	17.3	24.9	46.8	120.2	439.0
1919	73.0	71.5	24.5	16.3	14.4	17.0	24.2	44.8	105.0	393.7
1918	86.8	71.0	25.0	17.5	15.6	19.3	27.9	48.9	120.7	421.9
1916	106.6	71.2	20.0	14.2	15.2	18.4	27.1	49.2	120.5	411.2
1915	88.6	66.2	18.8	13.9	12.5	15.7	24.1	44.2	113.8	406.9
1914	101.3	68.6	18.5	14.5	13.5	17.0	23.3	43.7	113.7	412.8

Nonwhite Males

					Age (years)					
Year	0–1	1–4	5–14	15–24	25–34	35–44	45–54	55–64	65–74	75–84
1984	40.4	33.3	20.5	54.5	66.1	70.9	69.7	81.8	106.2	167.2
1983	49.7	33.3	19.8	51.8	68.4	71.5	77.6	90.0	111.9	185.5
1982	50.0	34.2	20.9	54.2	71.4	71.4	83.1	94.3	111.7	172.4
1981	44.2	39.3	23.4	59.0	77.6	79.8	93.0	100.2	121.7	172.3

	Age (years)									
Year	0–1	1–4	5–14	15–24	25–34	35–44	45–54	55–64	65–74	75–84
1980	62.2	41.1	25.5	69.0	85.5	85.2	101.5	112.9	132.0	217.7
1979	56.8	45.7	28.4	67.1	89.4	93.1	101.0	106.5	124.4	185.8
1978	71.4	44.9	28.2	74.9	92.7	101.9	99.9	117.4	126.6	205.5
1977	66.9	42.9	30.8	76.6	100.6	97.2	013.2	121.2	125.3	181.6
1976	75.2	43.3	29.0	76.0	101.2	98.6	105.2	117.2	127.5	185.0
1975	82.9	45.0	33.7	83.1	107.2	107.0	110.2	124.0	136.4	184.4
1974	93.3	44.5	32.6	87.8	105.0	106.4	115.6	127.7	148.0	165.3
1973	111.7	55.1	38.0	104.1	122.4	124.4	131.0	147.1	154.9	199.5
1972	103.0	54.0	34.0	109.4	124.7	129.7	134.3	149.5	163.7	209.6
1971	133.5	54.7	37.8	114.1	127.5	123.1	132.0	141.9	168.5	207.9
1970	142.4	53.1	36.6	121.0	133.4	134.5	146.9	152.0	160.9	204.1
1969	116.2	51.4	39.2	125.0	136.1	127.6	141.4	164.1	192.5	196.6
1968	138.6	56.5	39.3	120.6	143.1	138.3	148.6	163.0	218.2	195.0
1967	157.2	59.6	36.8	109.5	136.2	131.9	137.9	155.3	186.2	199.0
1966	184.5	58.1	38.6	109.3	129.4	132.0	145.3	157.3	198.8	214.4
1965	168.9	58.6	35.2	99.4	123.9	129.8	136.8	146.5	174.7	193.7
1964	166.7	55.3	36.9	94.8	118.7	125.0	133.5	137.1	171.6	170.1
1963	163.6	57.5	36.1	98.9	114.2	115.7	125.4	138.7	169.2	196.6
1962	172.0	52.9	35.4	96.1	109.4	111.6	123.6	136.2	167.2	182.8
1961	170.1	53.3	34.7	90.3	101.6	108.5	118.6	129.3	129.1	177.3
1960	204.3	60.0	38.6	98.8	106.1	110.4	127.8	129.1	142.8	206.8
1959	221.1	58.3	36.7	92.2	106.6	117.8	122.8	139.6	172.2	180.9
1958	238.2	56.8	34.4	95.7	109.2	113.4	114.8	136.0	176.5	203.7
1957	225.4	55.6	38.1	96.7	122.1	118.8	128.5	141.2	185.2	220.9
1956	238.3	56.2	36.5	106.7	120.3	131.8	127.6	145.5	179.9	208.6
1955	208.6	60.4	35.9	100.2	115.8	121.7	135.2	139.9	182.7	198.4
1954	236.1	59.4	36.9	100.1	116.8	108.8	129.2	128.5	174.4	227.4
1953	234.2	67.6	39.9	111.2	128.9	127.0	141.8	146.9	175.7	278.2
1952	263.7	68.7	38.3	113.0	127.6	130.8	148.0	153.8	174.1	268.2
1951	230.1	66.2	44.9	102.3	118.6	127.2	139.9	149.7	187.2	255.8
1950	245.5	65.0	41.8	97.4	110.1	119.2	129.8	143.4	165.6	223.0
1949	234.5	63.6	40.3	94.1	103.7	107.6	125.8	129.0	176.8	260.2
1948	240.0	61.5	39.7	99.8	103.4	118.4	141.7	145.0	179.4	275.7
1947	211.9	64.5	45.6	103.5	110.6	117.0	133.1	149.7	181.0	247.2
1946	207.9	76.4	49.7	96.3	105.6	114.1	132.7	147.9	171.3	225.3
1945	213.6	69.6	45.6	101.8	113.4	121.4	130.1	142.2	168.4	251.2
1944	200.7	75.0	51.6	106.2	105.6	112.3	134.6	128.0	168.0	230.8
1943	216.2	76.8	47.8	111.5	103.6	111.4	128.2	135.8	182.1	246.6
1942	212.2	67.2	48.2	111.0	118.9	128.3	140.9	138.9	173.5	242.1

					Age (years)					
Year	0–1	1–4	5–14	15–24	25–34	35–44	45–54	55–64	65–74	75–84
1941	239.2	62.1	48.0	119.8	135.4	144.9	155.3	166.4	198.3	301.5
1940	276.9	64.1	47.4	109.1	123.0	124.9	146.8	154.3	205.9	306.5
1939	219.6	66.0	50.9	103.4	113.6	122.8	148.2	151.1	181.6	262.3
1938	201.7	62.9	48.4	107.8	121.2	130.2	135.4	158.3	178.3	243.5
1937	221.2	79.0	48.5	119.0	132.9	153.3	166.6	187.6	224.0	341.2
1936	253.1	64.3	51.2	117.8	146.2	170.5	180.6	205.5	249.3	368.0
1935	204.9	65.4	49.6	112.2	132.1	150.2	147.1	173.3	218.3	318.8
1934	216.9	84.6	57.6	123.4	145.7	152.9	179.6	194.9	234.4	341.8
1933	205.7	69.7	58.4	114.3	131.6	137.6	152.4	173.2	212.4	341.6
1932	185.6	77.4	53.3	113.7	128.7	138.1	135.5	161.5	194.9	296.8
1931	179.8	69.1	55.6	108.6	129.2	136.6	153.5	163.1	208.3	247.9
1930	217.2	82.7	53.0	124.1	142.4	159.6	158.1	162.9	233.7	382.3
1929	205.8	81.5	58.2	128.5	150.4	161.7	163.2	167.1	210.1	402.2
1928	219.1	82.0	55.6	129.7	141.5	157.6	161.7	138.6	211.9	328.0
1927	229.3	97.1	63.7	140.2	150.6	169.1	165.3	155.8	203.7	392.3
1926	206.4	103.7	64.1	137.9	149.1	158.7	163.7	166.5	200.9	331.3
1925	188.6	102.3	64.8	138.6	137.2	155.1	156.5	145.0	193.0	343.9
1924	259.7	108.5	58.1	131.5	121.1	134.8	139.2	148.3	178.4	325.1
1923	217.1	102.7	60.6	127.1	124.0	125.6	132.2	125.6	190.0	287.5
1922	229.6	94.4	50.6	107.3	100.6	96.6	117.4	123.7	154.8	225.2
1921	208.3	87.7	57.6	122.3	98.4	100.1	103.2	98.4	146.8	228.2
1920	242.8	111.2	58.7	130.6	107.4	96.1	102.5	125.9	181.5	242.4
1919	208.2	109.4	64.7	120.1	105.7	111.3	109.4	114.2	197.1	256.1
1918	226.7	122.4	64.2	134.5	121.8	147.9	131.7	150.1	222.7	351.5
1916	276.2	134.1	54.1	124.5	128.9	148.0	127.3	151.8	189.8	293.2
1915	269.5	129.9	68.4	115.2	110.0	128.4	131.6	156.2	205.1	270.0
1914	375.3	120.7	59.4	123.1	140.5	138.1	131.2	136.0	172.6	333.7

Nonwhite Females

					Age (years)					
Year	0–1	1–4	5–14	15–24	25–34	35–44	45–54	55–64	65–74	75–84
1984	32.8	22.7	8.7	14.4	16.6	16.7	20.3	25.4	40.6	87.5
1983	34.5	24.5	10.5	15.0	17.4	16.7	22.6	28.1	46.3	95.0
1982	36.6	25.0	11.3	14.5	17.4	18.4	21.2	26.3	43.1	74.1
1981	37.0	26.5	11.3	14.2	19.4	18.9	23.0	27.7	41.2	82.2

Year	Age (years)									
	0–1	1–4	5–14	15–24	25–34	35–44	45–54	55–64	65–74	75–84
1980	47.6	29.6	12.4	15.7	19.9	20.9	24.2	24.4	55.5	123.0
1979	55.0	32.2	12.2	17.8	19.4	20.6	24.8	30.5	46.1	86.1
1978	65.5	36.4	12.6	19.5	20.1	23.4	27.4	37.8	48.5	92.6
1977	56.4	30.7	12.4	20.6	20.3	21.1	27.9	39.2	45.9	104.3
1976	64.3	30.7	12.4	19.2	22.7	22.8	28.4	34.5	46.9	93.5
1975	75.0	34.5	13.1	20.5	21.7	25.9	30.0	36.6	50.3	101.9
1974	74.8	35.0	14.2	20.3	24.9	26.9	31.8	39.4	55.2	91.3
1973	100.8	41.5	15.8	26.8	27.7	30.6	36.3	36.9	63.5	105.5
1972	83.3	38.0	17.9	25.3	26.4	31.4	36.4	40.1	66.4	110.6
1971	109.1	39-7	17.2	27.7	29.2	33.2	36.7	43.2	72.4	113.7
1970	114.8	41.1	18.1	25.5	28.6	32.8	36.6	41.2	70.0	126.5
1969	114.2	41.7	17.6	30.2	28.8	32.2	37.5	45.4	85.1	116.9
1968	118.7	43.7	17.8	24.1	29.6	35.4	34.7	50.4	85.4	120.0
1967	132.9	44.3	17.2	24.5	28.4	32.5	36.1	45.7	77.3	123.5
1966	147.5	49.3	17.5	25.1	31.3	33.6	42.3	46.7	91.1	138.5
1965	159.8	45.5	18.2	22.7	26.5	33.5	36.4	44.9	79.1	106.2
1964	136.7	46.2	17.9	20.3	28.0	29.8	31.3	46.9	73.9	144.2
1963	155.0	46.5	18.9	20.6	28.3	27.8	35.1	47.3	81.3	141.2
1962	160.6	49.8	18.6	19.5	23.3	30.0	32.1	45.9	86.0	139.2
1961	133.5	50.3	17.8	21.0	25.7	29.2	30.0	45.7	68.8	131.5
1960	173.5	51.5	19.9	19.6	23.1	29.3	34.8	51.0	75.8	146.2
1959	200.3	48.6	18.3	18.7	25.1	29.4	32.6	41.6	91.3	127.0
1958	212.7	55.9	18.3	19.4	22.5	27.8	31.1	45.7	103.3	147.5
1957	194.9	53.6	18.8	22.1	27.1	30.3	36.9	49.4	101.2	163.1
1956	193.4	47.6	19.7	21.6	24.2	31.4	33.4	52.7	101.5	155.3
1955	179.8	58.3	18.8	21.7	27.6	29.2	34.6	51.8	99.1	175.9
1954	217.9	55.3	17.3	21.1	24.9	29.7	35.4	48.4	97.2	186.9
1953	201.7	57.0	17.7	24.7	28.2	32.1	38.3	47.0	91.3	192.0
1952	222.0	60.8	20.1	24.8	28.6	28.4	40.6	52.5	100.6	203.7
1951	223.5	55.7	19.0	25.6	25.7	31.9	38.2	53.1	90.9	199.0
1950	207.6	58.3	20.4	22.1	25.8	29.0	30.9	47.8	94.6	166.0
1949	197.5	49.1	18.3	18.7	20.5	22.4	34.9	42.1	87.2	182.0
1948	190.4	57.2	21.6	19.9	21.4	24.7	30.6	48.9	91.2	178.4
1947	202.7	54.1	19.2	21.9	24.1	23.3	34.9	51.3	87.6	158.1
1946	198.6	58.0	24.3	24.1	20.2	25.6	33.2	44.4	84.8	180.7
1945	183.0	55.1	22.1	19.4	19.7	24.6	32.3	45.5	97.5	201.2
1944	185.3	66.1	21.3	18.1	21.8	23.6	29.2	48.3	83.2	197.5
1943	182.1	65.7	21.5	18.2	20.6	21.2	33.2	50.6	107.0	223.4
1942	201.5	57.2	20.7	20.9	21.3	25.0	29.9	50.3	98.2	200.0

Year	Age (years)									
	0–1	1–4	5–14	15–24	25–34	35–44	45–54	55–64	65–74	75–84
1941	214.7	57.6	21.0	21.3	24.1	26.5	35.6	52.2	104.8	178.2
1940	211.4	52.7	20.6	25.3	26.9	25.5	37.9	61.6	115.5	239.9
1939	166.8	57.0	18.9	23.3	23.6	24.1	34.7	68.0	101.0	189.4
1938	178.3	63.5	22.2	21.7	22.5	30.8	43.3	71.7	98.9	192.9
1937	206.4	63.7	25.8	22.4	26.4	32.9	46.2	76.1	118.0	211.6
1936	205.9	73.7	25.0	24.2	32.2	35.2	49.7	90.6	152.5	251.5
1935	179.6	69.2	24.3	20.8	26.3	30.8	48.9	71.2	114.7	213.4
1934	211.2	72.0	27.3	24.9	29.8	34.7	49.4	86.3	114.4	229.5
1933	181.6	69.7	25.5	22.0	24.8	33.3	44.1	80.5	113.3	152.9
1932	165.3	70.2	25.6	19.5	26.4	29.3	42.7	69.5	118.5	234.2
1931	170.0	74.0	25.3	22.0	28.1	31.6	44.7	81.7	124.0	243.4
1930	185.2	75.5	27.9	21.7	26.6	30.3	46.1	90.0	112.5	210.4
1929	194.4	80.6	29.4	24.5	29.6	32.2	47.0	84.0	106.6	192.6
1928	191.7	85.2	31.0	24.7	25.0	32.5	50.0	68.2	112.9	243.3
1927	182.6	81.8	30.4	20.7	23.5	33.1	43.6	69.1	116.3	209.1
1926	178.0	99.1	33.8	25.9	28.6	36.8	44.0	62.9	125.3	213.1
1925	227.2	98.1	30.1	30.4	27.6	30.8	41.4	70.5	97.6	254.0
1924	212.4	117.3	34.3	27.8	25.9	30.2	49.0	64.1	137.3	267.7
1923	180.3	103.7	30.2	23.0	24.5	21.2	33.0	61.5	109.9	255.5
1922	194.5	104.2	29.3	21.0	17.3	25.4	30.9	55.2	102.7	172.2
1921	188.0	88.7	27.8	16.1	15.8	24.4	27.9	57.1	126.5	203.7
1920	208.6	116.2	40.2	20.5	19.9	21.7	34.5	49.5	114.7	242.2
1919	188.4	104.3	33.7	18.6	25.2	22.5	34.9	55.2	97.8	276.2
1918	199.4	113.2	36.1	19.4	22.6	34.4	42.2	70.5	136.4	223.4
1916	208.4	125.8	37.7	20.5	19.5	25.7	26.9	55.1	80.6	231.6
1915	213.9	114.0	39.2	23.2	19.9	26.8	31.8	71.0	105.1	247.0
1914	322.7	118.8	41.2	19.1	19.0	27.0	51.0	57.3	109.8	295.1

REFERENCES

Barker RG: *Ecological psychology*. Stanford, CA: Stanford University Press, 1968.

Barker RG, Gump PV: Big school, small school: High school size and student behavior. Stanford, CA: Stanford University Press, 1964.

Basch MF: Perception, consciousness, and Freud's "project." *The Annual of Psychoanalysis* 3: 3–19, 1975.

Brenner MH: *Times series analysis of relationships between selected economic and social indicators*. Springfield, VA: National Technical Information Service, 1971.

Brenner MH: Mortality and the national economy. *Lancet* 1979: 568–573.

Brooke EM: *Suicide and attempted suicide*. Public Health Papers 58. Geneva, Switzerland: World Health Organization, 1974.

Colledge M: Economic cycles and health. *Social Science and Medicine* 16: 1919–1927, 1982.

Constantino JP, Kuller LH, Perper JA, Cypess RH: An epidemiologic study of homicides in Allegheny County, Pennsylvania. *American Journal of Epidemiology* 106: 314–324, 1977.

Doege T: An injury is no accident. *New England Journal of Medicine* 298: 509–510, 1978.

Dublin LI: *Suicide: A sociological and statistical study*. New York: Ronald Press, 1963.

Dunn HL, Shackley W: Comparison of cause-of-death assignments by the 1929 and 1938 revisions of the International List: Deaths in the United States, 1940. *Vital Statistics—Special Reports*, Vol. 19, No. 14, 1944.

Durkheim E: *Suicide: A study in sociology* (Spaulding JA, Simpson G, trans.). New York: The Free Press–Macmillan, 1951. (Originally published 1897.)

Easterlin RA: *Birth and fortune*. New York: Basic Books, 1980.

Farberow N: *The many faces of suicide*. New York: McGraw-Hill, 1979.

Faust MM, Dolman AB: Comparability of mortality statistics for the fifth and sixth revisions: United States, 1950. *Vital Statistics—Special Reports*, Vol. 51, No. 2, 1963a.

Faust MM, Dolman AB: Comparability ratios based on mortality statistics for the fifth and sixth revisions: United States, 1950. *Vital Statistics—Special Reports*, Vol. 51, No. 3, 1963b.

Faust MM, Dolman AB: Comparability of mortality statistics for the sixth and seventh revisions: United States, 1958. *Vital Statistics—Special Reports*, Vol. 51, No. 4, 1965.

261

Freud S: Beyond the pleasure principle. *Standard Edition* 18: 3–64, 1955. (Originally published 1920.)

Freud S: Mourning and melancholia. *Standard Edition* 14: 237–258, 1957. (Originally published 1917.)

Freud S: The psychopathology of everyday life. *Standard Edition* 6, 1960. (Originally published 1901.)

Gedo J, Goldberg A: *Models of the mind.* Chicago: University of Chicago Press, 1973.

Gordon RE, Gordon KK: Social psychiatry of a mobile suburb. *International Journal of Social Psychiatry* 6: 89–106, 1960.

Greenwood M, Woods HM: The incidence of industrial accidents upon individuals with special reference to multiple accidents. In *Accident research* (Haddon W, Suchman EA, Klein D, eds.). New York: Harper & Row, 1964. (Originally published in Report No. 4, Medical Research Committee, Industrial Fatigue Research Board, Great Britain, 1919.)

Grove RD, Hetzel AM: *Vital statistics rates in the United States: 1940–1960.* Washington, DC: U.S. Government Printing Office, 1968.

Hellon CP, Solomon MI: Suicide and age in Alberta, Canada, 1951–1977: The changing profile. *Archives of General Psychiatry* 37: 505–510, 1980.

Hendin H: *Suicide in America.* New York: W.W. Norton, 1982.

Henry AF, Short JF: *Suicide and homicide: Some economic, sociological and psychological aspects of aggression.* Glencoe, IL: The Free Press, 1954. (Reprint edition, New York: Arno Press, 1977.)

Herzog A, Levy L, Verdonk A: Some ecological factors associated with health and social adaptation in the city of Rotterdam. *Urban Ecology* 2: 205–234, 1977.

Holford TR: The estimation of age, period and cohort effects for vital rates. *Biometrics* 39: 1311–1324, 1983.

Holinger PC: Adolescent suicide: An epidemiological study of recent trends. *American Journal of Psychiatry* 135: 754–756, 1978.

Holinger PC: Violent deaths as a leading cause of mortality: An epidemiologic study of suicide, homicide, and accidents. *American Journal of Psychiatry* 137: 472–476, 1980.

Holinger PC: Self-destructiveness among the young: An epidemiologic study of violent deaths. *International Journal of Social Psychiatry* 27: 277–282, 1981.

Holinger PC, Klemen EH: Violent deaths in the United States, 1900–1975. *Social Science and Medicine* 16: 1929–1938, 1982.

Holinger PC, Luke K: The epidemiologic patterns of self-destructiveness in childhood, adolescence, and young adulthood. In *Suicide in the young* (Sudak US, Ford AB, Rushforth NB, eds.). Littleton, MA: PSG, 1984.

Holinger PC, Offer D: Perspectives on suicide in adolescence. In *Social and community mental health*, Vol. 2 (Simmons R, ed.). Greenwich, CT: JAI Press, 1981.

Holinger PC, Offer D: Prediction of adolescent suicide: A population model. *American Journal of Psychiatry* 139: 302–307, 1982.

Holinger PC, Offer D: Toward the prediction of violent deaths among the young. In *Suicide in the young* (Sudak HS, Ford AB, Rushforth NB, eds.). Littleton, MA: PSG, 1984.

Jenkins J, Sainsbury P: Single-car road deaths—disguised suicides? *British Medical Journal* 281: 1041, 1980.

Kaplan HB, Pokorny AD: Self-derogation and suicide—II. Suicidal responses, self-derogation and accidents. *Social Science and Medicine* 10: 119–121, 1976.

Klebba AJ: Homicide trends in the United States, 1900–1974. *Public Health Reports* 90: 195–204, 1975.

Klebba AJ: Comparison trends for suicide and homicide in the United States, 1900–1976. In *Violence and the violent individual* (Hays JR, ed.). New York: S P Medical & Scientific Books, 1979.

Klebba AJ, Dolman AB: Comparability of mortality statistics for the seventh and eighth revisions of the International Classification of Diseases, United States. *Vital and Health Statistics*, Ser. 2, No. 66, Washington, DC: U.S. Government Printing Office, 1975.

Klein GS: Consciousness in psychoanalytic theory. Some implications for current research in perception. *Journal of the American Psychoanalytic Association* 7: 5–34, 1959.

Kohut H: *The analysis of the self*. New York: International Universities Press, 1971.

Kramer M, Pollack ES, Redick RW, Locke BZ: *Mental disorders/suicide*. Cambridge, MA: Harvard University Press, 1972.

Lalonde M: *A new perspective on the health of Canadians*. Ottawa: Tri-Graphic Printing, 1974.

Lester D: Sibling position and suicidal behavior. *Journal of Individual Psychology* 22: 204–207, 1966.

Lester D: *Why people kill themselves*. Springfield, IL: Charles C Thomas, 1972.

Lester D: Temporal variation in suicide and homicide. *American Journal of Epidemiology* 109: 517–520, 1979.

Levy L, Herzog A: Effects of population density and crowding on health and social adaptation in the Netherlands. *Journal of Health and Social Behavior* 15: 228–240, 1974.

Levy L, Herzog A: Effects of crowding on health and social adaptation in the city of Chicago. *Urban Ecology* 3: 327–354, 1978.

MacMahon B, Johnson S, Pugh TF: Relation of suicide rates to social conditions. *Public Health Reports* 78: 285–293, 1963.

Maris R: The adolescent suicide problem. *Suicide and Life-Threatening Behavior* 15: 91–109, 1985.

Massey JT: Suicides in the United States, 1950–1964. *Vital and Health Statistics*, Ser. 20, No. 5, 1976.

Menninger KA: *Man against himself*. New York: Harcourt, Brace, 1938.

Murphy GE, Wetzel RD: Suicide risk by birth cohort in the United States, 1949–1974. *Archives of General Psychiatry* 37: 519–523, 1980.

National Center for Health Statistics: Annual summary for the United States, 1979. *Monthly Vital Statistics Report*, Vol. 28, No. 13, DHHS Pub. No. (PHS) 81-1120. Hyattsville, MD: Public Health Service, 1980.

National Center for Health Statistics: Advance report, final mortality statistics,

1981. *Monthly Vital Statistics Report*, Vol. 33, No. 3, Suppl. DHHS Pub. No. (PHS) 84-1120. Hyattsville, MD: Public Health Service, 1984.

National Center for Health Statistics: Annual summary of births, deaths, marriages, and divorces: United States, 1983. *Monthly Vital Statistics Report*, Vol. 32, No. 13. DHHS Pub. No. (PHS) 84-1120. Hyattsville, MD: Public Health Service, 1984.

National Center for Health Statistics: Advance report, final mortality statistics, 1982. *Monthly Vital Statistics Report*, Vol. 33, No. 9, Suppl. DHHS Pub. No. (PHS) 85-1120. Hyattsville, MD: Public Health Service, December 20, 1984.

Offer D, Ostrov E, Howard KI: *The adolescent: A psychological self-potrait.* New York: Basic Books, 1981.

Peck M, Litman RE: Current trends in youthful suicide. *Tribuna Medica* 14: 13–17, 1973.

Porterfield AL: Traffic fatalities, suicide, and homicide. *American Sociological Review* 25: 897–901, 1960.

Rogot E, Fabsitz R, Feinleib M: Daily variation in USA mortality. *American Journal of Epidemiology* 103: 198–211, 1976.

Rosenberg ML, Gelles RJ, Holinger PC, Zahn MA, Conn JM, Fajman NN, Karlson TA: Violence: Homicide, assault, suicide. In *Carter "closing the gap,"* Health Policy Project, Violence Epidemiology Branch, Centers for Disease Control, Atlanta, GA, 1984.

Schmidt CW, Shaffer JW, Zlotowitz HI, Fisher RS: Suicide by vehicular crash. *American Journal of Psychiatry* 134: 175–178, 1977.

Seiden RH: Suicide among youth: A review of the literature, 1900–1967. *Bulletin of Suicidology* (Suppl.), 1969.

Seiden RH, Freitas RP: Shifting patterns of deadly violence. *Suicide and Life-Threatening Behavior* 10: 195–209, 1980.

Selzer ML, Payne CE: Automobile accidents, suicide, and unconscious motivation. *American Journal of Psychiatry* 119: 237–240, 1962.

Shapiro J, Wynne EA: Adolescent alienation: Evaluating the hypotheses. *Social Indicators Research* 10: 423–435, 1982.

Solomon MI, Hellon CP: Suicide and age in Alberta, Canada, 1951–1977: A cohort analysis. *Archives of General Psychiatry* 37: 511–513, 1980.

Stengel E: *Suicide and attempted suicide.* Baltimore: Penguin Books, 1964.

Tabachnick N: *Accident or suicide? Destruction by automobile.* Springfield, IL: Charles C Thomas, 1973.

Teicher ID: Children and adolescents who attempt suicide. *Pediatric Clinics of North America* 17: 687–696, 1970.

Thomas L: *The lives of a cell.* New York: Bantam Books, 1974.

Toolan JM: Suicide and suicidal attempts in children and adolescents. *American Journal of Psychiatry* 118: 719–724, 1962.

Toolan JM: Suicide in children and adolescents. *American Journal of Psychotherapy* 29: 339–344, 1975.

Turner CW, Fenn MR, Cole AM: A social psychological analysis of violent behavior. In *Violent behavior: Social learning approaches to prediction, management and treatment* (Stuart RB, ed.), New York, Brunner/Mazel, 1981.

U.S. Bureau of the Census: *Historical statistics of the United States, Colonial times to 1970*, Bicentennial ed., Part 2. Washington, DC: U.S. Government Printing Office, 1975.

U.S. Bureau of the Census: *Statistical abstract of the United States*, 101st ed. Washington, DC: U.S. Government Printing Office, 1980.

U.S. Bureau of the Census: *Statistical abstract of the United States*, 103rd ed. Washington, DC: U.S. Government Printing Office, 1982–1983.

U.S. Bureau of the Census: *Current population reports*, Ser. P-25, No. 952, Projections of the population of the United States by age, sex, and race: 1983–2080. Washington, DC: U.S. Government Printing Office, 1984.

Vital and Health Statistics, Ser. 20, No. 16: Mortality trends for leading causes of death: United States—1950–69. Washington, DC: U.S. Government Printing Office, 1974.

Vital Statistics of the United States, 1961–1980: Mortality. Washington, DC: U.S. Government Printing Office, 1974.

Vital Statistics—Special Reports, Vol. 19, No. 13: Classification of terms and comparability of titles through five revisions of the International List of Causes of Death. Washington, DC: U.S. Government Printing Office, 1944.

Vital Statistics—Special Reports, Vol. 21, No. 7: Accident fatalities in the United States, 1943. Washington, DC: Department of Commerce (Bureau of the Census), 1946.

Vital Statistics—Special Reports, Vol. 43: Death rates by age, race, and sex, United States, 1900–1953. Washington, DC: U.S. Government Printing Office, 1956.

Wasserman IM: The influence of economic business cycles on the United States suicide rates. *Suicide and Life-Threatening Behavior* 14: 143–156, 1984.

Webster's new collegiate dictionary. Springfield, MA: G&C Merriam, 1977.

Wechsler H: Community growth, depressive disorders, and suicide. *American Journal of Sociology* 67: 9–16, 1961.

Weiss NS: Recent trends in violent deaths among young adults in the United States. *American Journal of Epidemiology* 103: 416–422, 1976.

Wolfgang ME: Suicide by means of victim-precipitated homicide. *Journal of Clinical and Experimental Psychopathology* 20: 335–349, 1959.

Wolfgang ME: *Patterns in criminal homicide*. Philadelphia: University of Pennsylvania Press, 1968.

World Health Organization: *International classification of diseases*. Geneva, Switzerland: World Health Organization, 1900, 1909, 1920, 1929, 1938, 1948, 1955, 1965, 1975.

INDEX